CASS LIBRARY OF AFRICAN STUDIES

GENERAL STUDIES

No. 108

Editorial Adviser: JOHN RALPH WILLIS
Department of History, University of California, Berkeley

# The History of Education in Ghana

# The History of Education in Ghana

From the Earliest Times
to the Declaration of Independence

## C. K. Graham
*University of Science and Technology,
Kumasi, Ghana*

FRANK CASS & CO. LTD.
1971

First published in 1971 by
FRANK CASS AND COMPANY LIMITED
67 Great Russell Street, London, WC1B 3BT


Distributed in the United States by
International Scholarly Book Services, Inc.
Beaverton, Oregon 97005


Library of Congress Catalog Card Number 77-169808


ISBN 0 7146 2457 8

*Printed in the Republic of Ireland by
Cahill and Co. Limited, Parkgate Printing Works, Dublin* 8.

*To the memory of*
*My Father,*
*The Rev. Charles Graham*

# Contents

# Preface

The word " education " is used in many parts of Africa to refer to formal instruction in European-type schools. Those Africans who have been to school are said to be " educated "; all others—whether they have learnt some trade or not—are regarded as uneducated. This is clearly a restricted use of the word. Education in the wider sense of the term has always been an important factor in the way of life of the African. Parents and the wider circle of kinsmen consider it a sacred trust to discharge their obligations regarding the child's " socialisation ". In fact, the entire community often takes part in it in various ways. Throughout the child's daily activities— and later in his adolescence—he is made aware of the material and the spiritual fundamentals of social life. The customs, traditions and values of his community, as well as the world view and meaning of life are all " taught " to the growing child. At the same time he attempts to take on more and more of the responsibilities and duties which fall to him. Thus, before the coming of Europeans, the people of the Gold Coast " educated " themselves. In a sense, their traditional education was fully capable of supplying the necessary elements to maintain the levels attained by their society in the economic, social, technical and cultural areas.

However, over the years traditional education—although effective when it was simply a matter of handing down experience from generation to generation, when techniques were relatively simple— came to offer little possibility for progress in the assimilation and spread of new experiences and knowledge. Also, European states which ever since the Age of Discovery have cast about for new territories to conquer, Christianise or to exploit economically, appeared on the Gold Coast scene before the close of the fifteenth century, and brought with them the more formal Western type of education.

My purpose in writing this book is to tell the story of the growth and development of European-type education in the Gold Coast, from the beginning of her contact with European civilisation, up to Independence. African scholars have often expressed concern that European historians or visitors to Africa have usually given jaundiced accounts of the history of African societies, and that what the Europeans wrote about largely reflected their own feelings and thoughts. This book is an attempt to redress the balance, for I have tried to interpret and set down the facts from the standpoint of the African. I have tried also to show the relationship of education to other aspects of social structure such as the economic, the religious and the political.

The vast literature concerning culture contact and social change in Africa tends to include some studies of the psychological factors. But the inter-personal processes that underlie relationships between Africans and Europeans are still too seldom analysed; and even where inter-personal processes have been considered, for the most part the literature describes relatively impersonal, stereotyped and superficial transactions. In this book an attempt has been made to analyse some of the interrelations between the various ethnic, occupational and political groups that helped (either directly or indirectly) in the educational endeavours in the Gold Coast.

I have also tried to draw attention to the crucial but often neglected fact that African teachers, catechists and ministers were the main channels through which ideas on education passed to the chiefs and people of the Gold Coast. I have tried to highlight the little known efforts of men like Joseph Smith, John Anderson, Amo, Capitein, Nkwantabisa, Philip Quaco, the Rev. Laing, David Asante, Attoh Ahumah—to mention only a few.

A common charge often levelled against European educationists is that they have neglected the agricultural and industrial training of Africans in the Gold Coast. This charge is certainly unfair; and I have endeavoured to show that whatever their other objectives were, the European educationists tried to experiment and find out what curricula would offer the best balance between a vocational education designed to produce the skills required in the country, and a general education needed for cultural sophistication.

In writing this book, I drew from many sources, including the archives in London of the Methodist Missionary Society, the Society for the Propagation of the Gospel, and the Public Record Office. Amongst the libraries where I found most stimulating material are the Senate House Library of London University, the Royal Anthropological Society Library, the British Museum Newspaper Library, and the Library of the London School of Economics. I am most grateful to them all.

I should like to acknowledge a particular debt of gratitude to Dr. P. T. W. Baxter of Manchester University, who opened up many new and fruitful lines of research to me. My grateful thanks are also extended to D. G. MacRae and E. Gellner—both Professors of Sociology at the London School of Economics, and the supervisors for my Ph.D. degree there—for their invaluable suggestions. I also have to thank my wife Esther for prodding me on to write this book.                                    C. K. GRAHAM

University of Science and Technology,
Kumasi
1970

# CHAPTER I

# EARLY EDUCATIONAL EFFORT 1600–1800

Although Portuguese influence on the Gold Coast is seldom remembered today, Portugal was one of the first European countries to make an impact on the economic and educational life of the country. The Portuguese were probably the first to open a school there, their aim then being primarily to convert the people at Elmina[1] to the Catholic faith. King John III had given instructions to the Governor at Elmina in 1529 " to provide reading, writing and religious teaching for African children ".[2] The medium of instruction was to be Portuguese; the teacher was to be paid 240 grains of gold a year for every pupil he taught, up to a maximum of fifteen. If the enrolment rose above that number he was to receive no higher remuneration, but if a pupil died or cut short his schooling, then the teacher was to receive a corresponding reduction in salary.[3] There are no available records to indicate the number of pupils and teachers in this school at this period, nor the progress the school made. It is probable, nevertheless, that only a handful of boys attended this school.

A little over a century later—in 1637, in fact—when the Dutch seized the Elmina Castle, they restarted the school in the Castle. Their aims were similar to those of the Portuguese, for they too wanted to help the children who were " qualified " to learn to advance in the Christian faith.[4] It is not clear what was meant by " qualified ". Perhaps the word refers either to children who had some sort of religious background or to children of mixed parentage.[5]

The Dutch Charter of 1621 (renewed in 1640) had also given instructions for the setting up of " Christian schools " wherever they traded, in accordance with the teaching of the Dutch Reformed Church.[6] It was hoped, therefore, that the children from the school at Elmina, apart from advancing in the Christian faith, would also become more and more favourably disposed to the Dutch authorities as well as accomplished in the Dutch language.

Let us now examine the nature of British policy in the Gold Coast colony at this period, and their trading and commercial interests, in order to see the extent to which education was

1

influenced by these interests. There is little doubt that trade and commerce sent the British to the Gold Coast. It was always taken for granted that some national advantage could be derived from trade and from prohibiting the export of slaves by other European powers.[7] British participation in West African trade in the last decades of the 18th century involved mainly the business of Liverpool, Bristol and London trading houses.[8]

The point is often made that the sole purpose of British presence in the Gold Coast prior to 1800 was to Christianise the Africans. This is not so. As Morel, a British historian, has put it: " it was commerce alone that sent the British and other European countries to the West Coast of Africa. Commerce was the ' fons and origo' of our presence there ".[9] Morel considered that " as a nation we should gain much and lose nothing in frankly admitting to ourselves that our presence in West Africa was due neither to a desire to mend the ways of priestly theocracies, nor to alter the tyranny of the strong over the weak . . . but the belief that West Africa constituted a vast outlet for the free and unfettered development of British trade, and an equally vast field for the cultivation of products of economic necessity to ourselves ".[10]

Of course, the British were not the only traders to the country during the three hundred-odd years that spanned the time of the earliest contact which the Gold Coast had with Europe and the beginning of the eighteenth century. The Fanti of Cape Coast and Anomabu, for instance, had for centuries trafficked with whites— with the Normans, Portuguese, Spaniards, French and the Dutch —in rubber, pepper, gold, ivory and in fellow Africans, receiving in return rum, guns and gun powder.[11] The main items of export were palm oil, ivory, guinea pepper, guinea grains, camwood, ebony, beeswax, gum copal, hides and gold dust.[12] Governor White also observed that " Cape Coast was the emporium of trade, probably owing to the number of free traders residing in that town ".[13] Cape Coast was the capital of the Gold Coast until 1877.

However, despite the fact that trading activity took place throughout the eighteenth century, trade and commerce appear to be among the neglected aspects of early Gold Coast social history. Their investigations are of paramount importance and basic to our understanding of the extent to which educated Africans were offered jobs in existing trading establishments in Fantiland, and therefore, to our understanding of Anglo-Fanti relations, especially regarding educational practices of the day.

The urgent need for literate interpreters had induced the Royal African Company to set up a school at Cape Coast Castle in 1694, and John Chiltman was appointed its first teacher.[14] This school

was shortlived. However, on his appointment to the chaplaincy at
the Castle in 1712, the Rev. John Jameson resolved to open a
" well qualified " school which would instil good principles into the
young mulattoes and some of the blacks even, and would, therefore, serve the Company's interests.[15] When Jameson died a year
later his school became moribund.

However, the school appears to have had a new head within a
short time. A letter from one James Wenden, dated November 15,
1712, reported that his brother, Thomas Wenden, " being appointed
Chaplain by the African Company to their settlement at Cape
Corso (Cape Coast) was willing to carry on a correspondence with
the Society, if he could do them any service in those parts. To
which end the said Company had desired Thomas Wenden to apply
himself to the Society for some of the ' thoughtful realities ' which
they gave to their poor, that he might dispose of them among the
inhabitants and soldiers there ".[16] After the Committee had considered Mr. Wenden's letter they decided that a " packet of the
Society's books should be given to Mr. Wenden's brother who was
going to Cape Corso in Guinea, not exceeding the value of 40s.".[17]

In the eighteenth century education was mainly a subsidiary
function of the Merchant Companies. The funds which helped to
run the Royal African school were irregular. In 1794, for instance,
the Committee in London contributed £60 towards the running of
the Castle School at Cape Coast and the following year the contribution was £37.[18]

The Company also supplied text-books to the school. This
practice was carried well into the nineteenth century. For example,
on appointing Charles Williams to the headship of the Cape Coast
Castle school in 1815, the Secretary to the African Committee
instructed him to take delivery of the following :

> 100 Books No. 1; 100 National Society School Books, No. 2;
> 100 National Society School Books No. 3; 100 Sermon on the
> Mount; 100 Church Catechism, Psalters (100); Slates (20); Copper
> Plate Copies (20); Arithmetical Tables for Madras Schools (20);
> Sand Boards (6). A further supply was to be sent as the Governor
> and Council might report them to be required.[19]

One distinctive feature of early educational practice was that it
mostly aimed to teach mulatto children. At this time, " if the father
of any person born in the country was an European, such a person
was considered as having a better right or a stronger claim to be
under European jurisdiction than ordinary natives ".[20] And it should
be explained also that before the twentieth century it was common
practice for Europeans to leave their wives and children in

England—largely because of the enervating climate and its attendant fevers—and, on their arrival in the Gold Coast Colony, to marry African girls according to local custom. In the words of J. L. Wilson:

> " the number of white females was then very small, for they tended to suffer more from the climate than the men; and because they had less to engage their minds, they seldom became sufficiently interested in the country as to be willing to make it their home. It was not uncommon for European residents to form connections with native women of mixed blood, of whom there were many about the forts. In the course of time they found themselves surrounded with large families of mulatto children. Before a connection of that kind could be formed with a family pretending to respectability, the European bound himself to make provision for the support of the consort (as the temporary wife was called), and the children; and in case he left the country, these engagements as a general rule, were scrupulously and honourably fulfilled."[21]

This Euro-African marriage was, nevertheless, not peculiar to the Gold Coast. It has been reported that in eighteenth century Senegal, for example, Europeans married Senegalese women. " When marriage according to Catholic rites was not possible or expedient, other methods were employed—celebrated with some formality, constituting family relationship of recognised status which often endured happily until the man returned to Europe."[22] Here, too, the offspring were usually educated in Europe, especially in France.

It was to the offspring of such mixed marriages that the early educationists turned their prime attention. And at that time, at Cape Coast for instance, a fund (known as the " Mulatto Fund ") was set up; towards this fund all resident Europeans were expected to make monthly contributions in proportion to their salary. The aim was to help to finance the education of the mulatto children, and to help support mulatto and African women by whom the resident Europeans had children.

Of course, there were a few Africans who married European women. Philip Quaco, Jacobus Capitein and E. Andoh (a soldier at the Cape Coast Castle) were among such men. Their children, who, of course, were mulattoes, might also have profited from the schools. (Some mulatto names which have come to stay in the country are Brew, Smith, Hesse, Swanzy, Butler, Hanson, Gomez, Bartels and Quist.)

It should be pointed out that, contrary to popular thinking, the emphasis placed on exclusive teaching of mulatto children was not

very widespread. Thus, although the Castle school at Accra concentrated exclusively on teaching mulatto children, the Cape Coast
Castle school, on the other hand, took on both mulatto and
African children. In 1740, for instance, of the 45 pupils in
Capitein's school only 11 were mulattoes.[23] Swanzy's remark, therefore, that the Cape Coast Castle School of the early nineteenth
century was " for the education only of whitemen's children " is
difficult to understand.[24] However, even where training was given
to mulatto children, the intention was mainly to enable them to
serve as soldiers at the Fort, and in any other capacity the African
Company would direct. Thus it was that when in 1815 a school
master was sent out to Cape Coast he was instructed " to take
to his assistance 3 mulatto writers who were in the service of the
Castle ".[25]

During this period (that is, before 1800), although the schools
were few and of limited size, there was a definite organisational
structure in existence. There was an executive authority made up of
the President and Council at Cape Coast Castle, who were accountable to the Committee of Merchants in England. This Committee
of nine was itself elected every year by the Freemen of the three
chief ports trading in Africa—London, Bristol, Liverpool, and was,
in turn, answerable to the Exchequer, the Board of Trade and
Plantations and the Admiralty (and, therefore, to Parliament). It
was the Committee and, to a lesser extent, the Society for the
Propagation of the Gospel which by the close of this period largely
financed the schools and paid for the maintenance of the school
functionaries.

This organisation, however, was very similar to that which the
Dutch had adopted in their schools about a century earlier. In the
latter, the executive body was the Secret Council which was responsible to the Directors in Copenhagen who, in turn, elected the
Chaplain and Superintendent of the School for the approval of the
King of Denmark. It was to the King, however, that matters concerning staffing and equipment were to be sent.

Before 1800, another feature of the educational process was that
of sending boys to Europe for education. It was felt that a

> most important assistance would be afforded to the influence
> of the Colony (in this case Sierra Leone) on the neighbouring
> nations, by giving instruction in England to some African chil-
> dren, who were either most promising in themselves, or most
> important from their African connections.[26]

It was also felt that the educated Africans would carry back to their
country " minds considerably enlightened " and would be parti-

cularly well instructed in the Christian religion. And since most of the Africans to be educated were the sons of chiefs it was felt also that in due course a large proportion of the kings and headmen of the surrounding countries would receive their education in England, and thus there was the probability that they would value the friendship and in a good measure adopt the views of the British Government. It was also envisaged that as " the Governments in Africa were in a great degree hereditary, these youths would succeed to power; and there would be a fair prospect of their carrying into effect in the countries which they would respectively govern, plans more or less similar to those inculcated in England and pursued in the Colony ".[27]

Among those Africans who had the opportunity of being educated abroad in the eighteenth century and who later excelled themselves was A. W. Amo of Axim.[28] He was sent over in 1707 and he lived with the son of the Duke of Brunswick-Wolfenbuttel. Later, he studied and lectured at the Universities of Halle, Jena and Wurtenberg, where he obtained his doctorate. This won him a citation which described him as " vir nobilissime et clarrissime ".[29] He was later awarded the title of Counsellor of State at the Court of Berlin. He spent altogether thirty-seven years in Europe and later returned to Axim.

Another African boy, Jacobus Capitein, was sent over to Holland at the age of nine by a Dutch trader, Van Goch. After nine years' schooling he entered Leyden University in 1737. He too was a brilliant student and was later ordained the first Protestant African priest. Later, he was sent to the Dutch Company at Elmina where he helped conduct services in the Castle. He was instrumental in helping to reduce the local language (Fanti) to writing, and he later had the Lord's Prayer and parts of the catechism as well as the Ten Commandments published in Fanti. These rudiments of the Christian faith, translated in Fanti, are an example of Capitein's unique contribution to missionary work.

His educational activities were no less remarkable. There were 45 pupils in his school in 1740; of this number four were mulatto boys, seven mulatto girls and five African girls.[30] It is interesting to note that in the Cape Coast area African and mulatto children were being given equal educational opportunities at this time. Equally revealing is the fact that girls' education was in no way lagging behind that of boys.

It has been said of Capitein that he prepared an orphanage for the teaching of baptised African children because he did not want the baptised African pupils to " contaminate " the mulatto children with their heathen background.[31] It seems rather incongruous that a man who was teaching both mulatto and African pupils should suddenly change his ideas and approach.

Nonetheless, by the time of his death in 1747, Capitein had succeeded in putting the school at Elmina on a strong footing. He had left behind a hard core of about 400 boys and girls who could play a useful role in their society. It has been said that it was from his school that he and other chaplain schoolmasters sent out into the African community of Elmina and Cape Coast those young people who had some knowledge of the Catechism, the Creed, the Lord's Prayer, the Commandments, and portions of the New Testament; young people who also attended and perhaps appreciated the church services held in the Castle.

Holland was not the only country to which boys were sent for education. In 1788, John Tarleton, the Mayor of Liverpool, informed the Privy Council that there were fifty-odd West African children, chiefly from the Gold Coast and Sierra Leone, whom parents and British traders had sent over to Liverpool to be educated.[32] In a report published at the close of the eighteenth century the Committee of the House of Commons had also indicated that there were about twenty-four Sierra Leonean children " of promise or important connections " who were studying in England.[33] It was also believed that there were over fifty West Africans studying in London and Bristol.[34]

Governor Melvie sent two boys (Aquah and Sackey) from Anomabu to be educated in London at the expense of the Committee, in return for a promise which the Fanti chiefs had made to expel the French from their soil.[35] The Committee later realised that they had made a wrong choice because Aquah was the son of a fetish priest, and Sackey was a chief's son.

Meanwhile, about £600 had been spent on them. So three years later, in 1756, the Committee decided that no more African boys would be sent to England at their expense.[36] Of course, the Committee had limited funds. Between 1750 and 1760, the annual grant made to them was £10,000 except in 1755 when £16,000 was granted; and from 1761 to 1795 the annual grant was £13,000 (except a £10,000 grant in 1764, and £15,000 in 1771 and 1781).[37] In his evidence before the Select Committee of 1816, Swanzy thought the cutting down of the Committee's grant from £23,000 to around £10,000 was unfortunate. Indeed, his considered opinion was that £40,000 was the right amount which could enable " the African Company to establish a school at each Fort, to pay proper teachers, to subsist such of the children of the natives in the interior as would be inclined to send their children for education . . . . and to enlist more soldiers, officers . . . . ".[38]

dant fevers—and, on their arrival in the Gold Coast colony, to

B

The Committee's decision to discontinue the practice of training Africans in England raises a number of sociological issues. It could be speculated that in the case of Aquah, the Committee might have assumed that because his father was a fetish priest, Aquah would still cling to traditional beliefs and values, even if he received western-type education. They feared that Aquah would discard certain aspects of western culture which his education might have given him. The Committee were thus unaware of the divergence between western and traditional norms which frequently tended to confront educated people in developing countries.

For, as the nineteenth century was to prove, educated Africans wished on the one hand to preserve their standard of living which was usually higher than that of their non-literate kin, and wherever possible, they liked to improve it; they also desired to be able to display the symbols of status which would gain them full acceptance by virtue of their education. But, on the other hand, the educated Africans faced demands for assistance of various kinds from numerous less fortunate members of the extended family. Some recent studies, however, indicate that although the extended family leads to a dispersal of savings, and the unemployed live parasitically upon their wealthier educated kin, this expectation on the part of a man's family could be a spur to further effort.[39]

Attitudes of educated Africans towards their non-literate kin were not only complex, but also tinged with ambivalence.[40] For while kinship bonds invariably linked them with their illiterate kin, their newly acquired status symbol—the prestige of their occupation—made them less inclined to adopt all the trappings of traditional life. There was every probability, therefore, that Aquah, with his training and western education, would not necessarily have blindly followed his father's priestly vocation and beliefs.

In the case of Sackey (the chief's son) different issues are raised. The Report from the Committee of the House of Commons had stated, inter alia, that " as the governments in Africa were in a great degree hereditary, these youths (i.e. sons of chiefs) would succeed to power, and there would be a fair prospect of their carrying into effect in the countries which they would respectively govern plans more or less similar to those inculcated in England, and pursued in the colony ".[41]

But in Fanti society, as among the Akans generally, inheritance passed not from father to son, but to sister's son.[42] The Merchant Company had wrongly thought that in the event of the chief's death or destoolment, it was his educated son—one who might be more inclined to co-operate with them because they had helped to finance his education—who would be enstooled.

Education in the seventeenth and early eighteenth centuries was nevertheless primarily the subsidiary function of the Merchant Companies, who simply considered the school as a source of supply of interpreters and clerical subordinates for the activities of the Company, and sometimes of soldiers to help defend the forts.

Writers on the subject of early educational endeavours seem to be generally silent on the conditions under which the African boys lived and studied in England. One such rare glimpse has been given by William Greaves, who at the close of the eighteenth century had a number of Africans studying under him. Because of the rare nature of his revelation we quote fully his statement contained in his evidence to the Sierra Leone Company.[43]

Greaves said he lived at Clapham (London) and had the care of the Africans then in England for education, as their schoolmaster. He had had other boys under his care but, at the time of his statement, he was charged solely with the education of the children in question. They had been placed under his care about two and a half years before. Their ages ranged from ten to seventeen. He instructed them in Reading, Writing and Arithmetic; one of the pupils excelled in mensuration. Almost all of the boys could speak and read English tolerably well. Pains were taken to give them information on general subjects, such as History, Geography, Natural Philosophy and Mechanics. He had not observed any " inferiority of capacity, allowance being made for the deficiencies under which they laboured when they came under his care ".

Greaves added that the boys " conversed together in their own language, but more frequently in English ". Some of the children, having learnt to read and write, had been put out to learn boatbuilding and it was proposed to place the others as " they got forward ", to learn different trades. They also learnt various useful arts within the school. Greaves pointed out further that the African boys retained a strong attachment to their own country, but did not appear impatient to return home till their education was completed, "being sensible of the advantages to be derived therefrom ". The students showed a great disposition to adopt the principles of the Christian religion, and several of them had written to their parents in Africa expressing their opinions on this subject. Books had also been prepared, principally on religious subjects, for their use, with the native language of some of them on one side and English on the other, which they read.[44]

Mr. Greaves's remarks were collaborated by Macauley and Lindham who also pointed out that some of the books prepared had been recently sent to the Colony, and it was hoped that by those means, with proper assistance, education might be facilitated among the Africans. Macauley and Lindham pointed out further that all the African children under Greaves had come for education at the desire and consent of their parents or other friends. They stressed that the intention of the Company had been to " continue the boys in England for seven or eight years, in order the better to prepare them, on their return to Africa, either to fill offices with the Company, or to promote civilisation in any other way, by means of the advantages which an European education would naturally give to them in their intercourse with their own people. Many of the educated Africans would succeed to power, being children of the chiefs of the country ".[45]

The Report of the Committees of 1785-1801, therefore, brings out clearly the nature and extent of the care and attention given to some of the African boys who were sent over to England to study, the range of subjects studied, and the duties which they were required to perform on their return to their own country.

One can safely assume that, before the end of the eighteenth century, trade and commerce did not open up much avenue for most of the educated boys who were in the Cape Coast area.[46] Unlike Sierra Leone, the Cape Coast area did not contain transported slaves, so enrolment in the school continued to be drawn mainly from mulatto children and children of the well-to-do African merchants and traders.

Some writers of Gold Coast history have stated that the local chiefs were not all that keen to give their children any education. Although this is largely true, available evidence shows that in the 1740s, for instance, King Poku of Ashanti sent twelve boys and two girls to the Dutch authorities to learn Reading, Writing and Music.[47] The boys were sent to the Cape Coast Castle school, and the Ashanti king proposed to pay for the children's subsistence with some elephant tusks.[48]

Apart from well-to-do merchants and traders and chiefs, there is proof that other sections of the African population were also keen to give their children education (contrary to popular writing on this period of educational experiment). Indeed, the records of masters like Quaco and Thompson (to be discussed later) indicate that frequent demands were made by the Africans themselves for schools.[49] The point really is that although adults did not desire instruction for themselves, they were glad to have it communicated to their children. This was the case particularly when it was not at their expense.[50]

The pattern of initial demand at this period was, therefore, not as random as is sometimes implied. Indeed, a definite process of selection, however limited, was at work, propelled largely by those who were peripheral to the indigenous society. Those selected were from among mulattoes, from children of African traders who were closely involved with the emergent coastal economy, and to a lesser extent from among the other Africans. During this period, the schools were not associated with mission activity as such. In fact, the missionaries only seriously came upon the educational scene during the first half of the nineteenth century, so until then the pattern of demand already noted remained unchanged. We shall now examine some of the factors that led to educational activity in contemporary England in order to help our understanding of some of the motives that propelled educational activities in the Gold Coast Colony in the eighteenth and nineteenth centuries.

In England, educational advance can best be gauged against a background of social disequilibrium. There were new inventions and new methods of production. The Napoleonic war had laid bare the evils which economic maladjustment could bring in its wake, and was also changing men's minds and hearts, picturing as it did a society in which all men had equal rights and were able to attain the fullest self-realisation. In England some people were amassing wealth and others were becoming more and more impoverished. The standard of living generally was not particularly high. There was a considerable degree of undernourishment among many sections and the problems of supplying food to the newly rising population had not been fully tackled and solved. And, as a result of the movement of large sections of the population, partly in search of jobs, the religious and social life of many men and women had been thrown out of gear.

It became apparent to many, therefore, that the machinery for adjusting themselves to these new situations was lacking. New systems of local government and social services (including, especially, education) had to be built up, therefore, to check further deterioration of living standards and morals. In fact, the Methodist revival, for example, had awakened many people to a zeal for Christian propaganda and there was also widespread desire among the young and the old to learn to read and write. It was largely because of these promptings that there emerged organised philanthropy aimed at developing a network of schools for the poor. The main stimulus then (as it came to be in the nineteenth century also) was " the hope of dealing with the sources of crime and destruction and civilising a class whose ignorance was a menace to society ".[51]

In England, in due course, there came into being a proliferation of schools. There were Day Schools and Boarding Schools which maintained, clothed, and educated the children until they were old enough to be apprenticed. Some of these Day Schools merely instructed the pupils, others provided the children with a free meal a day. Some even taught them to spin wool, mend and make shoes, sew and knit. Religious instruction, however, constituted the most important part of the curriculum. Some of the schools in England were, by and large, unhealthy; the drunkenness of some of the teachers was almost proverbial, their earnings were small, they punished harshly and regarded the lash as the only proper governing medium.[52]

One of the most serious obstacles to the early English elementary education—apart from child labour—was stated by the Census Report of 1851 to be not deficiency of school accommodation, nor even the poverty of many parents, but rather their indifference—the belief prevalent among the labouring classes that any instruction beyond a certain point could never be of any practical utility to those of their condition.[53] At this time " a parent in whatever station, would take himself and his own status as the standard up to which he desired to educate his child ".[54]

Although this verdict on the pre-nineteenth century English education may seem rather fastidious and exaggerated it reveals, however, that all was not well with the schools of the period. And with the rise of National schools at the beginning of the nineteenth century the motives underlying these schools vanished and they were merged into new establishments.[55]

It appears that the general feeling was not just for education for its own sake; nor was the prime desire to fit people into jobs. Rather, it was felt that over and above the idea of popular education as a human or religious duty, even a modicum of education would help to combat vice, irreligion and unsocial tendencies among the poor, who must be taught to live upright and industrious lives. All this goes to explain not only the strong emphasis that was placed upon religious education in the philanthropic schools for the poor, but also the place which was to be given to religious instruction in the schools in the Cape Coast area before the close of the eighteenth and nineteenth centuries.

We have already noted that at this time the Cape Coast school was being run by the Merchant Company; the pupils were being given rudimentary lessons to enable them to fill the limited clerical jobs available in the Castle. It seems that in England, too, before the nineteenth century, the State was slow to enter full scale into the educational area. The Government's policy then was generally that anything it did in the social life in England should give the least disturbance to the political structure and the " inherited fabric of social ideas ". And, in fact, from 1798, when the Day School epoch started with Joseph Lancaster, up to 1833, the whole of what had been accomplished in the work of popular education was the fruit of private liberality, incited mainly by religious zeal. It was only in the year 1833 that the Government first offered its assistance and contributed an annual grant of £20,000.[56]

We have so far discussed the pattern of demand for schools, the British policy and that of the Merchant Companies towards schools in the Cape Coast area, and some of the factors that led to the growth of English educational institutions in the period before 1800. Let us now look at the part that some outstanding educationists (Africans and Europeans) were able to play in the educational process at that time.

Formal education as we know it today was begun in 1752 when one of the early missionaries of the Society for the Propagation of the Gospel (S.P.G.), the Rev. Thomas Thompson,[57] came to Cape Coast. He had then worked for five years among the negro slaves in the plantations of America and the West Indies. Before his arrival at Cape Coast, religious teaching had been confined within the walls of the Castle. During his four years' stay (May 13, 1752 —February 17, 1756) he brought many changes into the life and activity in the Castle. His aim all the time was " to make a trial with the natives and see what hope there would be of introducing among them the Christian religion ".[58]

He travelled extensively on the Coast, studied the language of the people among whom he was working (i.e. Fanti) and made a bold attempt to understand and appreciate the meaning and significance of some local customs which seemed to him at first sight to be " ridiculous and sinful ".[59] In his *My Two Missionary Voyages* he tells of how, during his stay at Cape Coast, he performed varying types of work, sometimes acting as chaplain, reading prayers and preaching at various places, sometimes visiting the sick, distributing gifts of books from the S.P.G. and the Society for the Propagation of Christian Knowledge, and even lending his fellows his own books.[60]

Indeed, such was the zeal which he brought to bear on his work of teaching the Africans that after he had unsuccessfully advised the chiefs and people of Cape Coast to provide a classroom, he hired a room at his own expense and began to teach the few who were keen and interested.

The fact that Thompson's first approach was made to the chiefs and people, and not through the Merchant Company, bears testimony to his understanding of the local situation as well as his maturity of purpose and approach. His attempt was perhaps the first serious one ever to make the Cape Coast chiefs interested in Western-type education of their community.

The Rev. Thompson's school was intended for the children of mixed blood (mulattoes) as well as the children of some caboceers (important chiefs) and wealthy merchants. His efforts were not crowned with much immediate success. As he himself has put it: " Several of the young blacks came to me; but children growing weary of what is no longer a novelty, and the parents neglecting to keep them to it, and make them come duly, my hopes were quickly at an end of doing any good in this way."[61]

The Rev. Thompson's school was partly financed from fines which were imposed on officers and servants of the Merchant Government in Cape Coast Castle, who without justification failed to attend divine service on Sundays.[62] It does not seem probable that the fines alone could have made the running of the school possible. It is conceivable that the administration, the well-to-do merchants and traders, and some of the chiefs who had children in the school, might have made some contribution to its upkeep.

There are no available records to show how many of Thompson's pupils came from the rising merchant families, or from the families of chiefs, nor the number of mulattoes and girls. The demand for schools was of a rather limited nature and was placed on a relatively narrow base.

Apart from Thompson's contribution to the school, he was perhaps the first man to have attempted to bring Christian teaching from the Castle to the Africans, and to make the school the nursery of the church.

Thompson also made suggestions to the Committee of the Society for the Propagation of the Gospel for some of the young Africans at Cape Coast to be sent over to London to be educated.[63] Three boys who went over to England on his recommendation were Philip Quaco, Thomas Caboro and William Cudjo. These boys were educated at the expense of the S.P.G. at a school at Islington. Quaco, for instance, then a lad of fourteen, trained for ten years, obtaining the degree of Master of Arts at Oxford.[64]

Although it was a feature of the eighteenth and nineteenth centuries that boys were sent for further training in Europe, it can be said, nonetheless, that this foresight of the Rev. Thompson made possible continuity in the educational exercise. In fact, it was one of these boys, Quaco, the only survivor, who was to return to Cape Coast in 1766 to continue the educational process which Thompson had so diligently pioneered.

It is not clear whether or not any African scholar understudied Thompson, or served as his assistant in the school. If there was

one, then it makes it difficult to explain why the school closed
down on the departure of Thompson. It seems probable that when
Thompson returned to England because of ill-health the future
development of the school came to be closely related with the
Company. The fact that there was no trace of the Rev. Thompson's
school by the time Quaco returned was proof, perhaps, of the lack
of interest which the Africans might have shown in his work.[65]

On his return to Cape Coast from England, Quaco decided to
open a school in that town, primarily to teach the mulatto
children.[66] No sooner had he started teaching a group of children in private than the President of Council, Gilbert Petrie,
pleaded with him to take on the task of teaching children in
the Castle. Accordingly, Quaco reopened the Castle school to
the mulatto boys and girls; later he took on some of the " rougher
kind "—a reference possibly to the non-mulatto children (but more
probably to children of non-Christian parents). Philip Quaco's
school made slow progress. The selection of pupils was limited,
and the only children who were attending this school and who
might have been of pure African stock were four children who
were " the children of gentlemen "[67], a reference perhaps to the
growing section of African merchants and entrepreneurs. Enrolment in the school in the Castle also remained small throughout
the eighteenth century, never rising above sixteen. Between 1766
and 1789 the figure varied between 0 and 16. Indeed, there was
only one pupil in 1770 and 1771, no pupils in 1772 and two
pupils in 1775.[68]

Some writers of the social history of the Gold Coast have pointed
to Quaco's many setbacks as explaining the small size of his class
and the relative failure of his school in making progress. James
Swanzy, who had been living in Cape Coast between 1789 and 1799,
in his evidence before the Parliamentary Commission of 1816
testified to the fact that Quaco in his youth " used to do his duties
incomparably well ".[69]

It is true that Quaco's own countrymen might have shown a lack
of interest in his school. It is also true that the Missionary Society
which had sent Quaco over had, in a period of twenty-two years,
sent only two letters to him—a fact which would have disconcerted
any person.

It is often urged also that Quaco's unpopularity was partly due
to the fact that he had forgotten his mother tongue while he was
in England. If this was the case then it would have made communication between him and his countrymen impossible, and this
may have angered the Africans at Cape Coast. The Society for
the Propagation of the Gospel had urged him in 1769 " to endeavour

to recover his own mother tongue ".[70] It does not seem at all likely, however, that a man who was fully grown before setting foot on English soil could have completely forgotten his native language. Even Amo and Capitein who had left for Europe at a relatively early age, and who were there for many years, did not seem to have forgotten their mother tongue on their return to the Gold Coast. It is possible that a plausible reason for Quaco's obsession for speaking English was the fact that his wife was European, and he was consequently more prone to communicate his ideas in English than Fanti.

Quaco himself was a pleasant man; he was once described as " a man all of whose life was one great mass of obedience, perseverance and diligence . . . a truly educated native, with a strict adherence to the laws, customs and usages of his country as long as they are not repugnant to freedom, justice and humanity . . . a man who when seriously ill preferred to use native medicine ".[71] It becomes a little difficult, therefore, to understand the reason why such a man who set so much store by the customary usages of his country did not " re-learn " his mother tongue, even if he had forgotten it while he was studying in England. It seems more likely that the failure of Quaco's school arose largely because of lack of funds. Quaco's salary, indeed, had been in arrears of £369 at the time of his death.[72]

At that time many African teachers and headmasters had to supplement their salary with trading. Quaco himself had to do some trading in the course of his work to help maintain himself. When this was made known to the Committee of the Missionary Society (his employers), he was reminded in a letter to him that he had " painfully departed from the duties of his function by engaging so deeply in mercantile concerns ".[73] It is interesting to note that this " part-time trading " was to persist right through the nineteenth century. The Rev. Wharton of the Wesleyan Mission at Cape Coast had to write to the Missionary Society Headquarters in 1872 about " a regular system of trading carried on by a majority of the Mission agents in Cape Coast and one or two other circuits ".[74] Wharton called this a " pernicious system which had been progressing in a quiet and somewhat covert manner ever since permission was given some years ago to the wife of one of the school masters who had found commerce to be a more profitable concern than school teaching ".[75] The Rev. Wharton then determined to uproot this " growing evil ", although he felt sure that if he ever did several of his teachers would quit teaching.

It seems, however, that the failure of Quaco's school could be more properly set in the wider context of the general upheaval in the country particularly, and in the outside world generally. The Anglo-Dutch war had been fought in 1780 and this had led to the British defeat at Elmina the following year. The Napoleonic wars were being fought, with their damaging effect on trade and commerce in the settlements. Nearer home, there were the wars and rumours of wars involving the Ashanti and the Fanti on the coast. All these must have had an unsettling effect on Quaco's school.

Such were the distractions that by the 1780s, in fact, Quaco's school was on its last legs, having been reduced to a " pitiable condition ". Its survival is attributable to the timely aid given by a group of officials who had formed themselves into a Dining Club, with the name Torridzonian. They enabled the school to get funds for teaching, clothing and feeding the twelve mulatto children in 1788.[76]

Such had been the precarious position of the school that in the same year instruction was sent to the resident officers of the Company to the effect that fines of 7s. 6d. imposed on members of the Castle who failed to attend Sunday services without just cause should be " appropriated to the benefit of the charity school for mulatto children kept in the Castle ".[77]

However, if the condition of the Castle school was as " pitiable " as some have made it out to be, then it is rather difficult to see why at a meeting in London of the Committee of the Company of Merchants in 1788, " the existence of the school was viewed with satisfaction ".[78] The fact that it was at that meeting that they discussed " the issue of uniforms and books to the scholars—the latter consisting of Primers, Spelling Books, Testaments and Bibles "—makes it even harder to understand the reason why the school should give the Company of Merchants any satisfaction. It could well be, however, that it was the content of the instructions and the organisation of the school generally, that brought hope and encouragement to the Committee.

NOTES

1. Within a few years of their discovery of " A Mina " (The Mine) in 1471, the Portuguese had built a castle to protect their trade in gold. (D. Kimble, *A Political History of Ghana*, p. 15 n. See also A. W. Lawrence, *Trade Castles and Forts of West Africa*, p. 31.).
2. Antonio Brasio, *Monumenta Missionaria Africana*, Vol. 1, p. 502, quoted by D. Kimble, *op. cit.*, p. 62.
3. R. M. Wiltgen, *Gold Coast Missionary History, 1571-1880*, pp. 14-17.
4. *Ibid.*, pp. 14-17, 20-31.
5. Sir Alan Burns, *Colour Prejudice*, p. 22 (note 5).
6. N. R. Burr, *Education in New Jersey (1630-1871)*, p. 6.

7. C. W. Newbury, *British Policy towards West Africa* (Selected Documents: 1786-1874), p. 2. See also C.O. 268/35, John Russell to Doherty, 30.9.1840.

8. *Ibid.*, p. 3.

9. E. D. Morel, *Affairs of West Africa*, p. 22.

10. *Ibid.*, p. 22.

11. S. Baldridge, *White Africans and Black* (*Sketches and Impressions of Fourteen Months in Africa*), p. 112. See also G. E. Ferguson, *Mission to Attebubu*, p. 530.

12. P.P. 1816, Vol. VIIB, p. 12.

13. P.P. 1801-52, *Africa 3*, Miscellaneous Papers, p. 15.

14. K. G. Davies, *The Royal African Company* p. 280. See also E. Tylleman, *Guinea*, pp. 69-70; T. Astley, *A New General Collection of Voyages and Travels*, Vol. II, p. 600.

15. J. A. Wyndham, *Atlantic and Slavery*, p. 24.

16. S.P.C.K., Abstract Letter Box: Summary of Letters from 4833-5263 esp 4996.

17. S.P.C.K., Standing Committee Minutes 1713-18, p. 182. (Wenden appears in the Minutes as Wendy).

18. P.R.O. T/70/66, Royal African Company, 1.7.1720. See also Board of Trade Papers T/70/71, Committee to Governor and Council, 27.11.1794.

19. P.P. 1816, Vol. VIIB (Papers Relating to the African Forts), p. 13. Copy of letters from Secretary of African Committee to Charles Williams, schoolmaster, dated 9.10.1815.

20. P.P. 1801-52, *Africa 3*, Miscellaneous Papers, pp. 170 ff.

21. J. L. Wilson, *West Africa : Its History, Conditions and Prospects*, p. 153.

22. J. Hargreaves, ' Assimilation of 18th Century Senegal ', *Journal of African History*, Vol. VI, 2, 1965, pp. 177-184.

23. *Hague Archives*, Letters and Despatches to and from the Dutch West Indian Company, 15.2.1743. Quoted by F. L. Bartels 'Provision and Administration of Education in the Gold Coast 1765-1865 ' (unpublished M. A. Thesis 1949), p. 85.

24. P.P. 1801-52, *Africa 3*, p. 31 (Swanzy's evidence).

25. *Ibid.*, p. 23 (Cook's evidence, 12.6.1816).

26. Reports from Committees of the House of Commons (Miscellaneous Subjects), Vol. X (1785-1801), p. 742.

27. *Ibid.*

28. For a comprehensive account of A. W. Amo, read N. Lochner, ' Anton Wilheim Amo, a Ghana Scholar in 18th Century Germany ', *Transactions of the Historical Society, Ghana*, 3, 1957, pp. 169-179.

29. J. M. Trew, *Africa Wasted by Britain*, p. 48 ff.

30. *Hague Archives*, Letters and Despatches to and from the Dutch West Indian Company, 15.2.1743. Quoted by F. L. Bartels, *op. cit.*, (unpublished M. A. Thesis, 1949), p. 85.

31. *Hague Archives*, Letters and Despatches, 1.7.1745. Quoted by F. L. Bartels, *op. cit.*, p. 88.

32. B.T. 6/10, p. 245, Tarleton to the Privy Council, 16.4.1788.

33. Report from Committee of the House of Commons, Vol. X, 1785-1801, p. 742.

34. B.T. 6/10, p. 245, Tarleton to the Privy Council, 16.4.1788.

35. B.T. 70/30, p. 8, Melvie to Committee, 11.3.1753.

36. B.T. 70/29, p. 99, Committee to Charles Bell, 4.11.1756.

37. P.P. 1816, Vol. VIIB, pp. 109-110. See also P.P. 1801-52, *Africa 3*, Miscellaneous Papers, p. 109, for List of Annual Grants to Committee (1750-1807).
38. P.P. 1801-52, *Africa 3*, Miscellaneous Papers, pp. 20, 36.
39. P. C. Lloyd, *Africa in Social Change*, p. 191.
40. G. Jahoda, 'Aspects of Westernalisation: a Study of Adult-class students in Ghana'. *British Journal of Sociology*, Vol. XII, No. 1, March 1962, pp. 44-53.
41. The Report from Committees of the House of Commons, 1785-1801, Miscellaneous, Vol. X, p. 742.
42. A. Hannigan, 'The present system of succession among the Akan people of the Gold Coast', *Journal of African Administration*, 6, October 1954, pp. 166-71.
43. Report from the Committees of House of Commons, 1785-1801 (Miscellaneous), Vol. X, pp. 744-5. (Copy of Evidence on the Sierra Leone Company's Petition.)
44. Report from Committees of the House of Commons, 1785-1801 (Miscellaneous), Vol. X, pp. 744-5.
45. *Ibid.*, p. 745.
46. P.P. 1801-52, *Africa 3*, Miscellaneous Papers, p. 11 (List of persons employed by the African Company in 1813).
47. Colin Wise, *History of Education in British West Africa*, p. 1.
48. *Hague Archives*, Jacob de Petersen, 1.5.1744, quoted by F. L. Bartels, *op. cit.*, (unpublished M. A. Thesis, 1949), p. 85.
49. S.P.G. Letters, No. 8 (Quaco, 27.2.1766).
50. P.P. 1801-52, *Africa 3*, Miscellaneous Papers, p. 31.
51. Kay-Shuttleworth, *Social Conditions and Education of the People in England*, Vol. 1, p. 394.
52. Frank Smith, *A History of English Elementary Education (1760-1902)*, p. 41.
53. *Census of Great Britain (1851)*, pp. xxxviii-x1.
54. *Ibid.*
55. C. Birchenough, *History of Elementary Education in England and Wales*, p. 13.
56. *Census of Great Britain (1951)*, Education, pp. xvi-xix.
57. For a full account of Thompson's missionary activities, see his *An Account of Two Missionary Voyages* (London, 1758). Reprinted with introduction and notes by the S.P.C.K. (London, 1937).
58. *The Gold Coast Aborigines*, 8.1.1898.
59. W. E. F. Ward, *A History of the Gold Coast*, p. 194.
60. Thomas Thompson, *op. cit.*, p. 74.
61. *Ibid.*
62. J. J. Crooks, *Records Relating to the Gold Coast Settlements from 1750-1874*, p. 75.
63. S.P.G. Committee Minutes of 21.12.1752.
64. *The Gold Coast Aborigines*, 8.1.1898.
65. F. L. Bartels, 'Philip Quaque, 1741-1816', *Transactions of Gold Coast and Togoland Historical Society*, Vol. 1, Part V, 1955, pp. 153-171, 161-162. See also E. C. Martin, 'Early Educational Experiment on the Gold Coast', *Journal of the Royal African Society*, Vol. 23.
66. R. Wiltgen, *Gold Coast Mission History (1471-1880)*, p. 108. See also P.P. 1816, Vol. VIIB, p. 31. Here Swanzy in his evidence says "only white men's children" were taught by Quaco in Cape Coast Castle.

67. F. L. Bartels, 'Philip Quaque 1741-1816', *Transactions of the Gold Coast and Togoland Historical Society*, Vol. 1, Part V, 1955, p. 157.
68. S.P.G. Nos. 11, 17, 19, 20, 21, 24, 27, 30, 35, 36, 49.
69. P.P. 1816, Vol. VIIB, p. 31.
70. S.P.G. Records, p. 259.
71. *The Gold Coast Aborigines*, 5.3.1898.
72. S.P.G. Records, p. 259.
73. S.P.G. Letter Book, Vol. 1, pp. 61-65, Letter of 25.4.1795.
74. M.M.S., Box 1868-76, Wharton to Secretaries, 28.11.1872.
75. *Ibid.*
76. F. L. Bartels, 'Philip Quaque 1741-1816', *Transactions of the Historical Society of Ghana*, Vol. I, Part V, 1955, pp. 153-171, 161-2.
77. J. J. Crooks, *Records Relating to the Gold Coast of Africa*, p. 75.
78. *Ibid.*

# CHAPTER II

# EDUCATIONAL EXPANSION 1800-1850

During this period (especially before 1830), the Merchant Company continued to show interest in educational activities in Cape Coast in particular, and in the Colony generally. In the 1810s they made strenuous efforts to establish more firmly the Cape Coast School. Like the Sierra Leone Company of the eighteenth century, their aims were " to help train Africans who could either fill offices under the Company, or to promote civilisation in any other way, by means of the advantages which an European education would naturally give to them in their intercourse with their own people ".[1] The Select Committee of 1816, for example, was to report that the Company " took a great deal of pains to get a school master ".[2] In the end they secured the services of " a young mulatto who had lamed his hand, a man qualified to instruct ".[3] In Mr. Charles Williams's letter of appointment of October 30, 1815 his duties were spelled out for him. " On your arrival at Cape Coast, you will put yourself under the order of the Governor and Council, whose directions you are to follow implicitly, and who will give you all the necessary assistance in establishing a school for the instruction of the servants of the Company, natives of Africa ".[4]

The master-designate had qualified " in the art of instruction at the National School ", and the Committee entertained the most confident hopes that he would by diligence and zeal become the instrument of imparting to the African servants the advantages of education. His salary in the first instance would be that of a " writer "—£160 a year. It was the intention of the Company to increase that, provided that " within a reasonable time he succeeded in instructing the persons who would be committed to his care, in the arts of reading, writing and arithmetic, and in other respects conducted himself to the satisfaction of the Company ".[5]

Williams was further urged to make a report every quarter to the Governor and Council of his progress, the aid he required, and the difficulties he came up against. This would be passed on to the Committee for the appropriate action to be taken. It was stressed to Williams that " although the Committee anticipated the best

21

results from his exertion ", they nevertheless desired to inform
him explicitly that should the Committee be disappointed in
their hope, " they would feel it their duty to relieve the public of
what, in that case, would be a useless expense, by giving him his
discharge ".[6]

Williams was to take delivery of a supply of books, slates etc.
which had been recommended by Dr. Bell as necessary for the
instruction of persons under his system of education. Williams
acknowledged receipt of the instructions appointing him a teacher
and expressed perfect satisfaction with the terms and conditions.
He determined also to acquit himself to the satisfaction of the
Company and to acquire a reputation in their service.[7]

It has been recorded in the Parliamentary Papers of 1827, that
a school was first established at Cape Coast by the African Company in 1816.[8] This is perhaps a reference to Williams's school. It is
not possible, however, to assess Williams's part in the educational
experiment of the time because of unavailability of the necessary
records. J. G. Nicholls, however, in his evidence in 1842 informed
the Committee that he had letter books to prove that the Company
had maintained a school at Cape Coast for many years. He added
that there was an annual examination, and reports on the school's
progress were transmitted every year to the Committee.[9]

On the transfer of the several forts to the crown in 1821, a
liberal provision was made by Parliamentary grant, which included
salaries for two school masters, one mistress and four assistants;
the aggregate annual amount was nearly a thousand pounds.[10]
Books and other requisites for the schools, and a supply of clothing
for the children were also provided by the Government. Of course,
the schools were not concentrated on Cape Coast alone. As already
noted, a school master was stationed at Accra for instance. Later,
schools were opened at Dixcove and Anomabu by two assistant
masters.[11]

All the schools at the several places were reported to have been
in a state of " progressive improvement ". However, the ill-health
of some of the teachers coupled with the unsettled state of the
country consequent upon the approach of the Ashantis in the
1820s nearly suspended for a time progress of education. Perhaps
it was this that led the Rev. Dennys on his arrival at Cape Coast
in April 1824 to state that " hardly any improvement was
perceptible beyond what could be expected to be produced by a
common hedge school ".[12] This reference was a possible allusion to
eighteenth century Catholic priests and school masters of Ireland
who were thought to have kept schools out of doors so that the
schools might escape the attention of travellers and officials of the

Government. It is possible, perhaps, that M. G. Jones's quotation
from O'Hagan:

" Still crouching 'neath the sheltering ledge,
Or stretched on mountain fern
The teacher and his pupils met
Feloniously to learn."

was referring to the " hedge schools " in existence at that time.[13]
It could be said, however, that in general at this period, schools
began to spring up in the other important coastal towns. In Accra,
a school had been maintained since 1820, and in 1825-6 it was in
charge of an African teacher, who "although possessing some
qualifications which might make him useful as an assistant,
appeared ill calculated to act as master ".[14] It was also said that his
inattention to his duties was apparent, and opinions were entertained to his prejudice in other respects. The school had 94 boys
in 1820.[15]

## Trade and Commerce

We shall now examine the expansion in trade during the period
1800-1850, for any such expansion must have given a fillip to
educational development and direction. It is said that there was
an increase in trade in the second decade of the nineteenth century,[16]
the main articles of export at this period being palm-oil, ivory,
guinea pepper, guinea grains, camswood, ebony, beeswax, gum
copal, hides and gold dust. The principal exports from Cape
Coast, and Elmina in 1822 were native gold, ivory, palm-oil.
However, from 1823, trade was nearly at a standstill, recovering
a little in 1825. The amounts of gold exported were, in 1822—
10,896 oz., 1823—only 600 oz., 1824—2,011 oz., 1825—17,063 oz.[17]
The gold was only occasionally entered at the custom house,
therefore it was difficult to ascertain the true amount. Moreover,
the amount of trade at that time could not be correctly gauged
because a state of actual warfare or hostile preparation existed
during the whole of the period  since the forts were annexed to
the Crown in 1821. The amount of trade in these years, therefore, gave no real idea of the extent to which it might have been
carried out under more favourable conditions.

There were evasions also, through the Dutch possessions where
no duties were levied.[18] Cape Coast was situated between two of
these possessions, Elmina, seven miles west, and Moree, four miles
eastward, and nearly midway to Anomabu. Moree was not
occupied by the Dutch but their flag was occasionally hoisted there,
and under its protection goods were landed and afterwards

C

removed to their intended destination, which was occasionally Cape Coast town.[19] There had been instances when resistance was made by the native inhabitants when a seizure was attempted by the custom house officer. Duties were also evaded by goods which were being received through Elmina, which at that time was a free port, a fact which induced the traders of all nations, including Britain, to anchor there in the first instance. Indeed, Cape Coast in times of scarcity depended upon Elmina for supplies.[20]

Trade began to improve in the 1830s. In 1831 for instance, imports into Cape Coast were £130,851 and exports £90,000.[21] In the same year, at Cape Coast alone, 67 vessels handled trade worth several thousands of pounds sterling.[22] The items of goods imported into British settlements on the Gold Coast were: Manchester goods, guns, powder, lead, iron-bars, flints, rum, pipes, tobacco, beads, cowries, brass-wire, earthenware, soap, glass-ware, wines, provisions and perfumery. The items exported were gold dust, ivory, dyewoods, palm-oil, groundnuts.[23]

The increase in imports and exports is attributable to the re-opening of communication with the interior, owing to peace with Ashanti in 1831, to the protection afforded to traders throughout the entire country, and generally, to the increased facilities of communication, to the increased and increasing demand for goods, and to several comparatively new branches of commerce such as the trade in maize, palm oil, pepper etc., which had sprung up during the period of tranquillity which had for some years prevailed. Thus, in 1840 imports stood at £423,170 and exports £325,000. By 1841, palm oil, for instance, was assuming some importance, and, in fact, between 1827 and 1841 the quantity of palm oil exported from the Gold Coast to Britain rose steadily from 248 to 2,137 tons at an average value of £35 per ton.[24] And gold remained one of the most important revenue-earning items of trade.[25]

There was also considerable internal trading, largely because, with the cessation of the Ashanti war, paths into the interior had been opened. The kings of Ashanti and Dwaben,[26] for instance, had pledged themselves "to countenance, promote and encourage the trade of their subjects with Cape Coast Castle and its dependencies to the extent of their power ".[27] Many contemporary visitors to the Colony and Ashanti have noted the briskness of the trade and the wide range of articles displayed for sale. Cruikshank noticed " there was not a nook or corner of the land to which the enterprise of some sanguine trader had not led him; every village had its festoons of Manchester cottons and China silks, hung upon the walls of the houses, or round the trees in the market place . . . . one is at a loss to conceive whether there is any room for buyers among such a nation of pedlars ".[28]

One thing that stood in the way of smoother internal trade and commerce was the relatively poor condition of the roads and paths at that time. The cry was for more and better roads. This cry was to persist right up into the second half of the nineteenth century. " If a road was properly cleared leading direct to the interior from the coast," stressed a local newspaper in the 1880s, " the merchant of the coast could proceed direct there with his merchandise or open up trading stations there."[29] If that was done large quantities of ivory and other important articles of export in those regions, which could not be reached or brought down to the coast, and which were allowed to rot day after day, could be sent down to the coast and shipped to Europe.

The main centres with which Cape Coast did some trading (and their mileages from Cape Coast) were: Elmina (7 miles), Anomabu (11 miles), Dixcove (60 miles), Accra (75 miles), Kumasi (160 miles). And it took two hours to travel from Cape Coast to Elmina, and nearly twenty-four hours to Accra.[30]

Despite all the odds the Africans had to face (e.g. poor roads) the merchandise continued even in the last quarter of the nineteenth century to possess the same amount of fascination for the African minds as those of the English.[31] It was thought that the African traders were good traders, and their use of gold dust, for instance, was something approaching monetary use by the middle of the nineteenth century. The Select Committee on the West Coast of Africa was to report that " the people of Cape Coast were traders. Men and women all trade, the men went to Wassa, Aowin (at the back of Appolonia), to Ashanti and other distant parts . . . the natives in pursuit of a widely-extended traffic have a constant personal intercourse with the interior ".[32]

Nevertheless, the limited extent of the money economy, the largely undeveloped methods of inland transport, the limited range of goods produced and of demands to be satisfied, the corporate system of land ownership, and the whole network of social obligation, which set limits upon individual acquisition of property—all these were factors which were to impede economic expansion. But expansion in trade and commerce, limited as it was during the first half of the nineteenth century, was to have its effects on the growth of population. Into Cape Coast, for instance, came men from the north of the Gold Coast and from the Ashanti region of the country and from other coastal towns in search of work, and others came even from far away Sierra Leone. All these were factors which helped to influence the rate of educational growth and expansion in the Cape Coast area in the second half of the nineteenth century.

## The English Educational System

We shall now examine the extent to which the educational system in England was brought over into the schools on the Coast. We have already indicated that in 1815, when Charles Williams was appointed the school master of the Cape Coast Castle school by the Committee of the Company, he was informed that on board the ship proceeding to West Africa was a supply of books, slates, etc. recommended by Dr. Bell as necessary for the instruction of persons under his system of education. Mr. Williams was to employ the " Madras system "[33] in order to be able to remedy the short-comings which were so noticeable in the teaching done in the school. (In 1792 whilst Dr. Bell was the Superintendent of a Military Orphan School at Madras he employed and found the services of an eight year old boy helpful and efficient in teaching the younger pupils to write the alphabet in sand. Dr. Bell then, generalising from this instance, and considering the plan to be of almost universal application, ardently developed his idea. And on his return to England in 1796 he urged the adoption of his system as the most effectual means of rapidly extending popular instruction.)[34] The curriculum of Williams's school was, therefore, to be patterned on European lines and references were made to monitorial teaching methods.

An examination of the structure, organisation and curricula of contemporary English Monitorial Schools will enable us to assess the extent to which that system was " exported " into the educational system of the period before 1850.

The monitorial system was so called because of its use of monitors. The system originated from Joseph Lancaster. He opened a day school in 1796, and two years later his scholars had numbered about a thousand. In his perplexity to be able to provide sufficient teachers, he invented the plan of teaching the younger children by the older.[35] Under the technique of this system a master would teach a number of older and, if possible, brighter lads, each of whom would then seek to teach a small group of his subordinates, and by means of the monitorial organisation, a single school master could give instruction to hundreds of pupils.

There were variations of this system from school to school, but its essential features were that on a child's admission to school, a monitor taught him (together with nine other pupils); when he was absent, one monitor ascertained the fact, another found out the reason; a monitor examined him periodically and when he made progress a monitor promoted him; a monitor ruled the writing paper, a monitor made or mended the pens; a monitor had charge of the slates and books, and a monitor-general looked after the other monitors.[36]

Thus, in the monitorial schools, the master appeared to be left free to organise, to reward and to punish, and to inspire the monitors. The master was in sole charge of the school; he taught only the monitors, who were, in their turn, to pass on the instruction which they had received.

Because of their privileged position in this system, school masters had to measure up to certain standards of behaviour. The teachers (masters) were themselves taught. As Francis Place explained: " you would never succeed in education in general without arrangements to instruct teachers; they might be instructed with great facility, but they must be well instructed; they must be moral and competent persons, or they will not succeed, and good teaching will be delayed ".[37] In the charity schools particularly the teachers had to be churchmen. Also, they had to be strictly more than twenty-three years of age, and were expected to pass an examination in the principles of Christian religion. They were expected to be good, humble, and have an aptitude for teaching a fair writing hand, and an understanding of arithmetic.

But these were ideals not to be easily achieved. Lancaster and Bell had hoped that their monitorial system would provide a cheap, easily applied and rapid method of teaching the poor the basic elements of instruction. But those who entered teaching were generally persons who had tried other trades and had failed. These comprised semi-skilled craftsmen, shopkeepers, clerks. It is noteworthy that all these were occupations which called for a knowledge of reading, and writing, or offered opportunities to acquire such knowledge. At that time, teaching was regarded as a " respectable second best," although there were a few who thought they had a call to teaching as a religious duty.

In a balanced description of the Charity School another writer has noted the impossibility of denying that the masters and mistresses of the day were, as a body, ill-equipped for their work, or that they conducted themselves and their school satisfactorily only when they were subject to constant supervision and inspection. Among them were ignorant, lazy, dishonest and incompassionate men and women. However, in many cases, the masters tried to carry on their work faithfully and efficiently against the most serious of educational handicaps, those of a narrowly limited period of schooling and irregular attendance.[38]

In England it was perhaps in the 1830s and 40s—when it was

fully realised and insisted upon that education should be extended
to the poor through the medium of voluntary religious societies,
and that this education should be suffused with morality and
religion—that it became apparent that the chief need was for a
supply not only of efficient teachers, but also of religious and
humble ones.

It could be said, however, that in England (unlike the Gold
Coast where Training Colleges were conspicuously absent throughout most of the nineteenth century) teacher training, in a sense,
had assumed some importance after 1805 when Lancaster, for
instance, set up a department attached to his school at Borough
Road for the training of senior monitors who would take charge
of monitorial schools.[39] Lancaster, however, overran himself and
this proved to be " an exceedingly expensive establishment ".[40]

In the monitorial schools the pupils had first to learn to say
the catechism by heart distinctly and plainly. Catechising did not
mean " the bare asking of the questions and hearing the pupils
repeat the answers. . . . The clergy must condescend to be at the
pains of giving them an easy explanation of every part of the
catechism, to ask them the same question in other words, to
furnish them with plain texts of scriptures, to confirm them in the
doctrine they learn, and then close every instruction of the
catechism with some short exhortation for their delectation and
encouragement ".[41] Mrs. Trimmer has also explained that " once or
twice a week the scholars are catechised—that is they stand up in
classes and answer in rotation the questions in the Church
catechism and explanations of it. They learn, perhaps, besides,
chapters, prayers etc. by heart, and are sometimes taught
psalmody ".[42]

In addition to catechising, the pupils were at first taught to
read in a spelling book; the lessons consisted mainly of sentences
collected from the scriptures, most of which were in figurative
language. As soon as the pupils showed some measure of proficiency in reading and spelling they were made to attempt reading the New Testament " from beginning to end ". They were then
put to reading the Old Testament, and they had to go through that
in the same manner, generally, without regard to anything further
than improvement in the art of reading.

Much was done to inculcate moral training and habits of good
behaviour. Illustrations for teaching purposes were largely drawn
from the Bible and the catechism. In fact, it was once urged in
Lancaster's monitorial schools that " of the religious books, the
Bible alone, without note or comment should be read in the
schools ".[43] Of course, this was resisted by some on the grounds of

its being " incompatible with the principle on which the schools were founded ".[44] In all this, as in direct religious instruction, the master taught generally under the ministers' superintendence.

Before we indicate the extent to which, at this period, the schools in the Colony adopted some of these features, we shall examine further some methods employed in teaching subjects such as Reading, Writing and Arithmetic in contemporary English schools.

Reading was one of the chief ends of the monitorial schools : " Reading simply meant the power to recognise words and to string them together orally. The customary method was to begin with the alphabet and then learn to read by means of spelling. . . "[45] Reading was graduated. Pupils had first to learn to read and spell all monosyllables and monosyllabic words, then they proceeded to disyllables. Similarly, all syllables and words of two letters had to be known before they dealt with three-letter words, and when it came to reading of sentences, care was taken that these did not make too good sense, for fear that the children would memorise them rather than concentrate their attention on the individual words.[46]

Birchenough explains how reading of monosyllables went : " suppose the sentence was : ' the way of God is a good way '. This was first copied on slates, then from dictation, every word being spelled alphabetically. When the class stood up to read, the passage was attacked in the same way : T-h-e the, w-a-y way, o-f of, G-o-d God etc. It was next read in pauses : The way-of God-is-a good way : then it was read again without a stop. Then it was " spelt off book " thus : The t-h-e, way w-a-y etc. After- wards it was written from dictation, the monitor only pronouncing the words. As a further means of maintaining attention each boy would be required to spell only one letter of a word, and if any missed his turn, he lost his place in the class ".[47]

A typical syllabus runs as follows : Class I learns to read the alphabet and to trace the letters on sand. Class II spells and writes words and syllables of two letters, and writes them on slates. Class III spells and writes words and syllables of three letters. Class IV spells and writes words and syllables of four. Class V spells and writes words and syllables of five and six letters, and begins to read words of one syllable. Class VI speaks and writes words of two syllables and reads short passages containing disyllabic words. Class VII spells and writes words of several syllables and reads longer passages. Class VIII reads from the Bible.[48]

Writing and Spelling were combined with Reading, and in the early stages a sand tray was used. The pupils began with straight lines : I. H. T; then angular lines as in A, V, W; and then circular lines such as O, U, C. In the advanced classes, writing was based on special passages with moral purpose.

At this time Arithmetic had a relatively inconspicuous place in the curricula in England. Generally, it was taught only after pupils had shown proficiency with Reading and Writing. Arithmetic was also graduated. Class I learnt to cipher and to combine figures. Classes II to V learnt to add, subtract, multiply and divide simple numbers respectively. Classes VI to IX learnt the same rules for compound numbers. Class X learnt reduction, practice and the rule of three.[49]

Arithmetic was also taught laboriously. The figures were learnt by copying them. The teacher read out the sums to the class, then read out the full method of working it as well as the result of each step of calculation. The pupils then wrote down the answer as the monitor dictated it. In contemporary English schools, when the pupils had sufficiently practised this, " their skill was tested and those who were successful were promoted to a new group, and to a different kind of sum ".[50] There were, as already noted, twelve broad divisions, " starting with the learning of numbers, and proceeding through the simple and compound methods of addition, subtraction, multiplication and division to rule-of-three and practice ".[51]

The system of monitorial instruction itself met with a mixed reception in England. It tended to stress standardisation almost to a fault. By this system, according to one writer, " the squads of children goose-stepped to their stations, and they returned to their benches in the same measured manner. Singly or in concert they rose on command, and they sat down on command. They looked, listened and spoke on order; they removed their caps and showed their slates on order;—one might readily imagine that they scratched their heads on order. . . . It was a technique fraught with repetition, drill and rote, a hocus pocus whereby teaching and learning were reduced to a hollow formula ".[52]

This system had also a unique form of punishment and reward. Pupils who had done some " wrong " had their neck draped round with a heavy wooden slab, sometimes their legs were shackled and they were made to hobble to the point of exhaustion. On the other hand, children who merited praise were given cards of eulogy, tickets worth money at the school exchange, and occasionally, the honour of holding some office in the classroom or school.[53]

However, by the middle of the nineteenth century, this system was becoming unpopular in England, their methods had grown mechanical, and the catechising of the clergy had become perfunctory. " By this system of teaching the teacher was being induced to depreciate his social position for little else was required of him other than an aptitude for enforcing discipline, a nodding acquaintance with mechanical details for the preservation of order, and that sort of ascendancy in his school which a sergeant-major is required to exercise over a batch of raw recruits before they pass muster on parade."[54] Moreover, the meagre curriculum with reading as the chief accomplishment, their mechanical methods applied to unskilled assistants, and even their cheapness—all these conspired to fossilise the elementary school and make it unprogressive.

Nonetheless, it was a workable system. The method of teaching, rigid as it was, appeared to offer satisfaction to the pupils' love for activity with its constant change and movement. The system also brought out certain truths in child psychology. Pupils, like all children, like to be praised and rewarded and promoted; children love to hold office and feel responsible; children relish any activity which could bring about measurable results. All this the pupils had, and in abundance. Little wonder then that many English people of the day were impressed by it for " they saw that wild, turbulent, neglected and almost ruined children were suddenly converted to submissive, orderly and quiet habits ".[55] The monitorial system was also the first attempt to grapple with the difficulty of the shortage of teachers. Its abandonment came about largely because the role of the teacher began to be viewed as that of a moral regenerator and guide among the poor and ignorant, and not that of an ill-paid hireling drill-master.[56]

## The Monitorial System and Cape Coast Schools

To what extent was this system introduced into the structure and organisation of the educational system of Cape Coast before 1850? There is little doubt that the monitorial system had its advocates, even in the last quarter of the nineteenth century, among some educationists of the time. The Rev. T. B. Freeman, a Wesleyan minister at Cape Coast—a man of mixed West Indian descent once described as " a thorough Englishman in upbringing, education, tastes and pursuits . . . who laid deep and broad the foundations upon which stand today the splendid and extensive Gold Coast and Lagos Missions "[57]—had pleaded that the appointment of monitors could help solve the problem of the shortage of teachers. In order to keep up a supply of trained youths he urged that in the principal schools at the heads of " circuits ", each member should have an eye to selecting the most promising boys, fit to become monitors and irrespective (sometimes) of the actual wants of the school, to place them in that position and lead them on to future usefulness as teachers, giving them small wages of one or two dollars per month each to silence the claims of their parents who would otherwise take them from school to begin to earn a living.[58]

Freeman's plan appeared to have answered well the purpose for which it was designed and the expenses did not exceed five or six dollars per month on an average for each circuit.[59] Freeman, doubtlessly, saw in the monitorial system many essential features, namely its cheapness, character-training, as well as an opportunity to turn such monitors into pupil teachers who could later become qualified teachers. He believed that if a system such as the one he was advocating was not evolved, and if they did not lay hold of suitable lads whenever possible, and " hold them in hand ", the pupils might leave school prematurely to earn a living in the stores of merchants and petty retail traders. When that happened, he felt certain that the boys would lose their piety and would thereby become doubly lost to the church. Freeman's enthusiasm led him to employ " more monitors in the Wesleyan schools than were necessary ".[60]

However, in the period before 1850, no reliable records are available concerning the schools in the Cape Coast area to indicate the prevalence of the monitorial system, or which pupils (by name) were appointed monitors, or whether any of them were girls. The much famed African, Kwegyir Aggrey, was one of the pupils known to have been a monitor in the 1880s in the boarding school run by the Rev. and Mrs. Dennis Kemp, and he went to his first teaching job at the age of fifteen.[61] It would also be of interest to find out whether or not any other such monitors later on did assume important positions in the country.

It seems likely, however, that the system of appointing monitors was not practised on as large a scale as that done in contemporary English schools. The schools of Cape Coast, Anomabu, and Accra were comparatively small in size. The Castle School in 1822, for instance, had some 70 pupils only, supervised by two headmasters and three teachers. The ratio of pupils to teachers was, therefore, fourteen to one. In the schools on the coast, generally the size of the institutions did not make that system really necessary. If the system was adopted at all, it must have been copied on a rather limited scale. Only a handful of pupils of outstanding ability could have been chosen to assist in the classroom. But there is no actual evidence of this.

However, when the number of pupils in the Castle school, for instance, rose to 165, the staff also rose to six—the ratio of pupils to teachers, then, being about twenty-eight to one. It is likely that as the ratio of teachers to pupils dwindled over the years, some form of appointing monitors might have become necessary. And if African traders and merchants were helping to finance the schools,[62] as it has been suggested, then the employment of extra teachers should not have posed too serious a problem to warrant the appointment of monitors.

It seems probable, then, that the monitorial system was not employed in Cape Coast to any appreciable extent. Indeed, the reports of educationists at the time did not usually make specific mention of the system. What the records indicate, however, is that there was a system of grading of the classes, an essential feature of the monitorial system. Of course, the grading of classes is not necessarily a monopoly of the monitorial system—it was simply an expedient measure intended to make teaching reasonably easy.

A Report on the Cape Coast school in 1826, for instance, stated that, of the ninety scholars, twenty-two were in the first class, eighteen in the second, and the others nearly equally divided in the remaining three classes.[63] The Report explained that the first class had been from four to five years at school; the children in the second class had not been at school more than three years. These two classes spoke English tolerably well.[64] The third class could not speak English, although they understood it; the other two classes could neither speak nor understand it.[65]

And in 1844, a Report on the Castle school by the Colonial Chaplain made mention of pupils whose ages ranged from eight to seventeen, the first three classes comprising 110 boys.[66] No mention was made in this Report of the fact that the classes in English were divided into six, and the Arithmetic class into ten— a feature of contemporary nineteenth century monitorial structure.

It has been indicated by writers of educational history that, in the schools in the Colony generally, and in the Castle school in particular, the curriculum corresponded to the instructions in contemporary English schools for the poor; that emphasis was placed on religious instruction, by means of which it was hoped to instil into the pupils godly principles; that reading lessons were done by the alphabetic spelling method; that the Catechism was the principal reading book, and that with writing even, only special passages with moral purposes were chosen.[67] How far is this true?

There is little doubt that the Madras system, or Dr. Bell's system of instruction was introduced in the first decade of the nineteenth century. The letter of appointment of Charles Williams to the headship at the Castle school (October 30, 1815) had informed him that he was to take delivery of a supply of books, viz. Arithmetic Tables for Madras schools, Sandboards, etc.—all recommended by Dr. Bell, who was the exponent of the Bell system of instruction.[68] The fact that this consignment of books included one hundred copies each of the Sermon on the Mount, Church Catechism and Psalters, lent support to the idea that religious instruction was at the core of education at the time. Reading, Writing and Arithmetic were to be taught with diligence and zeal by him.[69] And in 1836, during Admiral Campbell's inspection of the Castle school he recorded that the main subjects taught were Reading, Writing, Arithmetic, Grammar and Geography.[70]

It was soon to become apparent that Reading and even Writing were largely based on passages with moral purpose. Bartels has indicated that of the five specimens available for his inspection three were quotations from the Bible about the Crucifixion and the Resurrection, the fourth from the speech of Theoderic, King of the Goths, and the fifth was a couplet on knowledge : " From Art and Science true contentment flow; For 'tis a Godlike attribute to know."[71] And by 1826, the boys who had been in school for four to five years " read the Bible fluently ".[72] In the Castle school Writing and Spelling were combined with Reading, and in the early stages it was evident that a sand tray might have been used as it was done in contemporary English schools. The letter offering appointment to Charles Williams had mentioned slates and sand boards,[73] which doubtless were to be used in writing lessons. The fact that writing was given such stress in the schools is indicative of the fact that it helped to meet the need for providing clerks in the administrative services in the Castle.[74] The only pupil in the Castle school in April 1770, in fact, had been ear-marked by the President of the Council, John Grossle, in consultation with Quaco, for the post in the Public Office as a " writer " to the Committee.[75] It is probable, too, that by the excessive use of writing the educationists were hoping to buttress religious teaching.

The system of " rewards and punishments " in schools must have been similar to that in the contemporary English schools. Although it is often said that detention of pupils after school was the only method of punishment approaching corporal,[76] nevertheless, there is evidence to suggest that flogging was systematically employed as punishment for talking and for other offences. And in the school days of Kwegyir Aggrey, for instance, " large was the pile of broken rods by the teachers' desk at the close of the day ".[77] Another interesting feature was the fact that the aristocracy of the towns in Cape Coast, Elmina and Anomabu, sent their sons to school, accompanied by a domestic servant to carry their books and to act as the whipping-boy.[78]

Other methods of punishment employed in England were used in Cape Coast, notably the hanging of wooden blocks around the necks of pupils. In fact, this was a common form of punishment in the Gold Coast schools right up into the twentieth century.

However, there was in the Gold Coast Colony an interesting system of rewarding pupils whose progress was satisfactory. Although there was no metallic currency under the old African Company, nevertheless, in 1816 some silver tokens of the value respectively of about 1/6d. and 3/- each were coined by direction of, and sent out by the African Company, as a reward to children for going to school.[79] For when the school was first established the people showed little desire to send their children. The introduction of currency also shows the extent of the Company's interest in the school's growth and development.

It is clear, then, that although the monitorial system itself was not imported in full force into the educational structure in Cape Coast, nonetheless, there were very close similarities in the content of the curriculum, in the grading system, and in the general organisation of the schools. It is also probable that in Cape Coast the length of lessons, the different classes, and the way in which the master distributed his time must have come close to that of contemporary English schools.[80]

There were obvious similarities between the Gold Coast schools and contemporary English schools. Dr. Madden, for instance, in his Report on the affairs on the Coast, has referred to the fact that the schools of the colony were established largely on the British and foreign system.[81] He was by no means convinced that the kind of instruction given was the best that might be desired, or such as was well calculated to enlarge the intellect of the children, or to teach them right habits of thought and action, instead of names and words learned by rote, which left no lasting impression on the mind. He thought there was too much time employed in the school in the mere exercise of memory, too much of a mere teaching of words, a neglect of the knowledge of things, and too little employment of the faculty of thinking.[82]

Dr. Madden noted also that in the boys' school which was kept in the Castle at Cape Coast, there were the same defects in the system of instruction.[83] He examined the children there, and after he had heard the biggest boy in the first class read very tolerably out of the Scriptures, and answered by rote every question put to him out of the Catechism, Dr. Madden asked the boy what his views on slavery were. When the boy answered that slavery was a good thing, Madden's opinion of the " poor " boy was that he had been taught to read and write well, but not to think.[84] Madden regretted to state that that defect in the system of teaching existed in most of the schools he had visited on the Gold Coast, in Sierra Leone and the Gambia.[85]

The boy's views on slavery should not have come as a surprise to Dr. Madden because the boy was living in a society where domestic slavery was part and parcel of it. Moreover, most domestic slaves at that time were not generally shabbily treated.

Nevertheless, Madden imputed the shortcomings to faults in the educational system, and the difficulty of finding fit and proper masters to instruct the children. Indeed, he was himself soon to propose the establishment of a Normal School in England for the exclusive training and instruction of school masters, themselves natives of Africa, who would be destined for these schools.[86] Dr. Madden's proposal is understandable if only because of the lack of teacher-training facilities in the Gold Coast at that time.

It is clear, then, that no attempt was made before the middle of the nineteenth century to introduce all the facets of the Charity School system into the schools in the Cape Coast area. However, available records do not indicate how far English games were played, English music cultivated, and English plays acted. This is an open field for research.

## NOTES

1. Reports from Committees of the House of Commons, 1785-1801 (Miscellaneous), Vol. X, p. 745.
2. P.P. 1816, Vol. VIIB, p. 13.
3. *Ibid.*
4. *Ibid.* Copy of a Letter from the Secretary to the African Committee to Charles Williams, Schoolmaster (30.10.1815).
5. *Ibid.*
6. *Ibid.*, pp. 13-14.
7. P.P. 1801-52, *Africa 3,* Miscellaneous Papers, Appendix No. 7, p. 47.
8. P.P. 1826-27, Vol. VII (Part 2), p. 22.
9. P.P. 1842, Vol. XI, p. 2; par. 13.
10. P.P. 1826-27, Vol. VII (Part 2), p. 22.
11. *Ibid.*, pp. 22-23.
12. *Ibid.*
13. O'Hagan, *The New Spirit of the Nation,* p. 16.
14. P.P. 1826-27, Vol. VII (Part 2), p. 24.
15. *Ibid.*
16. P.P. 1842, Vol. XII, Appendix pp. 1-15. See also P.P. 1842, Vol. XI, pp. 175-176, par. 3364-3367, 3397-3398, and p. 63, par. 1082-1085.
17. P.P. 1816, Vol. VIIB, p. 219.
18. P.P. 1826-27, Vol. VII (Part 2), pp. 28 ff.
19. *Ibid.*, p. 28.
20. *Ibid.*, p. 39.

21. P.P. 1842, Vol. XII, Appendix No. 3. See also P.P. 1842, Vol. XI, pp. 222-223, par. 3949-3953.
22. G. E. Metcalfe, *George Maclean of the Gold Coast,* p. 115.
23. P.P. 1842, Vol. XII, Appendix p. 43 (for List of Exports and Imports for 1831-1840).
24. D. Kimble, *A Political History of Ghana, 1850-1928,* p. 3 (notes).
25. G. E. Metcalfe, *George Maclean of the Gold Coast,* p. 116.
26. P.P. 1842, Vol. IX, par. 3467-3469.
27. T. E. Bowdich, *Mission from Cape Coast Castle to Ashanti,* pp. 143-5.
28. B. Cruikshank, *Eighteen Years on the Gold Coast, V*ol. II, pp. 33, 36. See also D. Kimble, *Political History of Ghana (1850-1928),* p. 3.
29. *The Gold Coast News,* 1885.
30. P.P. 1842, Vol. XII, Appendix No. 3, p. 15.
31. *The Gold Coast Times,* 15.11.1880.
32. P.P. 1842, Vol. XI, par 1088, and par. 3467-34-69.
33. P.P. 1816, Vol. VIIB, p. 13.
34. *Census of Great Britain (1851), Education,* p. xvi.
35. *Census of Great Britain (1851),* p. xv. See also P.P. 1842, Vol. XII, p. 89.
36. Salmon, *Joseph Lancaster,* p. 7. See also A. Meyer, *An Educational History of the Western World,* p. 283; Foster Watson, *The English Grammar Schools to 1660,* p. 16.
37. P.P. 1835, Vol. VII, Appendix and Index, p. 78, par. 923.
38. M. J. Jones. *The Charity School Movement,* pp. 96-109.
39. For a full account of the history of Training Colleges system see R. W. Rich, *The Training of Teachers in England and Wales during the 19th Century.*
40. P.P. 1835, Vol. VII, Appendix and Index, p. 77, par. 861.
41. C. Birchenough, *History of Elementary Education,* pp. 217-218. (He quoted from 'Welsh Piety', 1758.) See also Isaac Watts, *An Essay towards the Encouragement of Charity Schools, particularly among Protestant Dissenters,* 1728, *Works,* Vol. IV, p. 524.
42. Mrs. Trimmer, *Reflection upon the Education of Children in Charity Schools* (1792), quoted by Birchenough, pp. 218-219.
43. P.P. 1835, Vol. VII, Appendix and Index, p. 77, par. 864.
44. *Ibid.*
45. C. Birchenough, *History of Elementary Education,* p. 247 ff. (See Appendix.)
46. *Ibid.*
47. C. Birchenough, *History of Elementary Education,* p. 249. See also William Kempe, *The Education of Children* (1588) cited in T. W. Baldwin, *William Shakespeare's Petty School* (Urbana, 1943), pp. 9-10. It is stated here that " a child should learn the word ' merciful ' thus: m-e-r, mer; c-i, ci; merci: f-u-l, ful, merciful; n-e-s, nes, mercifulness."
48. C. Birchenough, *op. cit.,* p. 248.
49. Educational Record (1822), Vol. XVIII, p. 21; ' Monitorial Schools and their Successors '.
50. F. Smith, *A History of English Elementary Education (1760-1802),* p. 73.
51. *Ibid.*
52. A. Meyer, *An Education History of the Western World,* p. 283.
53. *Ibid.*
54. Educational Exposition, March 1853.
55. F. Smith, *A History of English Elementary Education 1760-1802,* p. 75.

56. Educational Exposition, March, 1853.
57. 'Gold Coast People', 26.10.1891, culled from *The Methodist Recorder*.
58. M.M.S., Box 1868-76, the Rev. T. B. Freeman to Missionary Committee, 2.6.1874.
59. *Ibid*.
60. M.M.S., 1850-1857, Report of the Deputation appointed by Missionary Committee and Conference to examine the accounts of the Cape Coast District, December 1856—July 1857.
61. W. M. Macartney, *Dr. Aggrey, 1875-1927*, p. 20.
62. Colin Wise, *History of Education*, pp. 8, 31.
63. P.P. 1826-27, Vol. VII (Part 2), p. 23.
64. *Ibid*.
65. *Ibid*.
66. C.O. 96/4, Colonial Chaplain's Report, 24.7.1841.
67. F. L. Bartels, 'Philip Quaque 1741-1816', *Historical Journal of the Gold Coast and Togoland*, 1955, Vol. I, Part V, p. 158.
68. P.P. 1816, Vol. VIIB, p. 13.
69. *Ibid*.
70. Cape Coast Archives, 297/135, Campbell to Wood, 8.2.1836.
71. F. L. Bartels, 'Philip Quaque 1741-1816', *Historical Journal of the Gold Coast and Togoland*, Vol. I, Part V, pp. 158-159.
72. P.P. 1827, Vol. VII (Part 2), p. 23.
73. P.P. 1816, Vol. VIIB, p. 13.
74. L. J. Lewis, *Year Book of Education (1956)*, p. 560.
75. Bartel, 'Philip Quaque 1741-1816', *Historical Journal of the Gold Coast and Togoland*, (1955), Vol. I, Part V, p. 160.
76. P.P. 1842, Vol. XII, Appendix No. 3, p. 89.
77. E. W. Smith, *Aggrey of Africa*, p. 34.
78. *Ibid*.
79. P.P. Great Britain, 1842, Vol. XI (par. 1490), p. 84. For a description of the coinage adopted at this time read E. J. Wright, 'Remarks on the Early Monetary Position in Sierra Leone' in *Sierra Leone Studies*, December 1953, New Series 1, pp. 136-146.
80. This pattern can be seen in other places too; K. Nesiah, writing on 'British impact on education in Ceylon' in *Year Book of Education (1958)*, pp. 121-122, states that "the schools were indeed a bit of England, with English games played, English music cultivated, English plays acted, and English manners held in high esteem".
81. P.P. 1842, Vol. XII, par. 9832-9834, 9844-9845.
82. *Ibid*.
83. P.P. 1842, Vol. XII, par. 9832-9834, 9844-9845.
84. P.P. 1842, Vol XII, Appendix No. 3, p. 19.
85. *Ibid*.
86. P.P. 1842, Vol. IX, pp. 666-667, par. 10250.

CHAPTER III

# THE ROLE OF THE ADMINISTRATORS, THE CHIEFS AND THE MISSIONS

Side by side with trade, commerce and population expansion went an expanding British interest in the Gold Coast. By the beginning of the nineteenth century, the onus of the ultimate control of the Coast was on the European traders " as a necessary condition to efficient trading on the coast ".

In fact, before the abolition of the Slave Trade in 1807, the English made little or no attempt to exercise any jurisdiction over the Africans.[1] This was, perhaps, due to the fact that they had absolutely no legal right to involve themselves unnecessarily with the way of life of the African population. It was only when their own interests, convenience or property were threatened by the outbreak of inter-tribal wars, with its consequent interruption of trade, that they took any action at all and made occasional attempts at mediation.[2]

The Ashanti Wars of 1808, 1811, 1816 and 1820 involved the Government in great expense. In 1824 the King of Ashanti, having failed to observe treaty conditions of the 1820 war, invaded Fantiland with 15,000 men. Macarthy, with 1,000 British soldiers and untrained Fantis, was defeated and killed. Two years later, in 1826, the Fanti refusal to pay tribute brought Ashanti down again. The Ashantis were defeated, and peace was made with the Ashanti king, who gave two hostages (his son and his nephew), and a sum of 600 ounces of gold was lodged in the hands of the British authorities as a guarantee for his faithful observance of the treaty.[3]

From 1750-1807 the Parliamentary grant to the African Company had averaged £13,431 per year; and from 1807, the grant had averaged £23,000 a year.[4] It is of interest to note that the expenditure in 1814, for instance, on white men's salaries was £14,789; black men's pay £1,176; pay of Castle slaves £1,692; hire of canoemen and labourers £1,899; fort's repairs and improvements £3,584; customary allowances to free natives £1,390; extraordinary presents to free natives £347; allowances for the sick and wounded, £458; extras, £1,597. Of the total expenditure of £26,938,

39

D

£15,073 (that is, over one-half of the expenditure for the year) was spent on Cape Coast alone.[5]

The implementation of Company and Crown policies was paid for largely by subsidies voted in the United Kingdom Parliament and by taxation in the Settlement. Grants to the Committee of Merchants between 1807 and 1821 varied between £20,000 and £30,000 a year. In 1823, however, the legislature granted £17,800.[6] Civil expenditure in the 1830s also fell to its lowest in the nineteenth century—no more than £13,500 in 1835—and when the Merchants were invited to run the forts again they received only £3,000-£4,000 a year from 1828 till 1843. Of course, the position changed gradually in the 1840s when the settlements were made to rely on customs to pay for local administration, as well as the cost of their own defence.[7] And Nicholls had occasion to point out that " the present Parliamentary Grant is almost insufficient to support the Forts . . . and with the £500 we found ourselves getting into debt every year, so much so that the Committee were themselves personally responsible on several occasions ".[8]

The British administration spent on education the following sums:—From January 1838-March 1840, £15 15s. per quarter; March 1840-September 1840, £17 5s. per quarter. For the three years 1838-1840, then, £345 10s. 8d. was spent on the school, and £257 3s. 5d. on teachers' pay.[9] It is interesting to note that at the same period over £2,409 was spent on military personnel and stores.[10] Thus by the end of the first half of the nineteenth century the Government's educational activities were confined to running the school in Cape Coast Castle and paying half the salaries of the school masters at the British settlements at Dixcove, Anomabu and Accra.

Throughout the nineteenth century the British administration continued to show interest in educational matters. On a few occasions they tried unsuccessfully to induce the Secretary of State to improve the Castle School, and raise the salaries of the teachers. The Colonial Office often came out with the comment that the governors had a tendency to make requisitions not with reference to the means of the community but with reference to their wants.[11]

By the beginning of the nineteenth century, however, the British administration was learning a lesson from their early experience on the West Coast, namely that separate traders were more efficient than monopoly companies and that administration by agents of the Crown was proving expensive in money and lives. They were also beginning to regard it as unnecessary for the protection of national interests.[12] There were even charges of extravagance.[13]

The several forts on the Gold Coast, previous to 1821, had been invested in the late African Company when at that period, they were transferred to the Crown. Only four of the forts had to be retained (the forts at Cape Coast, Anomabu, Dixcove, Accra). In 1821, the African Company of Merchants was abolished, and the control of the several forts and settlements then passed from the hands of this Company into those of the Crown, who then annexed them to the Sierra Leone Government.

Sir Charles Macarthy, Governor of Sierra Leone, was instructed to take over the administration of those forts and settlements. He arrived at Cape Coast in 1822, and proclaimed the assumption of control of the forts by the British Government. This was to have a profound and lasting effect on the pattern of development on the Coast, socially, politically and educationally. He made strenuous efforts to bring peace to the coastal peoples by dispensing justice more impartially.

In 1827, because of the expense involved in the Ashanti wars and the disasters attending the proceedings of Sir Charles Macarthy, the decline of commerce on the Coast induced the Government to withdraw all the public establishments from there and give up the administration of them to a Company of African merchants on the following terms (among others): that £4,000 a year was to be granted to the London Committee for the maintenance and re-parations of buildings and providing a sufficient garrison for the forts; that five of the merchants residing at the forts should form a Council of Magistrates for the regulation of internal affairs of the forts, and exercising all such powers as might legally be conferred upon them for the preservation of the peace, the protection of the forts, and the repression of the slave trade within their limits and influence.[14]

Sir Charles Macarthy's role in the establishment of British imperial influence is noteworthy. Although he had had definite instructions limiting his powers to the administration of British law and (as far as the Africans were concerned) strictly and ex-clusively within the forts themselves, Macarthy's enthusiasm in-duced him " to disregard the directions, and a kind of irregular jurisdiction had grown up, extending itself far beyond the limits of the forts by voluntary submission of the natives themselves, whether chiefs or traders, to British equity ".

Despite the fact that Parliament was full of praise for him for a job " practically and necessarily and usefully done ", they recommended the appointment of a Judicial Officer to be placed at the disposal of the Governor, " to assist, or supersede, partially or entirely, his judicial functions ". It was this that brought to the scene George Maclean[15]—a man who was to do so much towards the expansion and perpetuation of British justice—a man who was able to create social order out of social chaos.

It was this remarkable feat of Maclean's that made possible the Bond of 1844, the Bond by which Fanti chiefs bound themselves to mould the customs of their country to the general principles of English law.[16] In this Bond, the good sense of values of the chiefs and peoples comes clearly to the fore. For it is the only living document which bears permanent testimony to the fact that, but for the express recognition, acknowledgement and consent of the chiefs, the British could have had no claim in law to administer the first essentials of a constituted community, namely, the protection of individuals and of property.

In this Bond the Fanti chiefs and elders acknowledged the power and jurisdiction of the British and declared that the first objectives of law were the protection of individuals and property. They also admitted that human sacrifices and other barbarous customs were contrary to law. They promised that murder, robberies and other crimes and offences would be tried and enquired of before the Queen's Judicial Officers, and the chiefs of the district, and that they would endeavour to mould the custom of the country to the general principles of English law.[17] Of course, thirteen years before the signing of the Bond, in 1851 in fact, under Governor Maclean, a tripartite treaty of Peace and Free Commerce had been signed between the English and the Fanti on the one side, and Ashanti on the other. It can be said that with this peace treaty was started the constitution of the Council of Government as an arbitrator to the natives, and the extension of British influence might be said to have begun.[18] It could also be said that one major aim of making treaties with the chiefs was to solicit their assistance not only to help to relinquish the slave trade, but also to secure grants of land for cultivation.[19]

At this time, an interesting item of expenditure that was being made by the British Government was described as " Black Men's Pay ". This comprised the stipends or gratuitous allowances to the kings or caboceers and other free natives who were subjects of the British nation. In 1814 alone, this item accounted for £1,176, that is, about 5% of the total expenditure.[20] These chiefs and natives were expected, in return, to give whatever help they could to the British administrators.

This practice was questioned in the 1820s. For instance, Mr. Sewell, who was for many years resident as a merchant in the Colony, found it objectionable in so far as the chiefs considered the grant as a matter of right, and not as a reward for services performed, or as an incentive to future exertions.[21] In 1825 the annual amount of pay to native kings and caboceers was £548, reduced in 1826 to £481, which was distributed as follows : Cape Coast chiefs were given £223; Accra, £101; Anomabu, £98; Dixcove, £57.[22] Mr Sewell recommended that presents should be made to those chiefs who might be found to exert themselves in preserving the tranquillity of the country, in promoting commerce, and in affording facilities for obtaining a more intimate knowledge of the interior. He thought also that presents should be judiciously selected, and must not consist of such articles as had formerly been sent out, for instance, a heavy chariot, a gold repeater, and a turning lathe, nor of articles of clothing, such as a full dress military or naval uniform.[23] Sewell was also of the opinion that some of the chiefs thought that the English had made presents out of fear, and the arrogance of some chiefs was on the increase, to the extent that sometimes the presents were received with great indifference.[24]

The political developments prior to the second half of the nineteenth century gave considerable boost to trade and commerce, and this development, as well as peace with Ashanti, must also have had considerable effect on the educational activities of the time. For instance, in 1820, Joseph Dupuis, Consul of the British Government for the Kingdom of Ashanti in Africa, made a treaty with the King of Ashanti, by which the King bound himself not to destroy the town of Cape Coast, nor allow a gun to be fired in the town, nor suffer his troops to commit any act of hostility or degradation therein on the inhabitants or on their property.[25] This treaty and others which aimed to establish a peaceful trading settlement must have had considerable influence on the development of contemporary educational activities.

As British political interest widened, an attempt was made at enrolling sons of chiefs into the schools so that on the completion of their courses they might look after British interests. Indeed, the Sierra Leone Company of the latter half of the eighteenth century had also expressed the belief that by helping to train chiefs' sons, " when these youths succeed to power there would be a fair prospect of their carrying into effect in the countries which they would respectively govern, plans more or less similar to those inculcated in England, and pursued in the Colony."[26] This view was to be re-expressed by a British M.P. some one hundred and fifty years later. Explaining the reasons why sons, relatives and nominees of chiefs should be encouraged to be educated, W. Ormsby Gore emphasised the point that " education for the masses of Africans could not really succeed unless those whom the African recognised as his natural leaders were educated; . . . any permanent general advance of the bulk of African peoples could only be achieved by the leadership of their own chosen leaders ".[27]

And in the Ashanti treaty of 1820 the Ashanti chiefs pledged themselves to commit their children to the care of the Governor-in-Chief for education at Cape Coast Castle, in full confidence of the good intentions of the British Government and of the benefits to be derived therefrom.[28]

Some have expressed doubts as to whether or not that clause was, in fact, inserted in the treaty. Dupuis, for instance, believed that the British falsely inserted the clause in their copy, because a copy of the original treaty which the Asantehene had shown to him did not include it.[29] It is also possible that the clause might have been inserted in the treaty, but was never observed.[30] Nevertheless, whether the clause was inserted in the original or not, and whether or not it was observed after its insertion, it is noteworthy that some fourteen years later, the Ashanti king was to conclude another treaty under which two young Ashantis, Ansah (his son) and Nkwantabisa, a nephew, were to be sent over to England to be educated.[31]

An examination of the care and attention given to these lads shows the earnestness with which the British authorities regarded the practice of training chiefs' sons and relatives in England. There was little doubt as to the intentions of the British Government in sending them over, for, on the return of the two lads to the Gold Coast, they were made to stay at Cape Coast for nearly eleven years, during which time they lived under the protection of the Government.

On the eve of the departure of the two Africans to Kumasi, they were accompanied by the Rev. Freeman and the Rev. Brooking. And President Maclean instructed them thus: " From what you have seen and heard and learnt, you are fully competent to explain to the King of Ashanti and to the caboceers, captains and people the immeasurable blessings which will surely attend the introduction of practical Christianity."[32] Maclean added that their lives were to be exemplary. They must act uprightly and be orderly and virtuous. They must never attempt to interfere violently with the customs and prejudices of their countrymen, " for the abolition of human sacrifices and other barbarous customs and the removal of cruel and oppressive laws could only be the work of time and any rash and violent attempts at interfering with them would be productive of more harm than good."[33]

Maclean urged them further not to allow a day to pass without devoting a portion of it first to their religious duties and next to the reading of those books with which they had been provided.

They should also keep a daily journal for his perusal and information. They were to " guard themselves against sensuality and drunkenness, and by exerting themselves in the noble cause of Christianity and civilisation, they should prove that they were not unworthy of the trouble, care and expense that had been lavished upon them ".[34]

Governor Maclean informed the two Africans that they would be receiving an allowance of a hundred pounds each every year, part of which was to be used in procuring " such European articles of clothing and luxury as they were accustomed to ".[35] Finally, Ansah and Nkwantabisa were asked to visit Cape Coast periodically—every 20th May and 20th December—so that he could converse personally with them to satisfy himself as to their condition and welfare. Maclean urged them " to endeavour to comply with this ".[36]

The tone of Maclean's farewell address illustrates the extent of the interest the British administration took in sending Ansah and Nkwantabisa to England, the care and expense they were prepared to lavish on the Africans, the level of moral excellence they were expected to maintain, and the obligations they expected the Africans to discharge. By his speech, Maclean also showed his own concern for missionary and educational work.

It came as no surprise, therefore, that in 1843 the Methodist Church in the Colony sent Maclean a congratulatory letter, expressing their gratitude for the " handsome manner in which, in his capacity as Governor, he had at all times supported and aided them in the discharge of their Christian duties ".[37] The Wesleyans further attributed much of their success as a church to the noble manner in which he had used his widespread influence in recommending the church and its operations to the protection of certain kings and chiefs.[38] In fact, Governor Maclean was considered by some Africans to be " more than one hundred Governors ".[39]

There is no doubt that the British administration set much store by the training they had tried to give to the two Ashanti princes. Indeed, it was with great reluctance that Ansah, for instance, was permitted to leave Cape Coast. In his letter asking for permission to visit Kumasi (his home town), he stressed that he felt he had been " singled out from among his people [Ashantis] by Providence to be the instrument in His hands for their salvation ",[40] and that he was " very desirous to assure his father [the Ashanti king] and his tribe that he still cared for them ".[41]

It soon became clear to the British administration that the choice of Ansah for training in England was a mistaken one. For, as a son of the king, Ansah stood no chance of succeeding

to the Ashanti stool—inheritance in Ashanti (as in many other
Akan tribes) descended from father to maternal nephew—owing
to the matrilineal inheritance system of the Akan society. Indeed,
eventually it became obvious that the British Administration had
not benefited much from his training. In the 1870s the Government and the Fantis grew suspicious that he was intriguing with
factions in Ashanti. In 1873 the Fantis beheaded several members
of Ansah's household. In order to save his life, Ansah was sent
to Sierra Leone. On his return to Cape Coast some months later, he
continued to be regarded as a mischievous intriguer; so in 1884, it
was recommended by the Governor and Council that he should
be deported to St. Helena. However, he died at Cape Coast in
November of that year.[42]

The British Administration had desired to utilise traditional
political structures in the administrative process, and to use the
chiefs as the agents or foci of a moderate degree of controlled
social change. In this the British exhibited a clear misunderstand-
ing of the chief's role by wrongly supposing that chiefs were auto-
cratic rulers who could exercise a measure of arbitrary authority
and, therefore, could initiate "social improvements" among their
people. The British also erroneously thought that continuance in
the chiefly office was dependent only upon British approval, and
not upon the extent to which the chiefs discharged traditional
functions. In this respect, it is noteworthy that traditional concepts
of the conservative function of the chiefs were bound to conflict
with British ideas of using them as agents of change, and they
could not carry out the functions expected of them by the British
without at the same time imperilling their status with their subjects.

The case of King Aggrey of Cape Coast illustrates how educated
chiefs themselves could easily fall between two stools. The British
administration expressed pleasure at the installation of Aggrey,
possibly because he was an educated man whom they could use to
achieve their own ambitions, but " the influence of the heathen
chiefs was too great to admit of the choice of a Christian king ".[43]
Some of the non-Christian sections of the community could not
accept for their king a man who by his education and religious
beliefs had " disenfranchised himself from the protection of the
gods ". Accordingly they selected another prince who was considered more suitable for the throne than Aggrey. This prince
was called Kwesi Atta, though there is no record of his installation. Thus there were simultaneously two kings, one largely
supported by the educated and Christian Fanti section of the
community, and the other by most of the non-educated and non-
Christian section. Aggrey, however, proved to be a thorn in the

flesh of the British administration. For after the war of 1863, during which the Fantis and the British were disgracefully defeated, King Aggrey began to lose confidence in the ability of the British Government to protect them. Moreover, when at this time certain Fanti towns and districts, formerly under the British, were unceremoniously handed over to the Dutch, and their inhabitants indirectly threatened with annihilation by the Ashantis, King Aggrey sensed another impending danger. So he tried to win some Fanti Chiefs to his side to help him against the British administration. However, the chiefs refused, and so, single-handed, he pitted his puny strength against the full might of the British administrators.

He refused to recognise the Government's Law Courts, imprisoned people in his own gaols, and would not allow them to appeal to the British courts. He even refused to recognise the Governor, Colonel Coran. In short, King Aggrey's behaviour proved so unbearable to the British administration that in 1866 he was arrested and sent to Sierra Leone. However, three years later he was allowed to return to Cape Coast, but not to take the stool again.

Thus a chief considered efficient from the standpoint of the British administration ran the risk of being removed by his own people, whilst one deemed acceptable by his subjects was liable to be removed or exiled by the British.

Nevertheless, the education that the British tried to give the Ashanti princes is an indication that even before 1850 there was an attempt to continue the practice of sending native children over to England for studies.

It should be stressed again, however, that it was not the British Administration alone that took an interest in training chiefs' relatives in Europe. In fact, in 1843, a Netherlands Minister of State (in charge of Colonial Department) wrote to the Secretaries of the Wesleyan Missionary Society informing them about " two African youths, who were being educated in Holland and who would, in the course of two years, return to their native country ".[44] The boys were named in his letter as Akwasi Buakye, the son, and Kwamina Poku, the nephew of the King of Ashanti, who in 1837 " had placed these children in the hands of Major General Verwer "[45] The Minister stressed the fact that the " Netherlands wanted to be to these children, what Britain was to Ansah and Nkwantabisa ".[46] Moreover, he promised to correspond with the boys when they returned to their country, " on the best mode of ensuring their own welfare and of promoting the philanthropic and Christian views, with which they had been educated in Holland ".[47]

At the time, the Minister of State wrote to the Secretaries of the Wesleyan Society " both boys were learning to handle the turning-lathe, and one of them who was remarkably smart, was following public lectures for Civil Engineers at the Delft Academy ".[48] The letter from the Netherlands Minister of State is interesting for many reasons. It brings to light the fact that the education of chiefs' sons was regarded in some European countries as of paramount importance, that the news of the training of Ansah and Nkwantabisa had flashed far and wide as an achievement worthy of emulation, that much store was set by training Africans in mechanics and engineering, and that the educated sons or relatives of chiefs were expected to promote philanthropic and Christian views. It would reward study if an attempt was made to follow up the activities of Akwasi Buakye and Kwamina Poku on their return to Ashanti; so far, little is known about them.

Another attempt to educate the Africans came about when the chiefs were persuaded to send their sons to African schools  so that they could receive an education which might enable them to be of benefit to their own people directly if they returned to their families, or indirectly if they remained, by entering into connection with British interests. The schools which the chiefs' sons were to attend were to be of a higher standing than the ordinary schools. It was to be similar to the aristocratic schools which in 1854 were to be set up in Senegal, for instance, for the sons of chiefs. The Fanti chiefs, however (despite the fact that they were receiving grants from the British Administration), gave little or no support to that. It is noteworthy that in India, for instance, her rulers had also resisted a move to set up special schools for their sons, during the first half of the nineteenth century.[49] In Northern Nigeria too, the children of chiefs were among the first to attend schools.

British political expansion helped in clearing the way for missionary activities, which in their turn gave a fillip to educational expansion. Available records of the first half of the nineteenth century indicate that it took a great deal of effort before the Wesleyan Missionaries persuaded some chiefs to appreciate the need for schools. The journals of the missionaries of this period are full of accounts of their endeavours in this field.

The Rev. West once wrote to say that when he took charge of the Cape Coast District in the 1850s " there were being educated a few young men at the Mission House, the sons of country chiefs ". It was the Rev. Freeman who had first boarded them. There were " a few young women as well, the daughters of chiefs also being educated ".[50] And a Fanti Wesleyan minister also noted the difficulty he once encountered in persuading some chiefs and their subjects to patronise the schools. He wrote in 1842 : "I found the people so very much prejudiced against schools because the chief had sowed seeds of prejudice among the people."[51]

The Rev. W. Thackaray tells of how he had a long and pleasant conversation with King Amunu (Mr. Fynn of Cape Coast being the interpreter), during which he laboured to show him the powerful advantages of reading and writing. He did this by several illustrations : by comparing the advantages of "sending a letter instead of going oneself, or sending an oral message, pointing out that a letter could not alter itself, a messenger might deceive or forget or mistake or stumble over a stone; a letter could sometimes gain admittance where the writer himself may not ".[52] An African minister (the Rev. Addison) in a letter to the Missionary Committee tells how much of his time had been occupied in the streets and houses of the town " in endeavouring to remove from the minds of the natives the prejudices which had existed against education ".[53]

In due course, the chiefs began to see the need for providing schools. The Rev. Brooking, for instance, has recorded how in the 1840s, many villages felt the need for a school in the Gold Coast Colony. As he passed through a village called Akrofo not far from Cape Coast, many natives followed him to the outskirts of the village and entreated him to send them a teacher. They were themselves building a school-room by communal labour. When Brooking returned later to the village he noticed that the villagers had actually built a school-room with an apartment for the teacher, which they were prepared to furnish at their own expense.[54]

There was another town called Nyankomase where, at the chief's request, a school was to be set up. Such was this chief's interest and anxiety to introduce learning and Christianity that as soon as a teacher was sent to the village, he " immediately sent his own sons there, and intimated that if a night school were commenced, he would himself condescend to be taught the ABC ".[55] By 1850, therefore, demand for schools was being increasingly made by the chiefs of the Colony. Their desire was eminent and they exhibited an aptitude to learn, and were willing to be taught.[56]

However, openings for occupations remained very limited at the time. And the best that the chiefs could hope for their educated sons was for them to become their " private secretaries in constant attendance upon them ".[57] This was one means by which the chiefs tried to provide alternative roles for their children who could not traditionally succeed their fathers. John Ansah, for instance, the eldest son of Prince Ansah (i.e., the grandson of a

former Asantehene) had in 1889 tried to get himself appointed as
Prempeh's ambassador to the Governor, B. Griffith, who refused
to recognise him. He then went back to Kumasi where he was
reported to be acting as Prempeh's Prime Minister. He and his
brother (Albert Ansah) were members of the Ashanti embassy
which went in 1895 to the Secretary of State to establish the status
of Prempeh, the King of Ashanti.[58] The new role for the educated
sons of chiefs could have had its repercussions on the traditional
organisation, for the chief was normally surrounded by his elders
and linguists, the latter of which were his " private secretaries "
to all intents and purposes.

The linguist was not merely a spokesman to the chief. He was
the chief's confidant and aide-de-camp, the chief's mouthpiece in
every public function and in every judicial proceeding. Thus, it
was not to be expected that the linguist would be easily replaced
by the educated sons of chiefs. It seems more probable that,
despite the interest which the chiefs were patently displaying in
the educational process, and despite their faith in the value of
literacy, individuals who could be chosen for such a traditional
role as a linguist were not likely to be those who had necessarily
been to school.

It has been hypothesised by some that where Western educational institutions had been transferred to traditional societies
members eligible for chiefly or other traditional office would be
reluctant to use those institutions until such time as extended
European political control exerted pressure on modes of traditional
recruitment.[59]

It appears, however, that it is only direct pressure on modes of
traditional recruitment which will induce adoption of a new institution. Indeed, potential office holders will not use the new institution (education) when they are unsure of the aims and purposes
which the new institution is expected to achieve. Institutions often
set before people ideals they should pursue and ways to pursue
them, and if a potential office holder knows clearly the aims and
purposes of the new institution, and if the aims synchronise with
his own interests, he will be willing and ready to use it.

It is possible that the post of linguist was later kept separate
from that of the " private secretary ". The former might have
continued to serve the traditional functions, and the latter might
have served as a link between the non-literate chief and the
British administration. Continuance of the office of chief could
become directly dependent upon the discharge of traditional
function, and also upon the capacity of the chiefs to maintain

satisfactory relations with the European administration. The rise and fall of King Aggrey is illustrative of this hypothesis.

It was, however, to become common practice in the 1850s onwards for the British Government—as the Colonial Office had to admit in 1879—to deport kings (educated or uneducated) who stirred up disturbances or otherwise made themselves troublesome. By 1852 Governor Hill had deposed the King of Assin and had imprisoned him for life, because he was said to have taken a bribe from the Asantehene and had declared that he would throw off his allegiance to the English.[60] He was restored to his position four days later, after the Assin chiefs and captains had given an undertaking for future good conduct.[61] King Aggrey, the two kings of Sekondi and the King of Dwaben with some of his chiefs[62] were among those deported by the Government.

It was in the second half of the nineteenth century—in fact, during the 1870s—that considerable heart-searching was done both in the Colonial Office and among Gold Coast administrators concerning the proper relationship that should exist between the chiefs and the Government. " The summary treatment of Aggrey, though it emphasised that the British were not prepared to tolerate any local challenge to their authority, had left the jurisdiction of the chiefs still undefined, and had certainly not solved the problem of how to secure their voluntary co-operation in the new order."[63] The issue as to whether or not the chief's continuance in office was dependent more on his capacity to maintain satisfactory relations with the European administration than upon the discharge of traditional functions did not arise fully in the period before 1850, largely because the political ambition of England was of a limited range. It was in the second half of the nineteenth century that it became clear that the locus of power sometimes shifted from the uneducated chief towards those chiefs who had been to school. It would be of interest to find out whether King Aggrey's bold stand against the British administration induced the Government to prefer other educated men to hold traditional office.

## The Wesleyan Mission and Schools

To understand and appreciate more fully the work done by the Methodists in the educational field generally in the nineteenth century, one must know something of John Wesley's religious and educational philosophy. John Wesley's notion of education centred round his firm belief that all men are brothers redeemed by the love of God and the sacrifice of Christ; to him, therefore, all men are members of one family of whom God is the father. John Wesley believed also that any good education should have its foundations laid in the family.[64] He considered it essential that children should submit without questioning to their parents' and teachers' instructions. He had no faith in large public schools; " parents, if they had any concern for their children's souls ", he once said, " must send them not to any of the large public schools (they are nurseries for all manner of wickedness) but rather to a private school, kept by some pious man, who endeavours to instruct a small number of children in religion and learning together ".[65] Girls and boys must be given equal chance to educate themselves, he thought.

Wesley was not only a theoretician. In fact in 1739, after he had set up headquarters of London Methodism, he started to teach a few children at his own home to learn to read, write and cast accounts. Methodism, however, did very little in the provision of elementary education in England at this time. In fact, it was only in 1836 that attempts were made by the Methodist Society to assess the actual state of education in immediate connection with Methodism throughout Great Britain.[66] Indeed, there was a general awakening by the state and people at this time, following the extension in 1832 of the franchise to a largely uneducated electorate. It was in 1841 that the Methodist Conference also approved the General Plan of Wesleyan Education as a basis for all future operations of education.

The Wesleyans thus seemed to have a clear idea about the type of education to be provided for themselves and the Africans. They preferred to lay stress on a personal religion based on the Bible, an approach which called for certain intellectual requirements, and they believed that the individual must be taught to read and understand and search the Scriptures if he is to be able to make them a personal possession and so achieve salvation.

In contemporary England, many found in the Wesleyan Church the opportunity for the development of talents and the gratification of instincts that were denied expression elsewhere. The close and enthusiastic study of the Bible educated the imagination. " In chapel life working men first learnt to speak and to organise, to persuade and to trust their fellows. And in a world made almost intolerable by avarice and oppression, here was a refuge where men and things were taken up aloft and judged by spiritual and moral standards that forbade either revenge or despair."[67]

Methodism tended, therefore, to emphasise the importance of high standards of personal conduct, and it also helped to inculcate a new sense of responsibility towards social and educational reform. It was thus that Methodism was to play a major part in the early nineteenth century, and it is against this background that the Wesleyan educational and missionary activities in the Cape Coast area may be gauged. It is interesting to note that the Wesleyans came upon the educational and religious scene at Cape Coast only two years after they had made recommendations in England that English schools should be established wherever practical, and only two years before they formed an Educational Committee charged with the general supervision of all matters relating to Wesleyan education.

Before the Wesleyans came upon the Cape Coast scene in 1835, the Castle School at Cape Coast was certainly flourishing. Governor Charles Macarthy, for instance, had shown considerable interest in that educational venture. He had looked to the school to help widen the horizon of the pupils as well as prepare them for baptism, clerking and housework.[68] In fact on his orders books whose value totalled more than £350 had been brought to Cape Coast between 1822 and 1824.[69] These books had included 240 psalters, 240 prayer books, 120 Bibles, and 120 Testaments.

After Macarthy's death the Rev. A. Denning took over the teaching and divine service in the Castle School. He was successful in securing fourteen educated Africans to attend public worship in the Castle on Sundays.[70] These Africans were to emerge as the Bible Band which provided the foundation members of the Methodist Church in Ghana. The Rev. Joseph Dunwell, on his arrival at Cape Coast in 1835, spoke about " the advanced state of civilisation to which many of the natives have arrived ".[71]

Thus, by the 1830s when the Wesleyan Missionaries arrived at Cape Coast, there was already a school there. The Rev. Dunwell found also on his arrival in 1835 " an excellent school of about 140 boys who were very astonishingly proficient in Reading and Writing ".[72] Notwithstanding, the Rev. Dunwell conceived the idea of establishing a school connected with the Mission House where he could employ a good native schoolteacher for £3 per month, and two or three assistants for considerably less to be paid in cloth.[73] And by 1838, another Wesleyan minister, the Rev. T. B. Freeman, reported that there was in addition to the Government Castle School, a Wesleyan school, and a " good female school which ought to be continued ".[74]

In 1841 the Rev. T. B. Freeman reported again that there were nine Mission schools in the colony, three of which were female schools.[75] The school masters were appointed by the Wesleyan missionaries, and the salary of the teachers varied between £15 and £30 a year, according to their abilities. And all the school masters were Africans.[76] In 1844 the Senior Assistant Teacher at Cape Coast was receiving 13s. 9d. a month, and his four boy assistants were sharing 22s. 0d. between them.[77]

It seems rather strange that although there were Wesleyan schools as far away as Saltpond (about twenty-two miles away) and even Accra (some ninety miles away), the Wesleyan missionaries by the 1840s had established no school at Elmina (only seven miles away from Cape Coast). Elmina then had one Government school of about seventy pupils. The master was appointed by the Government on a salary of £100 a year. The assistant school masters were all Africans.[78] In fact, the first time that one reads of an attempt by the Wesleyans to open a school at Elmina was in 1872. At that time when the Rev. Rose went to open a school he was gratified to learn of " the deep interest several gentlemen had taken in it, by canvassing and sending the list of names of 80 boys and 27 girls ".[79]

By the 1840s, however, the Wesleyan schools were producing remarkably satisfactory results and the Cape Coast schools were gradually increasing in numbers.[80] At this time, too, George Maclean sent a warm report on the state of education at Cape Coast : " The people are beginning to see the advantages which young men who have been educated derive therefrom and the consideration in which when well conducted they are held, are growing more and more anxious that their children should also share in those benefits . . . they will themselves support the schools."[81]

It is often said that the main purpose that brought the Wesleyan missionaries to the Colony was not to open schools, but primarily to preach the Gospel; and that the Missionaries opened up schools not chiefly to spread literacy or to train their pupils to earn a living, but rather because of their conviction that schools were one of the best means of spreading Christian faith.[82] One is inclined to think that the critics of missionary education seem to want to have it both ways. If the missionary had considered it his duty to develop the material as well as the spiritual aspect of the African, the cry would have gone up that he was engaged in farming or trading, and that he should concentrate on his chief duty of evangelisation. And if the missionary had sought to bring spiritual enlightenment only, he would have been charged with neglecting material needs.

## The Basel Mission and Schools

During this period, when the Wesleyans were concentrating on opening schools on the Coast (their schools were at Cape Coast, Anomabu, Dominasi, Accra, Winneba, Manso, Saltpond, Komenda, Abasa), the Basel missionaries, who had established their headquarters in Accra by 1835, were moving to the much healthier Akwapim Ridge, largely because of the heavy toll on the lives of their missionaries in Accra. The Basel Mission opened up a boys' school there some two years later, and in 1847 they established a school for girls.

In their belief in the usefulness of Boarding Schools, the Basel mission opened such schools at Akropong and Christianborg between 1845 and 1850; the one for girls which was already established at Akropong was transferred to Aburi in 1854. Also, in their zeal to train African assistants for their schools, the Basel mission established a training school for catechists at Akropong in 1848 and another one at Christianborg two years later. These two institutions were, however, amalgamated in 1856 and sited at Akropong. It was this school which was re-organised into a theological seminary, with a four-year course, the first two years of which were mainly devoted to preparing for school work.

At this time also, two of the boarding schools had two advanced grades added to the curriculum, giving them a six-year course in all.[83]

As Carl Reindorf,[84] who was a product of the Basel mission system, has said, it was from among the boys of the Basel day and boarding schools that the most intelligent ones were selected every year. These were allowed to enter the middle schools. An active boy thus trained had no difficulty in obtaining an apprenticeship in a mercantile business or in a Government office. Other boys might become farmers or learn a trade in the industrial shops; but this was not the object with relation to the middle schools. Young men who had passed three classes of the middle schools and wished to become teachers or catechists, received a fourth class of preparatory teaching, which enabled them to enter special seminaries. And those who desired to become teachers had to stay in a teachers' training school connected with the theological seminary.

By the 1850s the Basel mission had published an elementary book of grammar and a dictionary, which helped in the production of primers and reading books for the schools. This also helped to make teaching more methodical, and it was this development which made it possible for the Basel mission to turn out at this time a steady stream of trained catechists and teachers, who helped to spread Christianity to practically every part of Akwapim.

It was the belief of the Basel missionaries that they could be more successful in their work both as missionaries and educationists in the rural areas, since they held that, unlike the urban areas where the indigenous merchant class and heterogeneous populations depended predominantly on an exchange economy, the rural areas would be more congenial to their purposes. They tried

E

to make a frontal attack on the traditional life of the small communities by placing the emphasis on establishing boarding schools, and thereby cutting their pupils off from the traditional setting, and by making vernacular the medium of instruction.[85]

It must be added here, however, that the African ministers and catechists were the main channels through which ideas on education passed to the chiefs and people, and their part in the exercise should not be minimised. An African Wesleyan minister (the Rev. Edward Addison), for example, wrote in the 1840s of how much of his time was "occupied in the streets and houses of the town in an endeavour to remove from the minds of the Africans the prejudices which had existed against education ".[86] And de Graft, also, after visiting many villages in 1841 wrote: " The chiefs and peoples all around have expressed the desire of getting teachers. Delay in answering their call is dangerous."[87]

By the mid-nineteenth century, therefore, there were in existence in the Colony generally, three types of schools: Government schools, Wesleyan schools and Basel mission schools. The Government and the Wesleyan schools were concentrated on the coastal towns, while the Basel mission concentrated on the rural areas. The early history of African education was certainly inextricably interwoven with the history of Christian Missions and the Government.

But modern education of the African began in the broader sense of the term almost from the beginning of European contacts. The traders were obliged to educate some Africans in European styles of life, but in due course the missionaries took on the task of educating the Africans. But whereas the interest of the trading companies lay in educating clerks first and foremost, the missionaries were rather more concerned with training teachers, artisans, and preachers. The chiefs played a useful role in this. And, as the second half of the nineteenth century was to show, it was the mission schools which became the chief agents of spreading Christian civilisation in the Gold Coast Colony.

NOTES

1. R. Robinson and J. Gallagher, *Africa and the Victorians—The Official Mind of Imperialism* (London, 1965), pp. 27-33.
2. W. W. Claridge, *A History of the Gold Coast and Ashanti*, Vol. I, p. 229.
3. P.P. 1842, Vol. XII, Appendix No. 3, p. 9. See also P.P. 1842, Vol. XI, p. 12, par. 205, pp. 80-81, par. 1414-1427, par. 1474-1478.
4. P.P. 1816, Vol. VIIB, pp. 109-110.
5. P.P. 1842, Vol. XII, Appendix 36. See also P.P. 1842, Vol. XI, p. 666, par. 10247-10248.

6. P.P. 1842, Vol. XII, Appendix No. 3. See also P.P. 1842, Vol. XI, p. 6, par. 101.
7. *Ibid.*
8. *Ibid.*
9. P.P. 1842, Vol. XII, Appendix 163, p. 59.
10. *Ibid.*
11. C.O. 96/4, Maclean to Hill, 18.2.1844.
12. C. W. Newbury, *British Policy towards West Africa, Selected Documents 1786-1874*, p. 2.
13. *Ibid.*
14. P.P. 1842, Vol. XI, p. 6, par. 101.
15. For a full account of Maclean's contribution see G. E. Metcalfe, *George Maclean of the Gold Coast (1801-1847)*.
16. C.O. 96/4 gives a full account of the 1844 Bond.
17. J. B. Danquah, 'The Historical Significance of the Bond of 1844', *Transactions of the Historical Society of Ghana*, 3, 1957, pp. 3-29.
18. C.O. 267/171.
19. C. Buxton, *Memoirs of Sir R. P. Buxton*, p. 448.
20. P.P. 1816, Vol. VIIB, p. 96.
21. P.P. 1826-7, Vol. VII (Part 2), pp. 26-27.
22. P.P. 1816, Vol. VII, pp. 89-91.
23. P.P. 1826-27, Vol. VII (Part 2), p. 27.
24. *Ibid.*
25. J. Dupuis, *Journal of a Residence in Ashantee :* Appendix III. See also W. W. Claridge, *History of the Gold Coast and Ashanti*, Vol. I, pp. 322-324.
26. Reports from Committees of the House of Commons, *Miscellaneous, 1785-1801*, p. 742. See also K. A. B. Jones Quartey, 'Sierra Leone's Role in the Development of Ghana 1820-1930' in *Sierra Leone Studies*, N.S., No. 10, June, 1958.
27. W. Ormsby Gore, M.P. on 'Education in the British Dependencies of Tropical Africa', *The Year Book of Education* (1932), p. 764.
28. Claridge, *op. cit.*, Vol. I, pp. 297-299.
29. J. Dupuis, *Journal of a Residence in Ashantee*, p. 35.
30. T. E. Bowdich, *Mission to Ashantee*, p. 416.
31. W. W. Claridge, *op. cit.*, Vol. 1, pp. 410-412. See also A. E. Southon, *Gold Coast Methodism—The First Hundred Years*, p. 37.
32. M.M.S., Box 1859-62, Governor Maclean's address.
33. *Ibid.*
34. *Ibid.*
35. *Ibid.*
36. *Ibid.*
37. M.M.S., Box 1843, letter to Governor Maclean from Leaders of Methodist Church.
38. M.M.S., Box 1842-1845, letter to Governor Maclean from Leaders of Methodist Church.
39. Daniel West, *The Life and Journals of Rev. D. West*, p. 162.
40. M.M.S., Box 1859-1862, Otu-Ansah's letter, 11.4.1860.
41. *Ibid.*
42. D. Kimble, *A Political History of Ghana, 1850-1928*, p. 269 (note 2).
43. M.M.S., Box 1859-1867, West to Secretaries, 16.3.1865.
44. M.M.S., Box 1842-1845, letter to Secretaries, 23.6.1843.
45. *Ibid.*
46. *Ibid.*

47. *Ibid.*
48. *Ibid.*
49. B. T. McCully, *English Education and the Origins of Indian Nationalism,* p. 185.
50. M.M.S., West Africa 1859-67, W. West to B. B. Boyce, 12.2.1863.
51. M.M.S., Box 1842-1845, de Graft to Secretaries, 4.3.1842.
52. M.M.S., Box 1835-41, the Rev. W. Thackaray's *Journal,* 22.3.1840.
53. M.M.S., Box 1847, Addison's letter to Secretaries of Wesleyan Committee, 13.5.1847.
54. M.M.S., Box 1835-41, Brooking to Secretaries of Missionary Committee 9.4.1841.
55. M.M.S., Box 1835-1841, Brooking to Secretaries, 9.4.1841.
56. M.M.S., Box 1835-1841, de Graft to Secretaries of Missionary Committee, November 1841.
57. B. Cruikshank, *Eighteen Years on the Gold Coast,* Vol. II, p. 113.
58. D. Kimble, *op. cit.,* p. 284 note (i).
59. *Ibid.,* Ch. 5. See also C.O. 96/25, Despatches of 23.10.1852 and 27.10.1852 from Hill.
60. C.O. 96/25.
61. *Ibid.*
62. C.O. 96/126.
63. D. Kimble, *op. cit.,* p. 458.
64. John Wesley, *Works,* Vol. VII, pp. 86-108. See also A. H. Body, *John Wesley, and Education,* especially pp. 145-158.
65. John Wesley, *op. cit.,* p. 83.
66. Minutes of Conference, 1836, Vol. VIII, p. 90.
67. G. M. Trevelyan, *British History in the 19th Century, p.* 160.
68. C.O. 267/56, Cape Coast Archives.
69. S.P.C.K., Reports 1823-25.
70. C.O. 267/93, Denning, 18.9.1826.
71. M.M.S., Box 1835-41. Dunwell to Secretaries, 2.1.1835.
72. *Ibid.,* Dunwell's letter of 8.1.1835.
73. *Ibid.*
74. *Ibid.,* Freeman to Secretaries, 10.1.1838.
75. *Ibid.,* 23.1.1840.
76. *Ibid.*
77. H. O. A. McWilliam, *The Development of Education in Ghana,* pp. 6-7.
78. P.P. 1842, Vol. XII, Appendix 3, pp. 90-92. (C. H. Bartels's Report of 18.3.1841 to the Committee on the West Coast of Africa.)
79. M.M.S., Box 1868-1876. Rose's reply to Laing, July, 1872.
80. M.M.S., Box 1842-1845. Martin's letter to Secretaries of December, 1845.
81. M.M.S., Box 1835-1841. Maclean to Colonial Office, 28.1.1840.
82. C. P. Groves, *The Planting of Christianity in Africa,* Vol. II, pp. 3, 224, Vol. IV, pp. 106, 316.
83. F. H. Hilliard, *A Short History of Education in British West Africa,* pp. 64-65. See also Noel Smith, *The Presbyterian Church of Ghana,* p. 168.
84. Carl Reindorf, *History of the Gold Coast and Ashante,* pp. 22-23.
85. A. W. Wilkie, 'An Attempt to Conserve the Work of the Basel Missions on the Gold Coast', *International Review of the Missions,* pp. 86 ff.
86. M.M.S., Box 1847, Addison to Secretaries, 13.5.1847.
87. M.M.S., Box 1835-41, de Graft to Secretaries, November, 1841.

# CHAPTER IV

# FIRST ATTEMPTS AT AGRICULTURAL AND INDUSTRIAL TRAINING

The point has been made earlier that no attempt was made before 1850 to introduce all the facets of the monitorial system into the schools in the Cape Coast area. Indeed, there were modifications. By 1850 positive attempts were also made to introduce other subjects such as industrial, agricultural and trade training to offset the apparently bookish nature of education. The real remedy for Africa was believed to lie in her fertile soil. It was urged that " missionaries and schoolmasters, the plough and the spade should go together ".[1]

In the questionnaires[2] sent round the schools in the British settlements before the mid-nineteenth century, an attempt was made to find out how far the educational system had been successful. There were questions to ascertain the quality of pupils, their mental qualities, or any tendencies in them towards obstinacy. Some of the questions tried to find out whether there were any trades or model farms, and to what extent the model farms, if any, were being developed.

In this way, the administration was beginning to find out the true position of existing educational institutions prior to 1850. The questionnaire provided perhaps the yardstick against which any future educational adventure could be measured. Moreover, the fact that some of the questions aimed to find out whether the funds at the disposal of the Missions were sufficient for the various school establishments, was proof also of the Government's desire to help the missions in their educational efforts.

It was, perhaps, on the basis of the questionnaire that in 1847 the Educational Committee of the Privy Council set out what appeared to be the first general statement of British educational policy in the Colonial areas.[3] The policy aimed, among other things, to inculcate the principles and promote the influence of Christianity; to accustom the children to habits of self control and moral discipline; to diffuse a grammatical knowledge of the English language as the most important agent of civilisation, to teach writing and arithmetic and show how the latter could be applied

59

to the wants and duties of a peasant in order to enable him to economise on his means, and give the small farmer the power to enter calculations and agreements. It also aimed to teach children how health could be preserved by a proper diet, cleanliness, ventilation and clothing, and by the structure of their dwellings, to give training in household economy and the cultivation of the cottage garden and common handicrafts, to teach improved systems of agriculture to avoid exhausting virgin soil.

The educational policy regarded as essential that pupils should be taught " the mutual interests of the country, and her dependencies, and the domestic and social duties of the coloured races ". A reorganisation of the structure and composition of the curricula and the classes was recommended. There were to be special elementary schools where pupils would be taught basic skills. On reaching the age of thirteen the boys were to enter Day Schools of Industry for six years during which period they would learn trades, gardening, and agriculture; and the girls, housewifery. Towards this end, three model farms were to be established, this being intended to help pupils develop habits of industry. Teacher training schools were to be opened up. The curriculum was to have an agricultural slant. Among the subjects to be taught were Chemistry and its application to agriculture, Agricultural Economy, Surveying, Practical Mensuration, Farm Management, and treatment of diseases.

The Committee rightly stressed that these were broad aims only, and that there should not be an indiscriminate introduction of its various aspects. The background of each colony had to be considered before any part of their recommendations were implemented. Credit must also be given to the Committee for their considered opinion that the work of education should be related to the conditions of life.

This scheme, broad as its aims were, had the support of influential opinion in England. For, a century earlier, in England, schools of industry had blossomed under the impact of the industrial revolution and the rise of the factory system. Their results had been widely acclaimed. Children had been admitted from an early age in England, and had been taught to spin, wind, knit, plait straw, sew, cobble shoes, and do gardening jobs. And the sale of the products of their labour had paid the expenses of the schools, as well as providing the children with meals.[4]

In the Gold Coast too, missionaries, administrative officers, and a few Africans had seen the need for giving some measure of agricultural and industrial training. A fuller examination of this will help correct the assumption often made regarding the imputed indifference of European missionaries and administrators towards these experiments in the education process. This examination is also necessary to disabuse those who hold the view that the prevailing academic education was an imposition on the Africans. We shall endeavour to show, on the other hand, that whilst European educationists were doing their utmost to introduce alternative forms of education, the Africans themselves were pressing for an academic type of education.

It must be pointed out at once that industrial training was a feature in many developing countries. In 1847, for instance, in New Zealand an Ordinance (No. 10 of 1847, dated October 7, 1847) had stated that " only those schools in which religious education, industrial training and instruction in the English language formed a necessary part of the system were to receive aid from public funds ".[5] Some policy makers, like Earl Russell, were even prepared to state that only a very " small part of reading and writing should be taught to children in the colonies. Rather, boys should be taught to dig and plough; as well as the trades of shoemakers, tailors, carpenters, masons; the girls should be taught to sew and cook, wash linen and keep clean rooms and furniture ".[6]

Of course, the recommendations of the 1847 Privy Council Committee were not fully implemented in the Gold Coast. The Committee, in their work, probably lost sight of the fact that the personnel and the machinery for implementing its recommendations would not be easily come by. Nevertheless, as H. S. Scott put it in 1938, " it is sad to think that eighty years ago there was actually in circulation a document which might and ought to have inspired those who were responsible for the administration of the Empire to do something which was, in effect, begun half a century later ".[7]

By 1840, little had been done to establish agricultural, industrial, or trade activities in the schools in the Cape Coast area. Nevertheless, the Europeans such as Dr. Madden, Governor Maclean, Governor Winniet, and the Revds. T. B. Freeman and J. Beecham showed considerable enthusiasm for some of these projects. Dr. Madden, for instance, recommended the establishment of a model farm at each settlement where a school existed, and in the towns, to afford the masters the facilities for teaching each child some trade or calling, at the same time as he was sent to school to learn to read and write. He believed that all the instruction that could be given them without teaching them habits of industry was of little value.[8]

The early missionaries also tried to emphasise training in agricultural and elementary technical skills.[9] One Wesleyan missionary of the time believed strongly that " if ever the Africans were to be raised in a temporal point of view, and if ever agriculture were to be introduced to the people as a whole, then agricultural and farming projects should be undertaken in the schools; that was not only the opinion of the missionaries and some of the leading men in society, but also the opinion of every European on the coast ".[10] These men were of the opinion that when the Africans saw what the land would produce, and when they were made acquainted with the profits accruing, that would provide sufficient inducement for them to take up agriculture.

It was this conviction as well as an inspiration he had had during a visit to the " plantations " established by the Danish Mission at Christiansborg that led, for instance, the Rev. Freeman, a Wesleyan missionary, to plead with the Secretaries of the Wesleyan Society in England for money to be given him to purchase a model farm five miles from Cape Coast, " to teach his boys practical agriculture ". And Freeman, during this inspired visit to the Danish Mission at Accra, is reported to have stated that the Wesleyan Mission ought to have some such establishment if only because it had a much greater hold of the country and a much more prosperous work.[11] The Rev. Freeman argued that although the farm would cost about £500, and its running expenses would also be £500, the sales from the farm (coffee, corn, yams) could easily meet these expenses. He was also certain that the management of the plantation would not place an extra burden on the hands of the missionaries.[12] The farm contained 100 acres of good land, eleven acres of coffee growing, some even bearing about 24,000 seedling plants fit for transplanting. It contained also a cottage for the supervisor, a carpenter's shop, blacksmith's shop, a number of small houses for the workmen and everything which was necessary to render it the most complete model farm. The owner, Mr. Swanzy, was prepared to accept £500 for it, although he had sunk £1,500 in it.[13]

So much did the vacillation of the Home Mission distress the Rev. Freeman that the following year (1842), he wrote again stressing the many advantages which could be derived from the purchase of the model farm. " The plantation, when acquired, could not only support itself ", he stressed in his letter, " but could also give them a surplus to assist in supporting the Mission schools, and any other future establishments."[14] " Not only myself ", Freeman pointed out painfully, " but also the merchants at Cape Coast, with President Maclean himself, and all my brethren (Christians) are aggrieved at the difficulties which we are encountering to secure money to purchase the farm."[15]

Freeman's belief was that the school (like the Church) should be both Christian and industrious; that its members, the young and the old alike, should develop a sense of the value of steady and vigorous industry, and to this end, they should be introduced to large-scale agriculture on well-organised plantations. The schools associated with agriculture would give a lead to the church members and the community generally.

Freeman had eventually to take over the farm without getting the approval of the Missionary Committee.[16] In place of a European resident manager, whom Mr. Swanzy, the owner, had employed at a salary of £150 a year, he posted one of his catechists with a yearly salary of £35. He also reduced the number of workmen to thirty at a monthly wage of 6s. each in order to effect the economy the Committee wished to see.[17] Two years later Freeman was authorised by the Committee to break up any small and unpromising schools at minor stations, and remove a certain number of the children to Cape Coast and other principal stations, where as boarders they could be more effectively educated than in the smaller schools in their native villages.[18]

In due course, Freeman closed one or two village schools and brought the scholars over into a boarding establishment at Beulah. The pupils worked at stated times on the plantation, and were taught by teachers from the Cape Coast school. Additional land was acquired, and by 1852 there were 4,500 cotton plants, 1,400 arrow roots, 23 olive trees and 225 vines running on 244 yards of trellis, besides cinnamon, black pepper, mango, ginger and other plants. The labour force was made up of about six men who were used for the hard and heavy work such as clearing the land. The twenty-three pupils divided into three working parties lent a hand. Seven boys aged from twelve to fifteen years spent four hours in the morning at school from six o'clock to ten, and two hours in the afternoon from two till four on the plantation, hoeing, cleaning, watering young plants under cultivation or in nursery beds, gathering cotton and other produce and generally training to transfer into the first group. The youngest, six of them, followed a similar programme but of a lighter kind.[19]

In Beecham's evidence of 1840 he expressed regret, as Freeman had earlier done, at the Wesleyan Committee's decision not to purchase the Napoleon Farm. He was of the opinion that it would have been an important arrangement for the employment of the Christian Africans, in teaching them agriculture, and in promoting their interests, and the interests of the inhabitants of that part of the coast generally.[20]

In 1841, when the Rev. William Thackaray was stationed at

Dominasi, he also started an experimental plantation to encourage the adult population to grow cash crops, and the pupils to cultivate an interest in farming. To achieve this, a site was acquired at a rental of £6 a year, and cleared of forest trees and brushwood. About one hundred pounds' worth of agricultural tools were to be supplied to the village chief for distribution to the Africans by the Committee of the Anti-Slave Trade Society. And some three years later a coffee plantation of one and a half acres was under cultivation. So successful did the farm and the school at Dominasi become that the village became a resort for Europeans in Cape Coast during the unhealthy season of the year.[21] The Rev. Thackaray's Dominasi experiment certainly pleased Freeman and many others. Not surprising, then, that on his death it was said of him that " during his brief sojourn in the colony he thoroughly gained the affection of the Africans, and the respect of all who knew him ".[22] The Rev. Freeman also noted that he never knew a person, who had lived and died, about whose eternal safety he felt more entirely satisfied.[23]

It became apparent in due course, however, that model farms could not easily be set up in most of the schools. So in 1850, a few gentlemen " connected with or inhabiting the Gold Coast, and others who saw the increasing necessity and the great importance of procuring cotton from other sources than the United States of America upon which England was mainly dependent ", formed an Experimental Cotton Plantation Association, with the intention of encouraging the cultivation among the Africans in general.[24] By means of this, they hoped that " the broad masses of the Africans would be taught habits of industry, and that occupation would, thus, be afforded those who were idle ".[25]

It is possible that the interest of this Association lay further afield. They might have hoped that perhaps, by this establishment, additional and valuable articles of exportation would be given to small African proprietors, and the agricultural population in the Colony, and eventually cotton might form a considerable item in the exports from the Gold Coast to England. The Rev. Freeman was himself one of the brains behind the project committee which was made up of the " most respectable people among the merchants and inhabitants of the Gold Coast settlement ".[26]

It is also noteworthy that the idea of establishing plantations in the Gold Coast was being advocated strongly by private individuals as well. In the 1840s, one E. I Graham, for example, wrote two letters from Epsom (Surrey) to the Rev. Freeman in an endeavour " to show to the chiefs and people of the country that Agriculture would be more productive to them than selling slaves ".[27] And to this end he was desirous of " establishing by means of private subscription a Native Mission. . . . under the Wesleyan Missionary Society in London ".[28] Available records do not indicate whether or not the proposal materialised.

Governor Winniet, also, had unsuccessfully pleaded with the Colonial Office, for the establishment of technical schools. In 1844 he pointed out that " there was only limited employment for educated boys (as teachers in the schools, clerks in Government and merchandise establishments), and consequently, the results of education, pleasing as they might be, were not so healthy as they would be if they were associated with various branches of mechanical knowledge ".[29] He also stressed the point that " model schools for the instruction and training of boys in the knowledge of various useful mechanical arts were most important desiderata ".[30] The Governor, however, did not make any effective suggestion as to how many more boys could be offered employment; nor was he sufficiently clear as to whether by " mechanical knowledge " he included the tilling of the soil.

As has been indicated elsewhere, it is not at all clear to what extent the respectable people among the Africans themselves helped in the effort to introduce agricultural training in the schools and church farms. H. S. Scott, for instance, has pointed out that " the African declined to accept the indigenous system of training as a foundation for his future education . . . he would regard any suggestion in the educational sphere to build upon the old as tantamount to a refusal to grant him the benefits and opportunities of the purely Western forms of training, to which he not unnaturally attributed the domination of the white ".[31]

By the middle of the nineteenth century, however, as we have noted, a Wesleyan project for the creation of a model farm school at Cape Coast and Dominasi was being seriously considered; and there had also been a recommendation by a Parliamentary Commission for the establishment of a model farm in each settlement and in the towns to afford the masters the facilities for teaching every child some trade or calling at the same time as he was sent to school to read and write.[32]

It is clear then, that when the European educationists (the administrators and missionaries) advocated agricultural and industrial training in the schools, they had at least a fourfold aim. Firstly, they believed that unless Christian education taught habits of steady industry through training in manual work true " civilisation " could never be achieved. Soil-tilling by organised labour on a big scale and selling its products was placed alongside Christianity as an instrument of civilisation. And in this context,

" civilisation " meant visible results, rather than the ideas that would produce them.[33]

Secondly, the educationists hoped by the establishment of farms to provide Africans with a worthwhile occupation on leaving school. Thirdly, they hoped to get supplementary money from the farms to finance establishments such as schools. Fourthly, the farms and large-scale agricultural projects were intended to be an example to the African community generally, and with the Africans' agricultural endeavours, valuable raw materials could be produced to improve home trade. In this way, the British educationists were anxious to use the schools as instruments for achieving economic expansion.

It must be emphasised again that whilst the English educationists were anxious to introduce agricultural and industrial training, the Africans themselves were hankering after academic subjects, mainly because they preferred a type of education that could help them to pass examinations which were, after all, set according to English standards. It is even possible that the Africans also saw through the ultimate objective of the educationists—namely, to make the Gold Coast Colony an eventual supplier of raw materials to Britain, and they were unwilling to encourage this.

Writers of the educational history of the Gold Coast generally do not explain the educated African's aversion to manual work. The important point is that he associated farm work in particular (and many other forms of manual work generally) with slavery. Indeed, the whole contact between Europeans and Africans was coloured by the continuance of slavery and slave-trading even long after 1807. To most educated Africans then, any attempt to free him from the state of slavery should entail not only freedom for his person, but also freedom from the servile work of cultivating the soil for his master. The very idea of cultivating the soil for oneself had the taint of slavery. Because of this background, therefore, if education was to mean much and to tear him away from this slavery, then it should also mean that he was to be free from the cultivation of the soil, and from many other chores performed with his hands.[34]

It seems, therefore, most unlikely that the bulk of educated Africans, especially the Christians at Cape Coast, would be " very anxious "—as the Rev. Freeman would have one believe—to engage in agricultural pursuits, and to request him to render them some assistance by taking out for them, on his return to the colony, a supply of seeds, implements of husbandry, and anything that would be useful to them in cultivating their native soil.

It is more probable that the Rev. Freeman himself wanted the seeds and implements to enable him, as he says, " to establish at the earliest opportunity, two farms as a means of teaching the Africans the best methods of cultivation and of showing them the very great capabilities of the soil ".[35] Of course, Freeman was conscious of this need of the country, but it is equally true that he was anxious to share his life-long love of nature. He was one who derived intense delight from the grandeur of the vegetation in the Gold Coast, and it is said that often did he express his heart's joy as he gazed on scenes of splendid, albeit wild, luxuriance. In his *Journal* Freeman has told of how his joys deepened when the African companions on his travels showed that they shared his enthusiasm.[36]

Thus, it is possible that when the European educationists wrote home for support in the agricultural experiment, as the Rev. Freeman did, they counted on the " verbal appreciation " of the Africans. For, if the Africans were in reality lending their full weight of support to the experiment, then it is difficult to account for the general failure of the scheme. As a Fanti missionary once noted in the 1840s, the Africans might have rather preferred the establishment of small gardens which boys could cultivate, possibly for their own consumption, whilst any extra money that accrued from the sales could be used in meeting expenses of running the school.[37] It is interesting to note that about one hundred years after de Graft's statement, a survey on African education produced on behalf of the Nuffield Foundation and the Colonial Office was to express similar sentiments : " The plans for a primary school should begin with a garden in which there is space for a small agricultural plot, nursery plots, team group gardens, and space for grass, flowers, and shrubs. A common agricultural plot is needed to demonstrate the basic principles of sound agriculture; experimental plots are necessary if the primary school is to be used as a demonstration centre for the district. . . ."[38]

It could be said then, that another reason for the failure of the agricultural experiments was the fact that the European educationists—missionaries, governors and other Europeans—did not appear to have heard the views of the cross-section of the African population on these issues. They had merely assumed that any education that seemed to have an agricultural flavour was bound to generate considerable African demand, especially since the Gold Coast Colony was, by and large, an agricultural community.

With this assumption the European educationists had ignored such vital issues as the kind of groups that were actually running the schools, the groups which were making use of the schools, the use to which education was being put, and the interests of the pupils themselves and their parents.

The failure of the experiment to introduce agriculture and trade into the school system has been given point in some recent studies of educational institutions which attempt to prepare students for an occupation. One major conclusion has been the assertion that there are often discrepancies between the ostensible aims and purposes of the new experiments, and the actual consequences which they tend to achieve.[39] As Friedrich Schneider put it : " Theory will furnish norms, goals, rules, and suggestions for methods. Yet practice can . . . test pedagogical ideas in reality, un-cover their exaggerations, faults, or untimeliness and thus stimulate improvements."[40] In the schools on the Colony then the " actual " consequences did not justify the aims and purposes.

These experiments—especially those undertaken by the Wes-leyans—failed also because the experiment called for constant supervision by those who had wider experience. But missionaries at this time were in short supply. And none of them could be spared to supervise some of the plantations which were as far away as 35 miles from Cape Coast. And at this time the Missionary Committee were also urging the Cape Coast Mission to reduce ex-penditure, especially for travelling. In 1856, for instance, a deputa-tion appointed by the Conference and the Missionary Committee " to examine the accounts of the Gold Coast District for the years 1854-1856 " had reported " a most unsatisfactory mode of keeping the accounts—a misleading and pernicious system of financial management ". And as a result of its findings drastic cuts were being urged " in travelling expenses, and in employing of the large number of paid agents, especially monitors in the Wesleyan schools, etc. ".[41]

Another source of difficulty was that although the missionaries themselves made secular demands for a model farm, they were always preaching to save souls from worldly things. This confusion of " teaching " could have led the Africans at Cape Coast to show disinterest in the Dominasi farm, for example—a fact which the Rev. Freeman reported to the Missionary Committee.[42] For these reasons practical agriculture ceased at Dominasi by the end of the mid-nineteenth century, and the plantation was made over to the chief of the town.

It is to the everlasting credit of the European educationists—whatever their other objectives were—that they tried to experiment and find out what curricula could offer the best balance between the vocational education needed to produce the skills required by a community such as the Gold Coast Colony, and a general education needed for cultural sophistication. It is not clear, though, to what extent they regarded the pupils as an important form of investment which could be rewarding to the national economy. Without doubt it was partly the very limited avenues for employing the educated ones as clerks and sometimes teachers, that led the European educationists to attempt introducing new subjects such as agriculture and industrial and trade training.

NOTES

1. Charles Buxton, *Memoirs of Sir T. F. Buxton*, p. 448.
2. P.P. 1842, Vol. XII, Appendix No. 3, pp. 87-117. (Report by the Investigating Commission for the Select Committee.)
3. *The Year Book of Education (1938)*, pp. 706 ff.
4. H. C. Barnard, *A History of English Education from 1760 to 1944*, p. 8. But M. A. Dalvi has, however, indicated in his *Historical Survey of Commercial Education in England 1543-1902* that "for a long time in England there was preference for classical studies and not commercial or industrial subjects".
5. P.P. 1847-48, Vol. XLVII, No. 130, of 9.12.1847.
6. C.O. 202/43, No. 132, Russell to Governor Gipps of New South Wales, 25.8.1840.
7. H. S. Scott, 'The Development of the Education of the African in Relation to Western contact', *Year Book of Education (1938)*, p. 711.
8. P.P. 1842, Vol. XII, Appendix No. 3, p. 19. See also *ibid.*, Appendix 41, pp. 101-104.
9. M. Read, 'Education in Africa: Its Pattern and Role in Social Change', *Annals of the American Academy of Political and Social Science*, CCXCVIII, March, 1955, p. 173.
10. M.M.S., Box 1842-45, the Rev. Allen's letter to Missionary Committee, 10.5.1842.
11. Daniel West, *Life and Journals*, p. 186.
12. M.M.S., Box 1835-1841, Freeman to Secretaries of Missionary Society, November, 1841.
13. *Ibid.*
14. M.M.S., Box 1842-5, Freeman to Secretaries, 17.4.1842.
15. *Ibid.*
16. *Ibid.*
17. M.M.S., Box 1842-5, Freeman to Secretaries, 9.5.1842.
18. P.R.O. CO/96/25, No. 20.
19. M.M.S., Box 1842-5, Freeman's Report on Beulah, 28.2.1842.
20. P.P., 1842, Vol. XI, par. 3646-3648; 7704-7705.
21. M.M.S., District Minutes (1840-65), Freeman's letter to *The Times*, 1.11.1844.
22. M.M.S., Box 1835-41, Freeman to Secretaries, November, 1841.
23. *Ibid.*
24. M.M.S., Box 1850-7, the Rev. T. B. Freeman's *Journal*.
25. *Ibid.*
26. *Ibid.*
27. M.M.S., Box 1842-5, Graham to Freeman, December, 1845.
28. *Ibid.*
29. C.O. 96/4, Cape Coast Archives (20.5.1844).

30. *Ibid.*
31. H. S. Scott, ' The Development of the Education of the African in Re-
    lation to Western Contact ', *The Year Book of Education (1938)*, pp.
    693 ff., esp. p. 697.
32. P.P. 1842, Appendix No. 3, p. 19.
33. T. F. Buxton, *Committee of the House of Commons (1837)*, p. 170.
34. W. E. B. Du Bois has expressed similar sentiments in his *The World
    and Africa*, p .18.
35. M.M.S., Box 1835-41, Freeman's letter to Sir T. F. Buxton, July, 1840.
36. T. B. Freeman, *Journal of Various Visits*, p. 35.
37. M.M.S., Box 1842-5, notes of de Graft of 4.3.1842.
38. *African Education—A Study of Educational Policy and Practice in
    British Tropical Africa*, produced on behalf of the Nuffield Foundation
    and the Colonial Office (1953), p. 99.
39. Stephen Cotgrove, ' Education and Occupation ', *British Journal of
    Sociology*, Vol. XIII, No. 1, March, 1962, pp. 38-39.
40. *Comparative Educational Review*, Vol. IV, No. 3, 1961, pp. 136-139.
41. M.M.S., Box 1856-7. Report of the Deputation appointed by the Con-
    ference and the Missionary Committee to visit and regulate the Mission
    in Western Africa, comprised in the Cape Coast District.
42. M.M.S., 1842-5, Report of 1845.

# CHAPTER V

# GIRLS' EDUCATION AND TEACHER TRAINING BEFORE 1850

It can be said that the position of women in society at any time determines the nature of their preparation for it. In the case of men there has always been a need to train them to earn a livelihood for themselves and their families and, sometimes, to accept public responsibility. The women's first duty in the eighteenth and part of the nineteenth century in England, for instance, was considered to lie " in contributing daily and hourly to the comfort of husbands, of parents, of brothers and sisters, and of other relations, connections and friends, in the intercourse of domestic life, under every vicissitude of sickness and health, of joy and affliction; and in forming and improving the general manners, dispositions and conduct of the other sex by society and example; and in modelling the human mind, during the early stages of its growth ".[1]

In England of the pre-1850 period, the aims of girls' schooling were, thus, not purely intellectual. Domestic skills were constantly demanded for girls from the poor home as a practical contribution for their future home-making. Indeed, Lancaster had even urged the need for female youth to make " all their own clothes, and even those of men and boys—cutting out the garments at first and finishing the work themselves ".[2] It was felt, nonetheless, that household duties must not be allowed to interfere with moral and intellectual cultivation. In traditional African societies also, the aim of girls' training was generally to make them good wives and mothers; and even at a very early age girls were expected to help in running the affairs at home.

It has been said that girls' education almost everywhere lagged behind that of boys, that mothers were usually reluctant to spare their daughters from household work, and that so long as education was thought of primarily as the gateway to types of employment which were only open to boys, one of its strongest attractions to the parent was lacking in their case.[3]

In the Gold Coast Colony during the period 1800-1850, however, interest was shown in education for girls. Although the Basel mission had no girls' secondary school at this time, a girls' boarding

71

school was opened at Akropong in about1850 and later transferred to Aburi in 1854. Long before the Wesleyan missionaries decided to open a girls' school at Cape Coast, one had been started in 1821. The school was under the charge of Mrs. Harriett Jarvis, the widow of an officer of the Company, and she taught mainly needlework. The fact that the salary of the Domestic Science teacher was £200—equivalent to that for an assistant headmaster—is indicative of the interest shown in this subject. Correspondence between Governor Smith and Harriet Jarvis gives an indication of the insistence on Domestic Science teaching. Some of the items listed for the girls were:

> 12 pairs of scissors
> 1 lb. cotton in Ball
> 1 lb. cotton in Hanks
> 1 lb. of cotton in Darning
> 800 Queen's needles
> 200 Darning needles
> 12 Silver Thimbles[4]

One of the main goals of needlework was to help train wives and mistresses for the resident merchants, and it helped eventually to turn out women who were largely " excellent managers in domestic concerns, and good and careful nurses ".[5] Mrs. Jarvis' school closed down some seven years later. But by September 1826 there was a female school at Cape Coast which consisted of twenty-four girls.[6] There were six girls in Class I, who understood the English language. These girls had been at school for between two and four years, and had been taught needlework. They were aged between eight and twelve years. There were two other classes.[7] It is interesting to note that " one half of the girls in the school were coloured, the offspring of Europeans who had been resident upon the coast ".[8]

It is difficult to understand why, soon after his arrival at Cape Coast in 1835, the Rev. Dunwell said he noted the absence of a girls' school.[9] Dunwell has noted also that he realised that this was a much felt need, and that he was much pressed upon by the Africans. " A female school is much wanted and the inhabitants press this subject upon me ", Dunwell wrote in 1835.[10] Dunwell, therefore, had to ask the Missionary Committee to send him any articles of clothing to be given to any girls who might decide to attend his school.[11]

One chief reason assigned for the relative paucity of girls receiving education was the want of clothing. Parents who desired their girls to go to school were obliged to provide them with dress, and many parents either had not the means nor the inclination to supply this.[12] (The girls were often helpful in domestic duties at home.) In Western Nigeria, too, in the second half of the nineteenth century, it was observed that girls' education did not commend itself much to parents : " A little girl from the time she was four became too useful to her parents at home to be spared for the purpose of education. Her services were utilised in conveying water, cooking, and carrying meals."[13] In the Cape Coast area, the British Administration were aware of this need, and in 1822, for example, they ordered the following items for use by the girls in the Girls' School :[14]

> 6 doz. straw bonnets
> 12 doz pairs of shoes (of different sizes)
> 12 doz. pairs of socks
> 6 pieces of pocket handkerchiefs.

Later they ordered in addition " 12 pieces of cloth for frocks, 3 pieces of cotton shirting, 1 towel piece, 1 dozen straw bonnets superior for Sunday attendance ".

By 1836 the Wesleyans had commenced a female school at Cape Coast. There were thirty girls who were taught by the wife of a Wesleyan minister, the Rev. Wriggley. It has been said that to her belongs the honour of opening the first important school of domestic economy for girls in the Gold Coast.[15] On Mrs Wriggley's death some five months after opening the school, Mrs. Elizabeth Waldron took over control. She was a mulatto, the daughter of an Irish employee of the Company of Merchants and an African woman. She taught the girls various branches of Reading and Sewing. The number of girls grew to about forty some four years later. They attended service in the Castle every Sunday, after which they visited the Wesleyan Mission House where they were examined in the Catechism by Mrs. Mycock (who had arrived on January 13, 1840).

The girls made satisfactory progress. They could repeat all the First Conference Catechism well; some of the elder girls could repeat the first three sections of the Second Catechism.[16] Great credit was due to Mrs. Waldron, through whose hands, it has been said, passed many influential women of the time.

Girls' education continued to make progress, and by the end of 1840 Mrs. Waldron had under her charge about eighty girls. In the same year, Mrs. Barnes—Mrs. Waldron's colleague—was also teaching Reading and Sewing to twenty girls at Anomabu, whilst Mr. John Martin was also running a successful school of twenty girls (and sixty boys) at Accra. There were three important girls' schools at this time.[17]

Progress continued to be made in 1841 too. The Rev. Waldron's diary of 1841[18] records the activities and progress of the Cape Coast girls' school in particular :

Feb. 12, 1841 :   The girls' school was ably conducted by Mrs. Waldron.

Feb. 13, 1841 :   The girls and Mrs. Waldron came to the Mission House. Questions were asked from the Conference Catechism, which they readily answered; they read correctly and some wrote a plain hand. We were pleased with them.

Feb. 25, 1841 :   The girls visited the Mission House. Mrs. Waldron examined them. They read and answered questions from the Conference Catechism. Mrs. Freeman presented each of them with a " work bag ", and several medals were also given to the girls in the 1st (upper) class.

Progress was made systematically, and by the end of 1850 foundations had been firmly and truly laid. But there were disturbing factors which, however, continued to check the expansion of the girls' education. Many parents still needed the services of their daughters at home, and they also seemed to value more highly bride-money, and the prestige which their daughters could bring to them on their marrying.[19] It was against such drawbacks that the educationists had to struggle. As further attraction to the girls and their parents, therefore, the educationists tried to board and feed them. The journals of the Wesleyan missionaries are full of reports of the care and meticulous attention bestowed upon the girls.

Some of these educated African girls were to prove to be useful instruments in the missionary endeavours. The Rev. Picot, for instance, has written about the use he made of some of the educated girls in collecting money for " God's work " in Cape Coast. When he found it difficult to collect the yearly subscriptions, he decided to ask " a few good looking, well dressed, well behaved educated young ladies, themselves the point of missionary labour to pump something from the officers ".[20] The Rev. Picot was sure that it would be impolite for a British gentleman " to refuse a lady " who called on him to make a donation.[21]

We have, in previous chapters, noted some factors that led to the expansion of schools in the Gold Coast Colony in the first half of the nineteenth century, the nature of the expansion, the structure and organisation of the educational system, the sort of curricula that was followed, the attempts made to introduce new ideas and experiments into the system, and the growth and development of girls' education. An attempt will now be made to examine the wage structure, facilities for teacher training and the quality of the teachers' work.

During the pre-1850 period, teaching was generally considered in many societies to be an ill-paid profession. In England, for instance, one of the important and significant teachers' complaints was that of low wages. In the words of Francis Place: " [in England] a master may be had at almost any price you please, but you would not have a competent one at a low price ".[22] At the time Place wrote, a master in London in a school containing six hundred children earned about £120 a year, although there were some who earned £80 or £90.[23]

Of course, the absolute amount of the salaries of teachers in England tended to vary according to the local situation of the school, the sex of the teacher, the rank of the certificate the teacher held and (to some extent) the denomination with which the school was connected.

In England the teachers had free houses or had their rents paid for them. Thus, inclusive of Government grants and all professional sources of income and rent allowance, the master in a Protestant school earned about £120 per year, and in a Church of England school £80. Uncertificated teachers in denominational schools earned about £85 and those in Church of England schools about £45. The salaries of certificated mistresses ranged from £55 to £75, and those of uncertificated mistresses from £25 to £50.[24] In fact, by the mid-nineteenth century, the average salary of some 20,000 teachers was just over £30 a year.

It is said that the teachers in contemporary schools in the Cape Coast area were poorly paid. To what extent is this a correct assessment, in relation to the salary structure of teachers in England, and especially in relation to the wage structure of other occupations in the Cape Coast area?

It is necessary to point out that the masters and teachers in the Cape Coast area were graded, according to their qualification, experience and competence. There were two grades of masters, and five grades of teachers. The salaries paid to them varied, therefore, according to the teacher's grade, his employer (Government or mission), and where the school was situated. This background knowledge is necessary in order to understand the apparent contradictory salary figures often quoted by educationists.

The annual salary of school master Grade I (a post always held by Europeans alone) was £300, and £250 for a Grade II master.[25]

European assistant master in Government schools at Cape Coast generally earned £200, and his African colleague £150.[26] But in Elmina, the Government appointed headmaster earned £100.[27] The masters in the Wesleyan schools who were all appointed by the Wesleyan Mission were said to be earning about £36 per year.[28] Perhaps by " masters " the Rev. Dunwell meant " teachers "; otherwise the discrepancy between the salary of African masters in Government schools will be too great. However, if one notes that a catechist was earning £35 a year,[29] then it is not difficult to believe that Dunwell was in fact referring to headmasters in Wesleyan schools and teachers. It is clear, then, that at the headmaster level, the salaries paid to those in the Cape Coast area— Europeans and Africans—were quite attractive. It is difficult to understand why it was reported that the Merchant Company early in the nineteenth century had found considerable difficulty in finding " a school master on a salary of £300 a year and a seat at the Governor's table ".[30] In fact, at that time a qualified surgeon earned about the same amount, and the Governor at Accra earned about £200.[31]

The salary of the teachers in the Wesleyan schools at Cape Coast ranged from £15 to £30, according to their abilities.[32] In fact by the 1840s the assistant teachers were paid considerably less than £3 a month in cloth.[33] In the Government schools the salaries ranged from £4 to £12 for the African teachers, and £60-£90 for the European teachers.[34] And according to McWilliam, by the 1840s the Senior Assistant teacher at Cape Coast was receiving 13s. 9d. a month (that is £8 5s. a year) and his four boy assistants were sharing 22s. (that is, £13 4s. a year) between them. This was clearly inadequate when one considers that a trained soldier was earning at this time £27 a year, a bell boy £13 10s., and a linguist £60.[35] Little wonder then that some African teachers had to quit teaching and enter commerce, or to supplement their income with trading as Quaco had done late in the eighteenth century.[36] If the teachers in the Cape Coast area had had their rent paid for them as was done in England, perhaps teaching would have become a little more attractive.

*Teacher Training in England*

It must be pointed out at once that even in England the proper training of teachers began to flourish only from the 1840s. It was realised then that no substantial progress could be made in popular education without properly qualified teachers. It was then that serious attempts were made to open up Training Colleges, and such was the need for teachers that by 1845 there were about twenty-two Church Training Colleges in England and Wales.[37]

Moreover, in England the following year, a scheme was drawn up by the Committee of Education to train pupil teachers. It recommended that stipends should be offered to selected boys and girls indentured as pupil-teachers for a five year apprenticeship, from the age of thirteen to eighteen. Grants were to be given to the teachers who trained them, and the pupil teachers were to be examined every year by Inspectors of Schools. The pupil teachers received nearly eight hours' instruction every week before and after school hours, and they were occupied over five hours every day in teaching or some allied activity. And at the end of their apprenticeship they were to compete for scholarships to be held at a Training College. An annual grant was to be given to Training Colleges in respect of each ex-pupil teacher student in training, and college-trained teachers were to receive proficiency grants from the Government, in addition to a salary paid by the school manager. As a further inducement, there was to be a pension scheme for teachers retiring after at least fifteen years' service.

In England, then, there were two classes of potential teacher-training students. The first was a certain number of young persons of superior merit, who on that account were selected from the elementary school to proceed to the Training Colleges—these were called " Queen's Scholars ". The second group was made up of other persons who would choose to enter a Training College on their own account. They received certificates of merit from the Government inspectors. For each " Queen's scholar " the Government paid to the training college £20 for the first year, £25 for the second, and £30 for the third year, and an additional £20 at the end of the first year if the student's progress was satisfactory. For each of the other students the Government paid sums ranging between £20 and £30.[38]

The measures were intended to ensure that the training colleges, so far as they were under government inspection, would receive, direct from the elementary schools, a constant stream of students, who gave promise of ability and showed an aptitude for learning. In addition to these the Government tried also to attract monitors —who might otherwise leave at the end of their schooling for other jobs—by offering gratuities of £10 to £20 a year to " the most eligible monitors as would consent to be apprenticed for five years to some competent master or mistress, and from £5 to £12 10s. to such as, without apprenticeship, would continue in the school till the age of seventeen ".[39]

By these means, it was thought that the monitorial system would be rendered vastly more effective and a source prepared from which an adequate supply of future able teachers might be drawn. In this way, the elementary school was designed to be a nursery to the training college, and inducements were held out to skilful monitors to look to teaching as the occupation of their lives. Those who passed one or more years in an inspected training college and received an annual inspector's certificate of merit were given £15-£30 grant, a salary of at least double the amount of grant, and a free-rent house.[40]

In this way, in England before the 1850s a way was found albeit temporary, of bridging the gap between the employment of monitors and the introduction of an efficient scheme for training teachers.

*Early Attempts at Teacher Training in the Gold Coast*

The Basel mission had earlier felt the need to train African assistants for their schools, and this had led to the establishment of a training school for catechists at Akropong in 1848, and another one had followed some two years later. In the Cape Coast area (and the colony in general), however, no such systematic effort was made at this time. Various sporadic attempts were made by the Wesleyan mission to train their teachers. Dr. Madden, for instance, had proposed " the establishment of a Normal School in England for the exclusive training and instruction of school masters, natives themselves of Africa, who should be destined for those schools ".[41] From 1845 to 1851, for example, at Akrah, there was a small training institution in which were usually four or five young men training to be teachers. This was not much of a success.[42]

With the aim of helping solve the problem of teacher-training it was planned that at the principal schools at the head of circuits, the Church members should select the most promising boys to become " monitors, who were to be led eventually to future usefulness as teachers ".[43] These boys " under training " were to be given " small wages of one or two dollars per month as an inducement to them and their parents ".[44] This practice, akin to that in England at the time, was later discontinued—a more efficient organisation for recruiting and training teachers was to be attempted in the second half of the nineteenth century.

Earlier, in 1842, a Seminary had been opened with the aim of preparing a few young men for pastoral duties and theological training.[45] The same year two students, William Hanson and John Ahumah Solomon, were sent by the Rev. Freeman to train. Later the number increased to six. It soon became obvious that these six teachers in training were not enough to meet the growing demand for schools at this time. For, as already noted, between 1842 and 1846, the Wesleyan mission alone increased the number of its schools (including the boys' and girls' schools at Cape Coast) from eight boys' schools and three girls' schools to twenty and four respectively with a total enrolment of 673 boys and 162 girls. And about sixty teachers of mixed quality were in charge.

There was always a clear need to improve their teaching ability, so the Rev. Freeman, for example, devised a system of " In-service Training " for the teachers under his charge. Freeman wanted, among other things, to know his teachers better. He also brought over some of his married teachers from England. Freeman then urged the teachers under " training " to " constantly read and study good books, in addition to the Bible "; accounts of such reading were to be shown to him. It was by such means that Freeman tried to sustain an educational system dependent on very slender resources.

It has been said of Africa in general that, with a few exceptions, the teachers were chosen carefully; and that, although they might be slenderly equipped with the knowledge and skill necessary for first-rate teachers, nonetheless, they were men of good, strong character, men whose life and example demonstrated the Christian truth and way of life.[46] In this sense, the African teachers of the Cape Coast (like other African teachers) shared the qualities of some of the teachers (masters) of the English charity schools who had to be morally fit, and churchmen.

Of course, good and efficient teachers were never easy to come by. A letter from the Secretary to the African Committee published in 1816, for instance, had revealed that it had for several years been the constant object of the Committee's endeavours to procure a chaplain (headmaster) properly qualified for the office, a man " whose character might enable them to rely with confidence both upon his exertions and his example ".[47] However, some of the good teachers in the Cape Coast area, such as de Graft and John Anderson, had been trained at the Monitorial School of the National Society at Baldwin Gardens in England. At this time, all the assistant teachers were products of the local school and generally it was the best of the scholars who were thus employed.[48]

Although before the turn of the eighteenth century there had been in England no effective system of training teachers, no educational technique for teachers to acquire and no proper system to inspect—the education which the Dame schools had provided being carried out by widows, bankrupts and discharged soldiers —in the nineteenth century in particular, serious efforts were being made to provide a means of free education for the " lower orders ".

(The impulse behind their efforts was akin to that which was later to send missionaries and educationists to the Gold Coast and other parts—the necessity of converting the "heathens" to some form of Christian morality.) And the serious lack of competent teachers was being fully tackled.

It is obvious that in the Gold Coast Colony, on the other hand, the first half of the nineteenth century did not witness any effective steps taken to improve the training of teachers. It should have been possible for the educationists to organise masters who would visit schools during the August holidays, spending a few weeks in each place, instructing the capable and replacing the incapable ones, as was the practice in England.

Moreover, in the Gold Coast, greater use could have been made of the pupil-teaching system. The aim of this system, introduced into England by James Kay-Shuttleworth—a system which had long been in full swing in Holland and Switzerland—was "to inspire students with a large sympathy for their own class; to implant in their minds the thought that their chief honour would be to aid in rescuing that class from the misery of ignorance and its attendant vices; to wean them from the influence of that personal competition in a commercial society which leads to sordid aims; to place before them the unsatisfied want of the uneasy and distressed multitude, and to breathe into them the charity which seeks to heal its mental and moral diseases ".[49] It must be said, however, that although during this period there was no teachers' college in the Cape Coast area, by the 1850s the Basel Mission on the other hand was sending out a steady stream of trained teachers from Akwapim.

Although there was no efficient system for teacher training before 1850, some of the African masters, especially those trained in Europe, made lasting impression on the educational scene. In fact, but for the indefatigable efforts of those African teachers and masters, the future of the educational exercise would not have been at all assured. As we have noted earlier, by 1850 all school masters and teachers were Africans,[50] a few of whom had managed to go over to the United Kingdom to improve themselves with higher education.

One such conscientious worker was Joseph Smith. After receiving an elementary education at Cape Coast Smith became a teacher in 1829. He later became school master at the Cape Coast Castle and served very well as the Rev. Dunwell's interpreter. At the invitation of President Maclean, Smith accompanied to England the two Ashanti princes (Ansah and Nkwantabisa) whom Maclean had had in the Castle school for five years. After teaching for a few years, on his return to Cape Coast from England, Smith applied to the Board of Government for financial assistance to go back to England for further training at a Seminary at Clapham in London. The Board, in its turn, recommended him to the care of the African Committee in England, which agreed to pay the expenses of the passage and to help give him " a complete learning requisite to promote Christian knowledge in the Colony ".

In 1836 the Trustees of the Wesleyan Church wrote a letter of recommendation to the African Committee of England. The signatories, all members of the Wesleyan Mission at Cape Coast, were John Hughes, H. R. Neizer, Thomas Hughes, John Mills, Elizabeth Smith, John Martin, Isaac Robertson, Hannah Smith, William Brown, John Aggry.[51] In their letter of commendation they indicated that Smith was " anxious to enlighten the minds of his countrymen, and that he desired further training as he did not have sufficient ability to carry his design into good effect ".[52] Smith left for further studies in England.

It is interesting to note that it was common practice in the nineteenth century for adults who were leaving for England to carry letters of introduction. In 1861, for example, the Rev. Laing's introductory note for Robert Ghartey said:

" The bearer, Robert Ghartey, is a class-leader and a local preacher of the Wesleyan Methodist society (Anomabu). And having sufficient cause to visit England, I beg to introduce him to your acquaintance as well as to the acquaintance of our friends in England. Mr Ghartey has been a local preacher of ten years' standing."[53]

On Ghartey's return he reported " the kindness he had received from the friends in England ".[54] And in 1872 the Rev. Waite introducing Mr. Sarbah of Cape Coast noted :

" He was one of our most active and useful members. He was formerly the Master of the School and was in our service for about 18 years. He is now a provision merchant, and supplies us very largely with cash. His visit to England is for the purpose of obtaining medical advice, and of getting what advantage he can by the change. He is thoroughly respectable and consistent and is both a class leader and local preacher."[55]

When Smith arrived back at Cape Coast in 1838, he did what he could to expand the frontiers of education and religion. He was on a salary of £54 a year.[56] Nevertheless, for five years (up to 1843), at a period when the forts had been handed back to the

Merchant Company by the British Government, Smith received considerable help from Governor George Maclean. The pupils in his school were studious; their ages ranging from eight to seventeen. The Colonial Chaplain's Report of July 1844 indicated the successful headship of Mr. Smith.[57]

The Report found that the first three classes—comprising about 110 pupils—spelt very well words of three, four and five syllables respectively; that in Geography and Grammar, the first class was beginning to make " tolerable progress ". The Report was, indeed, full of praise for Mr. Smith. " When it was borne in mind ", the Report stressed, " that the instruction imparted into these children and youth was in a language which was not their vernacular, then the degree of proficiency to which they attained could not but be highly satisfactory."[58]

Mr. Smith had impressed the Rev. Freeman four years earlier. Reporting on Smith's school in 1840, the Wesleyan minister had noted with satisfaction the excellent order and regularity which reigned in the school.[59] The school, at that time, had 162 scholars and was divided into five classes. On examining them, the Rev. Freeman noted the great ease and readiness with which the pupils had gone through their examination. Their answers to catechistical questions were in almost every case correct. The first class (i.e. Senior Class) especially, had become so well acquainted with Scripture history that they were capable (with closed books) of answering any reasonable questions which referred to any chapter in the Bible, which they might have read immediately before— whether referring to words or sentences. Freeman observed too that the first class had also gone through the whole of Murray's Grammar, and were quite capable of answering any questions on the subject.[60] The Report stressed that it would be doing Mr. Smith injustice if it neglected to state that the condition of the school both as to the requirements of the children and the discipline exercised among them reflected the highest credit upon him.[61]

The efforts of Joseph Smith were to have wide repercussions not only on his school itself, but also on the spread of Christianity. " But for the school ", wrote the Rev. Freeman in his Diary in 1840, " we should in all probability have found ourselves in the midst of a mass of ignorant people from whence we could select none to interpret for us those grand truths of Christianity."[62]

Mr. Smith himself seemed to have smelt the sweet scent of his success. In 1842, he had occasion to refer to the "prosperous state " of the Government school under his charge. There were over 170 children whose attendance he found " very regular ", and whose general conduct was such a source of satisfaction to him that he had not for a long time had recourse to corporal punishment. Smith felt certain that it was from among his scholars that the missions were supplied with interpreters, teachers and others who were of much assistance to the community in the diffusion of religious instruction.[63]

Such was the impressive role Joseph Smith played in raising the moral tone of the school under his care that on the eve of his departure to England in 1842, Freeman had to write to the Secretaries of the Missionary Committee in London stressing that " there was no man on the coast who knew so much about the general affairs as Smith did ".[64] Freeman added that " with him we did nearly all our business; he had been very upright and consistent in all things; he was a regular hearer at the Wesleyan Chapel and a man of unimpeachable moral conduct and of high principles, and a warm friend to the good cause of religion and education ".[65]

Joseph Smith's achievements as school master were all the more remarkable when one bears in mind the trying state in which schools were placed at that time. There was a general lack of proper classroom and teaching facilities, poor pay and a pitiful shortage of qualified teachers. Of course, all was not well with all the schools at the time. Dr. Madden, for instance, had had cause to refer in the 1840s to his conviction that the kind of instruction given in the schools was not the best that might be desired, or such as was well calculated to enlarge the intellect of the children, or to teach them right habits of thought and action.[66]

Nevertheless, the achievements of some contemporary English schools paled beside those of Joseph Smith's school. Smith's school was reporting regular school attendance, whilst the Census of 1851 in England, for instance, was revealing that even on the day of the Census itself 21% of pupils in England were absent from school.[67] Some boys in English schools tended to wander from one school to another, trying each for a short time and loitering at home for a longer or shorter period between each trial. The upshot was that a number of the children in England were ignorant of the simplest questions a child might be expected to answer. One inspector of a school in England had counted at the time " 74 blunders in an attempt by a boy to write down from dictation a passage containing 120 monosyllables ".[68]

It is not being suggested, however, that truancy was peculiar to schools in England, nor that all the schools in England coped with dullards. Doubtless, there was a fair amount of truancy in Cape Coast schools—as we shall explain later—and some of the pupils were dullards. But one important point being made is that some of the products in the Cape Coast schools, particularly in Smith's school, matched some of the best pupils in England. Dr. Madden, for instance, had affirmed that the intellectual capacity of the negro children was in no way inferior to that of the white children.[69]

It is sometimes argued also that the inspectors of the Church schools in England—whose report has already been referred to—were all clergymen, and so their opinion of the nature of schools might have been based less on the scholar's performance in the 3 Rs than on the moral tone of the schools and the formidable difficulties which the teachers had to face. The fact, however, remains that of the four inspectors who reported on Joseph Smith's school in 1842 three of them were clergymen with backgrounds very similar to that of the inspectors in England.

As to the reference to the difficult conditions under which the teachers in contemporary England had to work—a factor which is used to explain away the irregularity of attendance in some English schools, and the moderate successes achieved in some of them—it has to be pointed out that physical conditions were not much better, if not worse, in Smith's school at Cape Coast.

The point is that the successes which Smith won as a headmaster were due largely to his own zeal and earnestness of purpose. Proof of Smith's ability can be seen also from the fact that he held such important offices as Acting Secretary of the Council, Justice of the Peace, Acting Colonial Secretary and Customs Collector.[70]

Smith's case is not an isolated one. There was also one Mr. Anderson, reputed to be one of the best African teachers. He was said to have " conducted his school at Anomabu creditably ", and when he was transferred to Cape Coast it was said of him again that " under his charge the school at Cape Coast improved so much in a short time as to excite admiration ".[71] Anderson was soon to resign his headship—an incident regretted by all who were interested in schools—and to settle as a trader at Anomabu because General Turner, then in charge of the administration, had refused to appoint a second master " on account of his being a man of colour ". On Anderson's departure from the educational scene, the Rev. Denny at Cape Coast had to state : " hitherto it has but rarely occurred that African teachers have been found competent to take charge of schools, but there could be little doubt that when they combined a knowledge even of the elementary parts of education with respectability of character, persons in this class would under proper direction, prove eminently useful ".[72]

In a number of schools in the Cape Coast area, progress,

however, was hampered by irregular attendance, as already indicated. Poor health due to malnutrition and farm work was in
some measure to blame for the state of affairs.[73] It was partly to
get round this problem of malnutrition and irregular attendance
that the missionaries tried to attach a boarding establishment to
each school. In 1844, for example, for a period of six months,
eleven boys were boarded and clothed for £27 10s. and an unspecified number of girls for £22 10s.; at the same time another
boarding school under Elizabeth Waldron was being run at £55
a year.

Compulsory attendance was not and could not have been
achieved at this period in the Cape Coast schools and in the schools
in the Colony in general. (It was not achieved even in England
until a much later date.) British political control was of a rather
limited nature, and any such move could not have been carried
through. Persuasion, therefore, remained the most effective means
of attracting boys and girls to school, and ensuring some measure
of regularity in attendance. Moreover, a fair measure of regular
attendance could only be achieved where parents had assured
themselves of the tangible advantages which formal education
could give to their children. Indeed, in contemporary England
too, much of the irregularity of attendance was due to parents
who were largely indifferent to the benefits of education.[74]

The question of school attendance continued to engage the
attention of all those who had the interest of African education
at heart. The need for some measure of " compulsory attendance "
was to find expression in the Fanti Confederacy Ordinance of 1870
(article 25) which stated that " in districts where there were
Wesleyan schools the kings and chiefs should be requested to insist
on the daily attendance of all children between the ages of eight
and fourteen ".[75] This too was only a forlorn hope, for the chiefs
who were to enforce it could not have raised sufficient funds for its
supervision. In fact, in England too, it was not until the 1870s that
universal compulsory education tried to ensure regular attendance.

*Extent of Vocational Opportunities*

Before 1850 there was only a limited number of clerical jobs.[76]
The Forts could employ only a few hundred people and vocational
outlets for those who had completed their schooling were few. The
establishment at Cape Coast Castle by 1840, for example, included
two native doctors, one printer, eight carpenters, eight masons,
sixteen labourers, one house boy, five bell boys, two constables,
one gaoler, one school master, five teachers, and an " unspecified "
number of canoemen, messengers, hammockmen who were con-

stantly employed on the Coast and in the interior.[77] As has been indicated already, a high standard was required in those who were to be appointed clerks, or writers; they had to be of a reasonably high standard of education, of good morals and respectable appearance. A number of "native agents" employed to teach had the elements of their education in the Government school at Cape Coast, and although their qualifications varied in general, they offered useful service.[78] The educated boys were, of course, not interested in manual work, and commerce and office work to them became an eligible road to a position in society.[79]

At Cape Coast (and in the other coastal towns) education, before 1850, merely enabled young men to keep memoranda, copy papers and accounts, to superintend the discharging of cargo from vessels, oversee out-of-door works, and other such simple employment.[80] Education did not qualify the boys for conducting a merchant's business, although several acquired a sufficient knowledge of book-keeping to become first clerks to the merchants, and then to carry out business on their own account.[81] As has been noticed elsewhere in Africa, the aim of educating the African was not to produce equals, but useful citizens providing unskilled and semi-skilled labour in the economic co-operation between European capital, expert knowledge and skill, and African resources and labour.

Of course, contemporary English education was also found sometimes to be shallow. Kay-Shuttleworth, for instance, had pointed out that inspectors' reports indicated that many children who thought they could read, knew only the letters of the alphabet, or could at most merely pronounce monosyllables. Comparatively few of those who thought they had learnt to write were capable of writing a sentence legibly.[82]

The desire for money was also widespread in many countries. Among the contemporary English labouring classes, for instance, financial reward was the chief ambition. The Census report of 1851 indicated that material advantage and not any appreciation of the benefits of knowledge itself was the main aim of the nineteenth century educated person in England.[83] The Census of Great Britain of 1851 added thus:

" . . . practically, it is to be feared, the length and character of the education given in this country to the young are regulated more by a regard to its material advantage, as connected with their future physical condition, than by any wise appreciation of the benefits of knowledge in itself. It is hardly, therefore, matter for surprise, although undoubtedly it is for lamentation, that the working classes—seeing that the purely mental training which their children pass through in the present class of schools can rarely exercise an influence upon their future temporal prosperity and having for some generations past been tutored not to look beyond their station—should esteem a thorough education of this character to be not worth the time and money needful for its acquisition ".[84]

In the Cape Coast area too, before 1850 the wage for most workers was very low.[85] It was no surprise, then, that educated boys were keen to become clerks to the merchants. At that time a newly recruited soldier's pay was 25s. a month, paid in pieces of cotton handkerchiefs and rum; and because their value had depreciated the real income of a soldier was about 10s. a month. This was considered " disgraceful to the character of the British nation with the natives, and extremely unjust to the men ".[86]

At this period, too, servants' wages (i.e. wages given to men employed by Europeans at any kind of field labour) stood at two pence or three pence a day, and this was also paid in cloth.[87] Farm workers who were employed on the " plantation " near Cape Coast were also earning about 5s. a month; this was also paid in cloth.[88]

It is noteworthy that children were employed in large numbers on the plantation, and that they were receiving one-third the wages of the men (i.e. 1s. 8d.) Many parents preferred their sons to help on the farms or at home. In fact, of the one hundred-odd people who were working on the plantation near Cape Coast, a great many of them were children who were apparently well contented and well fed.[89] Employment of children both at home and on private and public farms was one of the factors which militated against educational expansion in the period before 1850. Perhaps it was this that led C. H. Bartels to report on the Elmina school that " whilst parents did not evince any reluctance to send their children to the schools yet they did not embrace the advantages offered to them so readily as they should ".[90] And the Select Committee Report of 1816 had earlier pointed out that the " natives would willingly allow their children to be educated in the English manner, if not attended with expense to themselves ".[91]

It is interesting to note that children in many contemporary English villages also continued their attendance at school till the age of ten or twelve, " but were then wanted to ' tent birds ' or to ' flay crakes ', i.e. to frighten crows from the corn. Sometimes the children went out with women to weed and hoe turnips etc. When parents were well off, the children might be kept longer at school,

G

but a few shillings a week extra, even for a part of the year, were great help to a family ".[92]

Nevertheless, during the first half of the nineteenth century, as noted, there were relatively little occupational openings for school-leavers in Cape Coast. And because they had no skills they probably became disillusioned. They found subsistence agriculture too rigorous.[93] Moreover, the Englishmen in the Cape Coast area before 1850 were largely middle-class. The range of their occupations were limited. Their jobs were purely administrative, not involving them in any manual work. They were the people who could be properly described as the " elite " in Cape Coast,[94] and they soon became models for the Africans, whose ambition came to turn towards the limited jobs and skills of the Europeans. The Africans, then, wanted to be clerks, because they had never seen the same dignity attached to the man skilled with his hands, to the artisan or the mechanic. Blamed for his hankering after the black-coated occupations, the African's fault lies only in adopting too closely the values of the British society.

The Africans at Cape Coast were in a dilemma, for, on the one hand, they were keen to copy from the English who were " the elite " of their society, and on the other, they found that a number of Europeans in Cape Coast were prone to many vices. On his appointment to the Cape Coast district as a missionary, the Rev. Dunwell, for instance, noted that some of the Europeans there were deeply sunk in sin.[95] In addition to this, until 1834, the Europeans at Cape Coast were also " holding slaves as pawns, buying and selling and disposing of them as property at their deaths, whilst the authorities even gave official sanction to the system ".[96] And an African minister, Joseph Smith, noted in 1843 that although some missionaries " have done well, there is abundant cause to lament that some behave in such a manner totally different from what they ought to do ", and he mentioned in particular the " haughty selfish disposition and abhorrence of coloured people " of a Europen minister by name John Watson.[97]

The educated Africans were faced with another dilemma. Although they formed one obvious source of African leadership, their very training in Western ways sometimes led to an uneasy acceptance or even rejection by their fellow Africans. Moreover, as the second half of the nineteenth century was to prove, especially in the Gold Coast Colony, the educated Africans (after having painfully assimilated themselves to Western values) were often denied the privileges enjoyed by Europeans. These dilemmas are yet to be completely resolved—perhaps they are not capable of complete solution.

*Conclusion*

The period 1800-1850 was, by and large, one of limited educational expansion. British political interests were shifting and even cautiously widening. Trade and commerce were also expanding. The chiefs were beginning to show some interest in education.

It should be pointed out that even at this date, the Wesleyan missionaries had a clear conception of the kind of education they desired for the Africans. The Rev. W. West summed this up when he wrote in the 1860s :

> " Our societies throughout the Gold Coast generally, are the fruit of our schools, and were these closed, and the teachers withdrawn, the societies would I fear in many places, dwindle away, and the people go back to their former ignorance and barbarism. . . . I do regard the schools as institutions in which the mind becomes early impressed with divine truth, it being the customary practice of the teachers to explain to the children the leading facts and first principles of the Gospel of Christ. They are as truly the nurseries of the Church as any schools at home can be".[98]

By the middle of the nineteenth century education was generally becoming a status symbol in the new society in which the chiefs found themselves, and they saw the need to help train their sons to benefit by this. In fact, even in the 1820s it was reported that " a few young men who had either been in England or educated at the public schools, were adopting the dress of Europeans, and approximating them in their manners. Some of them attended Church regularly and conducted themselves with decorum . . . of late, there was a sensible improvement, and an increasing taste was evident for imitating European manners ".[99]

There were broad similarities in the structure and organisation between schools in the Cape Coast area, and contemporary English Charity or Monitorial Schools of the period. Similar emphases were placed on religious teaching and the 3 Rs. But available records and evidence do not show that the monitorial method was practised to any appreciable extent.

At this period of educational expansion three parallel educational bodies were in being : the Government Schools (the oldest), then the Wesleyan Schools, and lastly, the Basel Schools. The Wesleyan educational efforts were confined to the colony—a pattern that was to persist throughout the nineteenth century—and the Basel schools were to be concentrated on the Ridge, some twenty miles east of Accra.

The Government and the Missions established the early schools partly to provide recruits into the lower sections of government and commerce. With regard to the Missions (and to some extent, the Government institutions) the curriculum was specially geared to teaching the Christian doctrine; for the Missions considered the schools as effective instruments to spread Christianity.

Government assistance to the schools came to the fore during this period, and not in 1882, as is sometimes alleged. The expenditure at the Castle School and its dependencies for 1838-1840 had shown an annual grant of £63. But gradually, the Government schools came to be absorbed by the Missions with no renewal of direct government ownership of any schools until late in the nineteenth century. In due course, a more typically English structure emerged—the expansion of the school system by voluntary agencies assisted by limited Government grants-in-aid.

This period also witnessed a climate of European opinion that seemed to favour new educational experiments. The Governors, European missionaries and merchants supported this, but the Africans at Cape Coast largely displayed a lack of interest. And the Missions had to provide the sort of education the Africans demanded in order not to jeopardise their interests as evangelists.

There was also a widening of the basis of recruitment. The improving economic situation, the expansion of British political interests (limited though it was at the time), the treaties made with the chiefs of Fantiland and Ashanti, the indefatigable efforts of the missionaries (persuading chiefs and their people, baiting children with boarding, feeding and clothing)—all these were factors. By the middle of the nineteenth century, however, the pattern of demand, though somewhat broader, had not changed significantly, for the expectations of the Africans themselves were a significant factor in reshaping the educational system.

The limited range of jobs open to the school-leavers to fill led to some measure of maladjustment, a factor which in the latter half of the century was to help sow the seeds of nationalism. It was also becoming evident by the mid-nineteenth century that education was a sure instrument of change—the African boy or girl who went to school was thereby being introduced to a world of thoughts, of achievement and of conduct outside the experience of his parents. And it was also becoming obvious that in so far as education paved the way to relatively higher paid jobs, it provided evidence that the formation of an elite is the result of the correlation between education and economic development. Indeed, western education of the African—even by the mid-nineteenth century— created an elite which, to some extent, stood apart from the masses. The class of elite, which was in the beginning relatively small, grew in number and importance, especially after the second half of the nineteenth century.

NOTES

1. Thomas Gisborne, *An Enquiry into the Duties of the Female Sex*, p. 12.
2. P.P. 1861, Vol. XXI (Part V), p. 15.
3. L. P. Mair, *Welfare in the British Colonies* p. 37. See also E. Evans-Pritchard, *The Position of Women in Primitive Societies*, pp. 43-56.
4. C.C. 267/54, Letter of 17.4.1821.
5. *Ibid. See also Census of Great Britain (1851)*, p. xxxvii.
6. P.P., 1827, Vol. VII (Part 2), p. 23.
7. *Ibid.*
8. *Ibid.*
9. M.M.S., Box 1835-41, Dunwell to Secretaries, 1.4.1835.
10. *Ibid.*
11. *Ibid.*
12. P.P. 1827, Vol. VII (Part 2), p. 23.
13. M. J. Walsh, 'The Catholic Contribution to Education in Western Nigeria, 1861-1926', p. 212 (M.A. thesis, London University.)
14. C.O. 267/56, No. 277, Macarthy's letter of 20.5.1822.
15. A. E. Southon, *Gold Coast Methodism—The First Hundred Years*, p. 39.
16. M.M.S., Box 1835-41, Brooking to Missionary Committee, 13.1.1840.
17. Beecham's evidence before Select Committee on West Coast of Africa. (Copy, M.M.S., Box 1842, 31.5.1842.)
18. Box M.M.S., 1835-1841, Waldron to Secretaries Missionary Committee, February, 1841.
19. *The Gold Coast Chronicle*, January, 1893.
20. M.M.S., Box 1868-76, Picot to Secretaries, 11.12.1873.
21. *Ibid.*
22. P.P. 1835, Vol. VII, Appendix and Index, par. 930.
23. *Ibid*, par. 927, 932.
24. P.P. 1861, Vol. 21, Part I, pp. 64-67.
25. P.P. 1801-52, *Africa 3*, Miscellaneous Papers, Arbuthnot's evidence, 2.7.1827.
26. *Ibid.*
27. P.P. 1842, Vol. XII, Appendix 3, pp. 90-92.
28. M.M.S., Box 1835, Dunwell's letter 8.1.1835.
29. M.M.S., Box 1842-5, letter of 9.2.1842.
30. P.P. 1816, Vol. VIIB, p. 15 (Cook's evidence).
31. *Ibid.* p. 20.
32. M.M.S., Box 1840, Freeman to Secretaries, 23.1.1840.
33. M.M.S., Box 1835, Dunwell's letter, 8.1.1835.
34. C.O. 90/1A, Minutes of Council; C.O. 267/56 No. 273, Macarthy's letter of 15.2.1822.
35. P.P. 1816, Vol. VIIB, p. 20.
36. S.P.G. Letter Box, Vol. I, pp. 61-65, letter of 25.4.1795.
37. H. C. Barnard, *A History of English Education from 1760 to 1944*, p. 102.
38. *Census of Great Britain (1851)*, pp. xxxiv-xxxv.
39. *Ibid.*
40. *Ibid.*

41. P.P. 1842, Vol. XII, Appendix No. 3, p. 19.
42. M.M.S., Box 1868-76, T. B. Freeman to Missionary Committee, 2.6.1874.
43. Ibid.
44. Ibid.
45. F. L. Bartels, The Roots of Ghana Methodism, Appendix B,, p. 350.
46. The International Review of Missions, Vol. XV, No. 59.
47. P.P. 1816, Vol. VIIB, p. 142.
48. P.P. 1842, Vol. XI, par. 3296, 7699-7770.
49. Kay-Shuttleworth, Four Periods of Public Education, p. 309.
50. P.P. 1842, Vol. 12, Appendix No. 3, p. 94.
51. M.M.S., Box 1836, Trustees of Wesleyan Church to Secretaries, 11.7.1841.
52. Ibid.
53. M.M.S., Box 1861, 11.7.1861.
54. Ibid., 13.12.1861.
55. M.M.S., Gold Coast 1868-76, Waite to Secretaries, 24.4.1872.
56. C.O. 96/4, Governor Hill to Colonial Office 20.3.1844. See also Colonial Chaplain's Quarterly Report dated 24.7.1844. These documents contain information about the headship of Mr. Smith.
57. C.O. 96/4, Colonial Chaplain's Quarterly Report, 24.7.1844.
58. Ibid.
59. M.M.S., Box 1835-41, T. B. Freeman's Journal, 23.1.1840.
60. Ibid.
61. Ibid.
62. Ibid.
63. M.M.S., Box 1842-5, Smith to Beecham, 18.1.1842.
64. Ibid., Freeman to Missionary Committee, 1842.
65. Ibid.
66. P.P. 1842, Vol. XII, Appendix No. 3, p. 19.
67. Census of Great Britain (1851).
68. Frank Smith, A History of English Elementary Education, p. 228.
69. P.P. 1842, Vol. XII, Appendix No. 3, p. 19.
70. For an account of Smith's future role in missionary activity and his conflict with de Graft, read A. E. Southon, Gold Coast Methodism - The First Hundred Years, pp. 24-31.
71. P.P. 1826-1827, Vol. VII (Part 2), p. 22.
72. Ibid., pp. 22-23.
73. C.O. 96/45, Bird's letter of 11.6.1859.
74. F. Smith, A History of English Elementary Education, p. 227.
75. D. Kimble, A Political History of Ghana, 1850-1928, Ch. 6.
76. B. Cruikshank, Eighteen Years on the Gold Coast, Vol. II, p. 185. See also P.P. 1801-52, Africa 3, Miscellaneous Papers, p. 11.
77. P.P. 1842, Vol. XII, Appendix 50 (showing disbursement of Parliamentary Grant for 1838-40).
78. P.P. 1842, Vol. XI, p. 190, par. 3613-3619. See also P.P. 1801-52, Africa 3, Miscellaneous Papers, p. 39.
79. B. Cruikshank, op. cit., Vol. II, p. 65.
80. Ibid., p. 60.
81. Ibid.
82. Kay-Shuttleworth, Public Education, pp. 238, 303.
83. Census in Great Britain (1851), Education: Report and Tables, p. xli.
84. Ibid.

85. P.P. 1842, Vol. XII, Appendix, p. 47. See also P.P. 1842, Vol. XI, p. 32, para. 523-524, and p. 90, para. 3616.
86. P.P. 1842, Vol XII, Appendix, p. 12.
87. *Ibid.*, pp. 13-14.
88. *Ibid.*
89. *Ibid.*, p. 14.
90. *Ibid.*, pp. 90-92.
91. P.P. 1801-1852, *Africa 3*, Miscellaneous Papers, p. 31.
92. P.P. 1861, Vol. XXI (Part V), p. 9.
93. Peter Hodge, 'The Ghana Workers' Brigade, a Project for Unemployed Youth', *British Journal of Sociology*, XV, No. 2, June, 1964, pp. 114 and 124. He notes here that: "it was to meet the dual task of providing young men with work and enabling them to take part in the execution of development projects that the Ghana Builders' Brigade was established in 1954".
94. P. C. Lloyd, *Africa in Social Change*, pp. 133-135.
95. M.M.S., Box 1835-41, the Rev. Dunwell's *Diary*, 23.4.1835.
96. P.P., Great Britain, 1842, Vol. XII, Appendix No. 3, pp. 29-33.
97. M.M.S., Box 1842-5, Smith to Secretaries, 18.2.1843.
98. M.M.S., Gold Coast 1859-67, West to Boyce.
99. P.P. 1827, Vol. VII (Part 2), p. 21.

# CHAPTER VI

# SOME CHIEF FACTORS IN EDUCATIONAL EXPANSION 1850-1900

It has been said that the third quarter of the nineteenth century marked the lowest depth of discouragement, as well as the beginnings of improvements in educational activity in the Gold Coast Colony.[1] This is largely true. By the beginning of 1850 commerce was steadily increasing throughout the whole country, and especially on the coast. The intercourse between the coast and the interior had also been greatly facilitated. The domestic comforts of the Africans were increasing; they were building better houses. There was progress also in cultivation, and all this helped the spread of education. Many of the principal African merchants, if they could not read and write themselves, were employing clerks of sorts to transact their business for them. By the beginning of 1850 there was much more demand also for labour, particularly that of mechanics and artisans. The country was sometimes in a peaceful and quiet state though, of course, the Ashanti wars raged periodically, disrupting trade and commerce, and educational and religious endeavours. It is against this background that one has to examine any further educational strides made in the Gold Coast from the 1850s.

The second half of the nineteenth century saw, nevertheless, an unprecedented expansion in educational activities. The Missions (Wesleyans, Catholics, Basel and Bremen) whipped up their efforts, and the Government's financial assistance to the schools increased. The Government's increased interest in the schools was largely attributable to the political expansionist policy which it was to embark upon more intensively at the time.

One factor which in its turn radically helped the growth of education at this period was, then, British political ambition (occasionally given a jolt—as we shall see later—by the Ashanti invasions). One aspect of British policy had hitherto been the avoidance of the use of armed force. However, by the end of the 1860s the need for defence (not diplomacy or courts) was paramount. For instance, after a truce in 1863 and the accession of a new Asantehene in 1867, Ashanti policy towards the British hardened. Moreover, the cession of Elmina to the British by the Dutch in 1871 sparked off a series of Ashanti demands to Elmina Fort and to the Asin, Akim and Denkyera States, and a full-scale invasion of the Fanti coast had to be resisted in 1873.

Just before the turn of the mid-nineteenth century, many people in Britain had also begun to express some anxiety about the Colonial settlements. In 1845, for instance, Dr. Madden had pointed out that the settlements appeared to be ill-chosen and ill-governed, and he had called for a new policy which would render the colonies efficient and beneficial to commerce and advantageous to the inhabitants. He had further stressed the point that in some of the settlements such as they had on the Gold Coast—where the monopoly of trade was in the hands of a few individuals, and where their jurisdiction was injuriously oppressive to the natives and unsatisfactory to all who were employed under it, because of the narrowness of the means placed at the disposal of the local administration—another system of government should be adopted, having in view the general extension of British commerce, and not the particular interests of any individual merchants, and the promotion of African civilisation, instead of the enlargement of their settlement at the expense of the natives' territorial rights.[2]

Despite what had been called " mis-statements in Dr. Madden's Report which a longer residence, affording him time and opportunity for more minute inquiry would have enabled him to correct ",[3] there were some British statesmen who shared his views.

Indeed, five years before Dr. Madden made his suggestion, Lord Russell, in a letter to the Governor of Sierra Leone, had also pointed out that the general object of British policy towards West Africa was to provide for the establishment of peace, innocent commerce and for the abolition of the Slave Trade.[4]

Before this time it was unclear what place there was for British settlements on the Coast to further these stated aims, or what role the British Government was to play in their administration. Indeed, the uncertainties and shifts in British policy were not so much a result of any failure to appreciate the nature of British interests in Africa. It has been said that the long exchanges between the Colonial Office, Foreign Office, Board of Trade, and between Colonial Governments and their agents, revolved around methods.[5] And as a result of representations such as those by Lord Russell and Dr. Madden (and others), the Gold Coast was given its own Governor in 1850, and Britain, hoping to gain more revenue from trade duties, took over the Danish forts. All this was to have a salutary effect on the educational experiment of the period.

At the beginning of 1850 when the forts and settlements were separated from Sierra Leone, trade was beginning to expand. Palm oil was the main export, but this fluctuated. Gold dust which came mainly from Ashanti was the second main export item, and other primary export products were ivory, gums, copal, monkey skins. The most valuable imports were textiles, wines and spirits, gun powder, guns, hardware, tobacco and beads.[6] All of these were traditional items in the coast trade, and the very simplicity of the list is indicative of the fact that there had been little expansion or diversification of the demand for industrial products.

Moreover, with the abolition of slave-trading, a complete change in economic roles and social stratification gradually emerged. And despite the fact that some of the slaves remained in the former master's employment, a potential labour force was to emerge slowly but surely, with the possibilities of wage employment. A system of credit emerged, and the group of independent merchants came to include some mulattoes and other well-to-do Africans. They often placed orders for goods on consignment from English shippers; they then received them on credit, and disposed of them from their trading stations, often accepting primary produce in exchange. Thus developed the operations of African middlemen and petty traders who were to prove so helpful to the European merchants of this period.[7]

This increased credit, as well as the introduction of shipping services, which had started between Liverpool and West Africa during the 1850s by the African Steamship Company, made it possible for the small-scale businessman to enter the direct import-export trade. In this way, there emerged " a new class of traders who, satisfied with smaller profits, were by their enterprise and personal exertion, doing more to push and extend the trade than was ever attempted by the few monopolists who formerly engaged in it ".[8]

Demand for European goods was also growing in the second half of the nineteenth century. English firms, consequently, began to appoint their own paid agents, some of whom were Africans. Some of these independent and flourishing African traders were S. C. Brew, George Blankson, James Bannerman, Samuel Ferguson, F. C. Grant and R. J. Ghartey.[9]

Trade continued to show an upward swing between 1850 and 1875. And although the structure of the economy did not alter too significantly, the emergence of the well-to-do African group was also to have a salutary effect on the educational development of the period. Trade and commerce continued to show marked improvement from the 1870s right up to the end of the nineteenth century, although there were some inevitable fluctuations. The trade figures for the period 1879 to 1893, as set out in the Statistical Abstract (No. 317) presented to both Houses of Parliament, were as follows :[10]

|         | 1879 | 1880 | 1881 | 1882 | 1883 |
|---------|---------|---------|---------|---------|---------|
| Imports | 323,039 | 337,248 | 398,124 | 392,582 | 382,582 |
| Exports | 428,811 | 482,058 | 373,258 | 340,019 | 363,868 |

|         | 1884 | 1885 | 1886 | 1887 | 1888 |
|---------|---------|---------|---------|---------|---------|
| Imports | 527,339 | 466,424 | 373,530 | 363,716 | 432,112 |
| Exports | 467,228 | 496,318 | 406,539 | 373,446 | 381,619 |

|         | 1889 | 1890 | 1891 | 1892 | 1893 |
|---------|---------|---------|---------|---------|---------|
| Imports | 440,868 | 562,103 | 665,781 | 597,095 | 718,853 |
| Exports | 415,926 | 601,348 | 684,305 | 665,064 | 772,107 |

Governor Griffiths' Report to Lord Knutford, whilst quoting figures similar to those above, gives the trade figures of 1875-1878 period as follows :[11]

|         | 1875 | 1876 | 1877 | 1878 |
|---------|---------|---------|---------|---------|
| Imports | 364,672 | 446,088 | 327,272 | 394,153 |
| Exports | 327,012 | 465,268 | 387,002 | 393,457 |

It is interesting to note that the principal items of import were beads, cotton goods, gun powder, guns, pistols, hardware and cutlery, silk goods, spirits and tobacco. The principal exports were gold dust, monkey skins, palm kernels, palm oil, rubber. These figures also completely dispel the delusion that the resources of the country and its people had been diminished by a period of depression prevailing for many years. One thing that the figures succeed in underpinning is that the average imports from 1875 to 1889, for instance, were £398,090, and the exports £406,682, showing a total average annual trade of the Colony as £804,772.

Of course, the table also shows that exports fell sharply from 1885-1889, but in 1890-1891 imports showed marked improvements. Total revenue also showed increases in that period. The chief items of exports were rubber (£313,817), palm oil (£126,857), palm kernels (£185,349) and gold dust (£86,186). The chief imports were cotton (£218,696), spirits (£81,719) and tobacco (£21,753).

It is obvious, then, that in the 1890s trading operations expanded, but the small African traders who were unaccustomed to partnership outside the family, or to the impersonal mechanics of the joint-stock company, suffered. *The Gold Coast Echo,* a local paper, wondered why some of the well-to-do young men, interested in trade and commerce, did not see the necessity to " put their money together and combine to start a business of their own ".[12] There is no doubt, however, that reserves of capital were lacking to the African businessmen, so a few of them became starved out of the business, and began to eke out a precarious livelihood by perhaps farming, fishing and petty trading.

At this time gold mining was being developed in the interior and money currency was being widely used. Another important development of the last quarter of the nineteenth century was the establishment of the Bank of West Africa; this event was hailed by many: *The Gold Coast News*, for example, welcomed the Bank's establishment, indicating that some of the current money-saving devices of the Africans were " to put money into the ground and in the walls of their houses. The educated and the civilised portion of the community sent the greatest part of their money to England to their friends or agents for safe keeping ".[13] The paper stressed: " All these methods have disadvantages, namely the long wait to draw, probability of not finding it easily (or at all). The incentives to extravagance among our young men would also be less if there were the facilities to save their earnings."[14]

The development of gold-mining in 1874 and the establishment of the Bank of West Africa, and a standard of money currency widely used—all this led to a broadening of the basis of trade which helped to provide financial aid to the more enterprising merchants. Eventually, therefore, there emerged a fully fledged group of traders and merchants by the turn of the twentieth century. Moreover, in 1890, the first export of cocoa (80 lbs) was made, which by the close of the century had risen to 536 tons. It has to be pointed out, nonetheless, that cocoa did not assume cash-crop importance till the 1900s.

The growth and expansion of the economy, as already indicated, did encounter periodic setbacks, often due to the wars with Ashanti.[15] A Wesleyan missionary in the 1870s, for instance, has recorded his impressions of the effect of the Ashanti invasions. In a letter sent to the Secretaries of the Wesleyan Committee in London, the Rev. Wharton wrote in 1873 : " I need hardly inform you that in consequence of the very excited and disturbed state of Cape Coast, and other towns on the sea board, commerce is at a deadlock, and I am unable to procure a sufficiency of cash to meet the requirements of the District. Occasionally, I succeed in getting from £10-£40 out of which I have to make small advances to our agents who are now in great straits, in consequence of the scarcity and dearness of food. We are now approaching the close of June Quarter when the teachers and others are paid, but I have no prospect of being able to meet their claims."[16] The Rev. Wharton had written one month earlier stating : " our interior schools are at present closed. . . . The Ashanti invasion of the Protectorate has been so far exceedingly damaging to Christianity and commerce."

During the Ashanti war of 1863 a Fanti Wesleyan minister, Laing, also wrote thus: " This war, I am afraid, will seriously affect our work. Some of the towns in which we have stations connnected with the Cape Coast circuit, have been deserted. . . . Famine has already begun to threaten this country."[17]

Misunderstandings between the Fanti communities themselves also had ill-effects on the stability of the coastal regions. The Rev. Alfred Taylor wrote in 1868 about the effect of the misunderstandings between the Dutch and English sections of the Fanti community. Cape Coast then was in a great state of excitement. " All trade is stopped and even farming is at a standstill. All the men are taken from their employments and businesses for the camp. . . . All this must very considerably affect every department of our work."[18] And the Rev. W. West echoed these misgivings when he wrote to the Secretaries of the Wesleyan Society the following year : " The unsettled state of the country during the past year has had the effect of disturbing our own affairs, and as the prospect of a settlement of differences between the Fanti and the Dutch is as yet very remote, a return to quiet and prosperity is not for the present to be hoped for."[19]

But although the economy suffered periodic setbacks, the generally improved state of the economy gave a realistic meaning to the pressure of the Africans for more schools and for clerical forms of employment. There was little need for skilled artisans because of the lack of any industrial institutions.[20] There was evidence too that the skilled artisans were receiving lower wages than the clerks.[21] No wonder, then, that there was a distaste for anything savouring of labour among upper standard boys who thought that to be a scholar was to be a gentleman, and to be a gentleman precluded the possibility of gaining a livelihood except by the pen.[22]

The period 1850-1900 was one which also saw the chiefs, missionaries and Governors playing an ever greater role in educational ventures. The chiefs from many villages near and around Cape Coast made demands for more and more schools. The missionaries, at first, were responsible for whetting the appetite of some chiefs for the schools.

The missionaries believed strongly that " unless they could by education lay a good foundation for a better social and a new spiritual life, missionary work would continue, as far as the masses of the people were concerned, surface work only ".[23] The missionaries were aware also that if they were to realise this goal then they would have to seek the assistance of the traditional rulers.

The Rev. W. West has pointed out that when he took charge of Cape Coast district towards the close of 1857 there were " a few young men at the Mission House, the sons of country chiefs, whom Mr. Freeman with the concurrence of the Committee had taken to board and educate. There were also at Mrs. Waldron's a few young women, the daughters of chiefs, and two or three of the children of an African Minister Brown. . . . The cost to the Mission at that time for their board and lodging was £37 or £38 a year ".[24]

The response from the chiefs remained encouraging. A Wesleyan African minister, for instance, has recorded that in 1870 he had a call from an educated chief, one James Simons, from a village called Donasi (a place not far from Cape Coast, with a population of 300), pleading with him to establish a school in his town. The chief promised to recruit twenty-five children himself and the General Superintendent of the Wesleyan Church had given permission for a teacher to be sent over, on condition that the chief would supply a teacher's house, a school room, and would also pay £12 every year to support the school. The chief gave his consent to this demand.[25]

The chief of Odumtu (now Nyakrome), a town forty miles from Cape Coast, had also promised to provide a free house for a teacher's residence if a school would be established in his town. The townsfolk had also promised to build a temporary school house for the school. The school was opened the same year with thirty-one pupils.[26]

Another African minister tells of how the chief of Swedru, a town about thirty-five miles from Cape Coast, had on his own initiative invited him to establish a school for the town, and send them a teacher.[27]

The Basel mission's educational expansion, which was much slower—the first schools were opened in 1843—also began to speed up at this period. By 1880, they had established 45 schools with a total enrolment of over 1,200. Indeed, up to the last decade of the nineteenth century, the Basel mission's educational work expanded considerably. In 1889 there were more than 92 schools, both boarding and day, attended by about 2,500 pupils. And by the close of that century, the number of schools rose by about 60% to 154, and the number of pupils by 200% to nearly five thousand.

Like the Wesleyans, the Basel mission also used their schools not only to provide secular instruction but also as training ground in Christianity.

The Government's assistance to the Basel mission was negligible. It rose from £60 in 1861 to about £175 in 1887. However, so advanced was the system of education that the Basel missionaries devised—there had been six years in primary school, followed by four years in the middle school—that as early as 1870 the educational system that existed throughout Ghana in the 1960s had been established.

Both the Wesleyan and the Basel missionaries particularly were attracted by the prospect of proselytisation in Ashanti long before 1900. The Rev. Thomas Freeman of the Wesleyan mission had managed to reach Kumasi in January 1839. But the Ashantis were opposed to the establishment of schools, mainly for fear that it might lead to rebellion and political unrest in Ashanti. He had to call off this first attempt, but returned to Kumasi in 1841. He was accompanied by the two Ashanti princes—Ansah and Nkwantabisa—whom the Wesleyans had educated in England. During this second visit, Freeman was warmly received, and the Ashanti king gave a small parcel of land to the Wesleyans to build a mission.

The Ashanti people were not anxious to deliberately stand in the way of the mission's activities, but neither were they anxious to do anything concrete to support the development of formal education in Ashanti. Because of this, notwithstanding the elaborate and courteous exchanges between Freeman and the Ashanti king from 1839 onwards, the Wesleyan missionaries had limited success with the station they had managed to establish in 1843. It became clear later that although some Ashantis were anxious to embrace Christianity, they lacked the courage to come forward openly.[28]

However, when in 1876 the Wesleyans decided to resume the mission which had closed down because of the Ashanti war at that time, the Asantehene indicated that they would accept the mission on condition that the missionaries would help the peace of the nation and the prosperity of trade as they had once done. The Wesleyans were also told not to expect the Ashantis to select children for education as their children "had better work to do than to sit down all day long idly to learn ' hoy, hoy, hoy ' ".[29]

The Wesleyans returned to Ashanti in 1884, when the Rev R. J. Hayfron was appointed to Kumasi. Some progress was then made in some outlying towns such as Bekwai. But it was not until Prempeh I was exiled in 1896 that real opportunity offered itself to the Wesleyans to whip up their missionary and educational activities in Ashanti.

The fact that the Wesleyans were forced to suspend and ultimately abandon their earlier efforts in Kumasi in the 1860s led the Basel mission to adopt a cautious policy and to make no serious attempt at establishing a mission there until the problem of Ashanti aggression had been finally settled.

The Basel mission, therefore, turned their attention from the Kumasi area. They reached Abetifi in the late 1870s. By 1878 they had finished a mission house, had dedicated a small chapel and had opened a boys' school. More missionary stations were opened, and by 1890 there were seven outstations and eight Basel mission schools. It was in 1881 that the Basel mission made serious attempts at educational and missionary work in Kumasi in Ashanti. The first Basel evangelist to visit Kumasi had returned earlier with the impression that they had to " wait for better hints from the Lord ".[30]

The Basel missionaries were able to penetrate into Attebubu and Nkoranza in northern Ashanti in 1895, and a firm Basel mission station was established in Ashanti in 1896. A change in the attitude of the Ashantis was noticeable at this time. And Ramseyer of the Basel mission was able to report that Kumasi was a Basel mission station, that all the towns were open to the Basel missionaries, and that many requests were then being made to them to settle among the Ashanti.

The growth of Basel mission educational activity was relatively fast. Whereas there were only two schools in 1896, there were fifteen schools by the close of the nineteenth century in Ashanti.

The Roman Catholics began work in 1881, when the first Fathers set foot in Elmina. In the following year their first school was opened at Elmina. Some three years later, they started a girls' school, and in the course of time they opened more schools in such places as Agona, Komenda and Shama. In 1890 they opened a senior boys' school at Cape Coast, and during the 1890s, after starting more schools on the Coast, they extended their educational and missionary efforts to Keta. Like the Wesleyans and the Basel missionaries before them, the Catholics made attempts at developing industrial and agricultural training. Thus, at Saltpond they set up an Agricultural and Book-binding Centre, a Printing and Carpentry Centre at Cape Coast, and a Woodwork Centre at Elmina.

The Bremen Mission started their activities in 1847 at Peki Blengo in the trans-Volta area, but because they were not successful there, in 1853 they directed their attention to Keta. Some three years later, they were able to open a station at Waya and another at Ho in 1857 and by 1881 they had established themselves in six out-stations. By the close of the nineteenth century they had opened up twenty schools attended by 591 children. Nevertheless, this apparently modest achievement had been paid for with appalling loss of life, for between 1847 and 1894, no less than sixty-four missionaries and their wives had died.

In the 1850s the distribution of schools and the enrolment of children and teachers showed that the Wesleyans had the highest number of schools, followed by the Basel missionaries. The Bremen, Catholic and Government schools numbered only eight in all.[31] The table is as follows :—

| Controlling Body | Schools | Enrolment | Teachers |
|---|---|---|---|
| Government | 3 | 507 | 16 |
| Basel | 47 | 1285 | 79 |
| Wesleyan | 84 | 3057 | 106 |
| Bremen | 4 | not available | not available |
| Catholic | 1 | 150 | 3 |

All in all, education at this period did not become essentially part of a coherent Government policy. The pattern that emerged was a group of Government aided schools as well as a large number of unaided ones, some of which from time to time asked the Government for money. There was no definite pattern of school distribution, either. Schools sprang up wherever the need was expressed for them, and wherever the townsfolk showed a genuine desire to help in their running.

The co-operation that existed between the chiefs and the Wesleyan ministers was not confined to the Cape Coast area. In 1876, for instance, a Wesleyan minister in Accra (some 60 miles from Cape Coast) convened a meeting of chiefs and elders to place before them the need for more educational institutions in the Accra area. He hoped by this means to gain their co-operation and get them to influence their people to send their children to school.[32]

Of course, the missionaries began to expand their educational activities largely through their own resources. In fact, in the early 1850s when Governor Hill arrived at Cape Coast, he concentrated on the few existing Government Schools and withheld financial aid from the Wesleyan educational efforts. It is noteworthy that at this time in England, self-help was a favourite motto with leading men in all classes. Trevelyan, for instance, has explained that " self-discipline and self-reliance of the individual Englishman, derived indeed from many sources, but to a large extent sprang from

H

Puritan tradition to which the Wesleyan and Evangelical movement had given another lease of life ".[33] And H. G. Grey had also
pointed out that the surest test of the soundness of measures for
the improvement of an uncivilised people was that they should
be self-supporting. He was certain that the people for whose
benefit any schemes were attempted, were likely to be more aware
of the value of such projects when they themselves provided the
money.[34]

The Rev. Freeman, as a result of Hill's attitude to the Mission
Schools, was therefore bound to make the church independent of the
government. The Cape Coast school expanded quickly, and with
its in-service training, became a model upon which other schools
were founded and expanded. In fact, from 1835 when the first
Wesleyan missionary arrived at Cape Coast, until some forty-five
years later, the Wesleyan Mission established in the country some
eighty-four schools with a total enrolment of over three thousand
pupils.[35] The Rev. Freeman had recorded the existing Wesleyan
schools at the beginning of 1850 as follows :[36]

| | School Teachers | Day Schools | Day Scholars | | Total |
|---|---|---|---|---|---|
| | | | Boys | Girls | |
| Cape Coast | 13 | 4 | 148 | 108 | 256 |
| Anomabu | 8 | 3 | 148 | 40 | 188 |
| Dominasi | 11 | 7 | 196 | 9 | 205 |
| Akra | 12 | 4 | 181 | 55 | 236 |
| Total | 45 | 18 | 673 | 212 | 885 |

The table shows that on an average, to every teacher there were
twenty pupils, and that one-quarter of the pupils were girls, whilst
at Cape Coast alone the girls numbered just over one-half the
total number of girls in the four day schools. Girls' education here
has never lagged seriously behind that of boys. Figures taken from
the Blue Books of 1851, 1861 and 1867 also indicate the extent
of the Wesleyan efforts over that period.[37]

| Year | Cost | Number of Boys' Schools | Number of Girls' Schools | Enrolment | | |
|---|---|---|---|---|---|---|
| | | | | Boys | Girls | Total |
| 1851 | not known | 22 | 2 | 725 | 267 | 992 |
| 1861 | £1,186 | 27 (some were mixed) | 3 | 1,061 | 236 | 1,297 |
| 1867 | £670 | 23 (some were mixed) | 2 | 736 | 183 | 919 |

These figures indicate a number of interesting facts. Firstly, it is clear that boys' training fluctuated, reaching its peak in 1861, and that for girls dropped steadily during the period. Secondly, there was also a sharp drop in money actually spent by the Wesleyans on their schools; it was nearly halved during the period 1851-1867. The figures reflect, therefore, both the rapid expansion of the 1850s, and the unsettled state of the country in the early 1860s.

The 1860s were, indeed, a dark chapter in the educational history of the second half of the nineteenth century. There had been the earthquake of July 1862, a mutiny in the Gold Coast Artillery; the Ashanti invasion of 1863, and the fruitless expedition of the British to the Prah the next year. Trade, as already noted, was halted as a result, and faith in the invincibility of the British administration began to wane and fade away.

It is interesting to note that in England too, during this period, funds for running English schools were also whittled down—from £813,441 in 1861—by £76,000 in 1866.[38] It is possible that this development could have affected the extent of the country's participation in the education expansion in the Gold Coast.

## NOTES

1. *The Year Book of Education (1938)*, p. 713.
2. P.P., 1842, Vol. XI, especially par. 9032-9046, and 9105-9110.
3. *Ibid.*, Sewell's evidence of 3.5.1842. See also par. 10878.
4. C.O. 268/35, Russell to Doherty, 30.9.1840.
5. C. W. Newbury, *British Policy toward West Africa, Select Documents, 1786-1814*, p. 2. See also ' British Attitudes towards East and West Africa 1880-1914 ' by H. D. Perraton in *Race*, Vol. VIII, January, 1967, No. 3, p. 223.
6. B. Cruikshank, *Eighteen Years on the Gold Coast of Africa*, London, 1853, Vol. II, pp. 41-42.
7. B. Cruikshank, *op. cit.*, Vol. II, pp. 33, 36.
8. C.O. 96/42. Ord to Labouchere, 31.3.1857. See also Bevin, H. J., ' The Gold Coast economy about 1880 ', *Transactions in the Gold Coast and Togoland Historical Society*, 2, 1956, 73-86.
9. J. E. Casely-Hayford, *Gold Coast Native Institutions*, p. 95.
10. P.P. 1894 (Stat stical Abstract No. 317 to both Houses of Parliament).
11. Report on the Economic Agriculture of the Gold Coast, London, 1890, No. 110, *Colonial Report No. 110* of January, 1891. These figures tallied with the Gold Coast Year Books (1884-1895) and J. S. Kettie, *Year Book 1898*, p. 200.
12. *The Gold Coast Echo*, 16.1.1888.
13. *The Gold Coast News*, 2.5.1885.
14. *Ibid.*
15. M.M.S., Box 1868-76, Wharton to Missionary Committee, 10.6.1873.
16. *Ibid.*, Wharton to Secretaries, 8.5.1873.
17. M.M.S., Box 1859-67, Laing to Secretaries, 12.6.1863.
18. M.M.S., Box 1868-76, Alfred Taylor to Secretaries, April, 1868.

19. *Ibid.,* West to Secretaries, 23.3.1869.
20. W. J. Rottman, *The Educational Work of the Basel Missions on the Gold Coast,* Appendix AI to Special Reports, H.M.S.O., 1905, XXX, Part II, p. 300.
21. I. M. Wallerstein, *The Road to Independence. Ghana and the Ivory Coast,* p. 241.
22. W. J. Rottman, *op cit.,* Appendix AI, XXX, Part II, 300.
23. M.M.S., Box 1868-76, W. Penrose to Secretaries, 26.4.1875.
24. M.M.S., Box 1859-67, W. West to W. B. Boyce, 12.2.1863.
25. M.M.S., Box 1868-76, Solomon to Missionary Committee, 26.9.1870.
26. *Ibid.,* Solomon to Missionary Committee, 26.4.1875.
27. *Ibid.*
28. Reindorf, *History of the Gold Coast and Ashantee,* pp. 242-243.
29. Findlay and Holdsworth, *The History of the Wesleyan Methodist Missionary Society,* Vol. 4, p. 175. " Hoy, Hoy, Hoy " is a corruption of " Holy, Holy, Holy "—a reference to the teachings of the holy scriptures.
30. CO/96/122.
31. M.M.S., Box 1850-7, the Rev. Freeman's *Journal,* Record of Schools as at May, 1851. For a full list of Methodist schools between 1852 and 1856, see F. L. Bartels, *The Roots of Ghana Methodism,* Appendix, p. 351.
32. M.M.S, Box 1868-76, Penrose to Missionary Committee, 26.4.1875.
33. G. M. Trevelyan, *English Social History,* pp. 509-510.
34. H. G. Grey, *The Colonial Policy of Lord John Russell's Administration,* Vol. II, p. 281.
35. C.O. 96/143. See also H. O. A. McWilliam, *The Development of Education in Ghana;* he gives the number of schools as 83.
36. M.M.S., Box 1850-7, the Rev. Freeman's *Journal;* Record of schools as at May, 1851. For a full list of Methodist Schools between 1852 and 1856, see F. L. Bartels, *The Roots of Ghana Methodism,* Appendix, p. 351.
37. *Blue Books, 1851, 1861, 1867.*
38. J. W. Adamson, *English Education (1789-1902),* p. 231.

## CHAPTER VII

# GOVERNMENT OFFICIAL POLICY IN EDUCATIONAL EXPANSION, 1850-1900

The development of education became the official policy of the Government from the 1850s onwards. In 1852, for instance, seeing the need to expand the social services generally, the Governor convened a meeting of the important chiefs, and urged the imposition of a Poll Tax of 1/- per head to be used on the judiciary, health, and other pressing social welfare projects and for the better education of the inhabitants of the forts and settlements.[1] The introduction of the Ordinance had referred to the benefits which many had derived from the Castle school at Cape Coast and to the need for the benefits of superior education to be more widely diffused to meet the wants of the advancing society.[2]

Encouraged by the chiefs' initial reception of the Poll Tax of 1852, Governor Hill proceeded to pass the Ordinance of 1852 " to provide for the better Education to the Inhabitants of Her Majesty's Forts and Settlements on the Gold Coast ". Hill's faith in the improving qualities of reading, writing and arithmetic led him to make provision in the Ordinance for the daughters of the better class of Africans whose education had been neglected.[3] By the provision of the Ordinance it was also hoped that teacher-training colleges would be set up.[4] The Ordinance of 1852 had drawn a distinction between " educating " and " training " teachers. The newly-trained teachers were to possess techniques for teaching as well as a general education. Girls were also to help in this teaching experiment.

Before the Ordinance was passed, the missionaries had been largely responsible for carrying the burden of education, aside from the Cape Coast Castle school (which cost the British administration some £100 a year), and the Dutch Government school at Elmina.[5]

Although the Ordinance and the Poll Tax failed to receive the support of the chiefs and people in the Colony, by these efforts the Government clearly signified its desire to enter the educational field directly through the provision of schools. Indeed, despite the failure of the Poll Tax Ordinance, by 1856 the British authorities had managed to open more schools—including one girls' school at Cape Coast—in the Colony.

The British administration showed renewed interest at this period. In 1854 the Governor and Council appointed a trained European school master and his wife (Mr. and Mrs. C. J. Vinall) to the school at Cape Coast, on a salary of £200. Illness and death deprived the school of their services after a short time. And in 1856 the appointment of Inspector of Schools was made. This inspector was " to perform financial duties . . . to receive reports from head-masters; to make himself familiar with and present to the Government the needs of the schools in matters of books, stationery, condition of school buildings and furniture, to inspect and superintend the schools, and to ensure the requisite supply of goods and efficient teachers by his own personal training of persons for such duties ".[6]

However good the intent that lay in the appointment, in practice the inspector's work was made utterly unfeasible, largely because of the poor state of the roads; he had, therefore, to concentrate only on the school at Cape Coast. As Governor Pine was later to point out, it would have made for more effective supervision if the District Commissioners of the various areas had been made to carry out the school inspection. Moreover, the Education Ordinance would have succeeded, if the Administration had co-operated with the chiefs and the educated Africans to a greater extent than it did.

The general lack of support by the local people for the Poll Tax Ordinance forced the Government to begin to see its educational role in a more limited fashion in later years. And it was not until some thirty years later that the Government was to make another serious effort to help finance mission schools through its grants-in-aid policy.

It should be pointed out that in England in the 1880s too, the story of national education was mainly one of conflict and frustration. The extent to which English thinking influenced those who framed the 1852 Gold Coast Ordinance, is not easy to assess. But interestingly enough, in the England of the 1850s, there were some who were also urging the imposition of local rates in order to help check the danger of bureaucracy in the centralised English education system. There were others too who were advocating the introduction of local rates on the grounds that it would help get round the existing religious difficulties. Public money, it was argued, should be used only to provide secular instruction, and religious instruction should be provided and paid for by the Church.

Of course, in the Gold Coast the manner of collecting the tax easily lent itself to abuse. It was disclosed at one time that collectors were inexperienced and the ordinance regulating its collection was unsatisfactory.[7] Some of the clerks were found to be very incompetent and almost useless. And at Cape Coast a clerk who was the cashier was found to be keeping sums of money for a fortnight before he handed them over to the Collector, who was Treasurer for all the receipts of the settlement and had no Bank to deposit them in.

Although the Poll Tax and the Education Ordinance of 1852 did not meet with much immediate success, the Government continued to show a rather cautious interest in educational matters. In 1870, Governor Ussher invited Dr. J. A. B. Horton to draw up a scheme for the establishment of " a good school of a higher class than hitherto " which would encourage the Fantis to educate their children. The same year Dr. Horton outlined his suggestions. He recommended that Government Day Schools should be opened in Cape Coast, Anomabu, Winneba and Accra; he also recommended the setting up of an academy for more advanced pupils; the employment of well-trained teachers at liberal salary rates and the establishment of a Board of Education with its own inspectors.[8] Dr. Horton's recommendations did not see the light of day, for he had fallen out with Governor Ussher over the publication of the former's letters which appeared to have accused Governor Ussher of helping in the Fanti Confederation.

Four years later, however, a token grant of £50 was made by the Government to the Wesleyans, and twice the amount was made to the Basel mission. The Africans were also to be " induced to tax themselves for educational purposes ".[9]

The relationship that existed in educational matters between the missionaries and the British administrators generally remained warm and intimate. And because the communication between the Rev. Grimmer, a Wesleyan minister, and Governor H. J. Ussher typifies this relationship, we quote fully their correspondence on this subject. Grimmer had received a copy of Dr. Horton's newly published book on *Letters on the Political Condition of the Gold Coast*—intended for private circulation only—in which the Governor had expressed his opinion of the state of education in the Colony. Grimmer then wrote in 1870 as follows:

" I received from the author, yesterday, a copy of his book, and I see that your excellency complains, and justly I think, of the low standard of education existing and lest any future action on the part of the Ministers in charge of the several Wesleyan stations in those towns where it is proposed to establish Government schools should induce your excellency to think that they

are opposing your efforts to raise the people, I deem it necessary to bring before you the following facts."[10]

He went on to stress the fact that the present inefficiencies of the
schools stemmed from the absence of a good Grammar School
from which teachers could be selected, of promising youths
who were morally and intellectually qualified to teach, and of
adequate funds (since only voluntary contributions supported the
missionary school). And finally Grimmer asked Governor Ussher
whether it would be practicable for the Government to assist existing schools, as was being done at the Gambia.[11] About two weeks
later (on November 8, 1870) Governor Ussher replied to say that
Grimmer's remarks " respecting assistance to be given to schools
of the Wesleyan denomination were deserving of attentive consideration ".[12] The Governor further trusted that Grimmer would
understand that " although he was anxious to extend education
under the rule of the established Church, he was most desirous of
testifying to the usefulness of the Mission schools and to afford
any assistance in his power to them ".[13]

The Rev. W. Penrose also wrote to Governor Stratham in 1875
thus :

> " Knowing the interest you take in education, we feel it our duty
> to bring under your notice our school work. . . . As the Mission
> (Wesleyan) is supported by voluntary contributions, the demand
> upon our Mission funds year after year for the maintenance
> of our schools is necessarily large ; and as this is one of the
> most important of Her Majesty's stations in this colony we feel
> ourselves justified in making application for a Government Grant
> to assist our school work."[14]

The demand for education continued to grow. *The Gold Coast
Times,* one of the local newspapers which had emerged at the time,
was urging every young man who was earning a " reasonable income to aim unswervingly and strain every nerve to procure a
good education for his children ". And in 1879, for example,
scholars at Elmina sent a petition to the Administrator at Cape
Coast for a school to be set up at Elmina to train their boys and
girls.[15]

In 1880 Governor Ussher raised the grant to the Wesleyans from
£50 to £200. The Government was at the time spending £300 on the
Castle school.[16] As noted earlier, more demands for bigger grants
were made by the Missions. But the Government was prepared to
consider increases in grants to them provided that a system of
testing their efficiency could be devised.[17]

It was largely due to this development that the Education Ordinance was passed some two years later. Under the guidance of Lord Kimberley, the Government enacted this Ordinance to provide for Government-financed and denominational schools which were to receive grants-in-aid according to their efficiency. By this Ordinance, there were to be two categories of primary schools : Government Schools, which were to be maintained entirely from public sources, and Assisted Schools, which were to be set up by the Missions or private individuals, but were to receive financial aid from the Government according to their efficiency. A Board of Education was set up to control and supervise the system and the Principal of Fourah Bay College, the Rev. M. Sunter, was appointed Inspector of Schools. His time, in practice, was shared between all the West African Settlements.

The grants were to be based mainly on such subjects as Reading, Writing and Arithmetic, and girls were to be examined in needlework. Grants could also be got for such "optional" subjects as History and Geography. The local Boards were to assist in the administration of the grants-in-aid system whenever these were considered necessary.

Although the proposals were not put into effect immediately, owing to shortage of staff, they gave legal recognition to the partnership between the churches and the Government; the sum of £425 was voted at once for distribution to the Wesleyan, Basel and Bremen missions.[18] The Educational Ordinance of 1882 also stipulated the establishment of Industrial Schools at each of the important places in the Colony. This provision could not be implemented until some three years later. The delay caused considerable dismay. "It is now three years since this ordinance (1882) came into operation," wailed a local paper, "but we have neither seen nor heard of the institution of any during this period."[19]

It has been said that the 1882 Ordinance bears too close a resemblance to the English Education Act passed in 1870, and that this in itself is proof that the introduction of the Ordinance in the Gold Coast was a reproduction of the structural characteristics of English education which had emerged as a result of the English Education Act of 1870. How genuine is this claim?

The Elementary Education Act of 1870[20] had provided for School Boards to be set up in England in areas which were short of schools in order to "fill up the gaps". The Education Department had the task of causing Boards to be formed where necessary, the country being divided into school districts. The aim was to enable the districts to collect returns which would show the number of schools, scholars and children requiring attention in each district.[21] Also essential to the Bill was a compromise on the religious issue. The Bill guaranteed the right of withdrawal from religious instruction on grounds of conscience in all public elementary schools, including those run by the churches. In the established schools supported by local rates, no catechism or religious formula distinctive to any particular denomination was to be taught. School Boards which were to be directly elected were empowered to raise a rate in order to finance their activities.

School fees were not to be abolished. But the School Boards were to be empowered to give free tickets to parents who genuinely could not afford to pay for their children's education.

Successful as the Act was in 1870, in later years it became clear that there were considerable omissions which led to unforeseen consequences.[22] The working of the School Boards led to unexpected expenditure commitments; a strain was therefore put upon the local finances, and little provision was made in the Act for the training of the large staff of teachers required for the national schools.

Similarities between the Gold Coast Ordinance of 1882 and the English Education Act of 1870 are obvious. For one thing, they had similar aims. The Ordinance of 1882 had stressed the " need for a superior system of education to meet the wants of an advancing society " whereas the Act of 1870 had been intended " to bring elementary education within the reach of every home ". Both of them made provision for the establishment of Boards, intended to assist in the administration of the grants-in-aid system whenever necessary.

Since the grant-in-aid system was one of the important provisions in the Gold Coast Ordinance, let us first find out the extent to which it was patterned on the English grant-in-aid system.

According to this system, every school in England, according to its size (and provided that a certificated teacher was employed), had to be given 4s. 6d. to 6s. 0d. a head, with additional sums according to the number of pupil teachers and assistant teachers. The school managers of all schools were to pay 21s. 0d. to 22s. 6d. for every scholar who attended the school during 140 days in the year preceding, and who passed an examination individually in Reading, Writing and Arithmetic.

In the Gold Coast too, during the year 1888 the system of granting Government aid to schools according to the amounts earned by the pupils by proficiency, attendance etc. was continued. During that year, the Basel mission schools earned £351 18s. 0d.; the Wesleyan schools £229 13s. 0d.; the Catholic schools

£77 5s. 0d.; the Bremen mission schools £28 7s. 6d.; the total being £687 3s. 6d.[23]

The grant-in-aid system had been found in England to have many disadvantages.[24] Inspectors had revealed that as a result of this system, there was over-pressure on the pupils, due to anxiety to produce results. There was an improvement in the 3 Rs but the other subjects were neglected. The position of teachers in the eyes of school managers, and therefore, their very livelihood, became dependent on the amount of grant earned by their pupils. There was a temptation for teachers to falsify registers and hood-wink inspectors by making pupils learn off their reading books by heart. When inspectors attempted to check this, there often emerged a feeling of distrust and hostility between them and the teachers.

The system of payment by results was carried too far and was too rigidly applied, and it had to be modified in the interests equally of the scholars, of the teachers, and of education. It had become apparent that teachers were too intent on the measures by which the maximum grant could be obtained, and too little sensible of the value of those intellectual influences which a school ought to exert, but which were incapable of exact official measurement.

If the grant-in-aid system which was introduced in Britain in 1861 had been found to have had these drawbacks, then why was the system introduced into the Gold Coast educational structure some twenty-odd years later?

The answer lies partly in the fact that, despite the setbacks of the system, it was a measure that did enable many schools to obtain public support which otherwise they would have had little prospect of getting. It was also felt that the examinations could exercise very profound influence over the efficiency of the schools, and would also tend to make a minimum of attainment universal. Effective elementary teaching, it was thought, could never be given to most pupils until real examination was introduced into the day schools. It was also realised that teachers were often tempted to cram " elder " classes, and that the system of grants would induce them to attend more closely to the younger pupils.

Minor amendments were made in the Gold Coast Education Ordinance of 1882 the following year.[25] A major one followed some four years later. In this new Ordinance, in place of the Local School Boards, the administration of all Government-aided schools was to be placed in the charge of managers who were empowered to appoint local managers whenever necessary. This essentially meant that the missionaries were to have sole responsibility for the schools in so far as there were no other alternative organisations which could perform the functions given to the missionaries.

The Education Ordinance of 1887 also advocated the establishment of Central School Boards empowered to formulate rules for
the inspection of schools as well as the certification of teachers.
It was also stipulated that grant-in-aid schools should take on all
children without distinction of religion or race. Moreover, no children should receive any religious instruction to which their parents
or guardians took exception.[26]

There were to be Industrial Schools in which a proportion of
pupils, to be fixed by the Board of Education, devoted not less
than ten hours a week to manual work (that is, any kind of handicraft, manufacturing process, agricultural work, or household
work in the case of girls) on a regular or approved plan.[27] It is
odd that agricultural work for boys was stressed so constantly, but
only needlework and household work were mentioned for girls—as
if women did not go to farm. This was, perhaps, an English view.

The new Educational Ordinance passed in 1887 was an attempt
to raise the standard of the educational work of the various missions.[28] The educational rules which were issued in the Ordinance
have been described as " a modified version of the English education Code of 1885 ". It has been pointed out that so faithful was
the reproduction that section 9 of the instructions on Music tests
was followed not by section 10, which had to be omitted because
it could not be enforced in Ghana, but by section 11—number,
words and all.

The Ordinance was, nevertheless, an attempt to expand the
limited curricular proposals and to widen the basis upon which
grants could be made. Drawing, Industrial Instruction and Physical
Exercises were included in the curriculum. Moreover, Singing,
Elementary Science, Bookkeeping, Shorthand and Mensuration
were made optional subjects for which grants could be earned.
There was provision for additional subjects to be approved for
grants, provided the school in question could present for approval
a graduated scheme for teaching. It is clear then that the Ordinance
was rather flexible, allowing every school to lay on extra subjects
according to the availability of staff and interest.

In the Gold Coast Ordinance, the grant payable to each scholar
present at the yearly inspection (and who passed in the 3 Rs) was
six shillings. If a scholar failed in one subject, the grant was
reduced to four shillings, and failure in two of the subjects reduced
the grant further to two shillings. Grant in respect of industrial
subjects was higher. The senior pupils were to receive a grant of
ten shillings per head, and the juniors five shillings. It was
essential, though, that the Board should have approved the course
of instruction.[29] In this way, encouragement was to be given to

industrial training.[30] The Ordinance did not, in any way, attempt to place restrictions upon the establishment of schools. Any such new schools were to abide by the rules embodied in the Ordinance only when they applied for grants.

It can be said, then, that the grant-in-aid system in no way circumscribed the pattern of education in the Cape Coast area nor in the Gold Coast generally. By 1887, for instance, of the total cost of education in the Gold Coast Colony the Government's share was less than one-tenth.[31] And in the grant-aided schools, no rigid examination of progress was noticeable. Flexibility became the watchword for the Inspectors. In 1888, for instance, some £687 3s. 6d. was spent on grants-in-aid. But when, later, the Ordinance proved to be much more workable, Government grants also rose remarkably to £1,673 in the 1891-1892 period; £3,400 in 1895-1896; £3,581 in 1896-1897 and £3,511 in 1898.[32] The Government had good reasons to increase its aid to the schools at this time. The paying of school fees, for instance, was largely unpopular with African parents. An African minister has pointed out that when in 1865 parents of school children were being asked to pay " for each scholar a small sum of one penny per week for the education of their children, some agreed, but many did not seem to be willing ".[33] And C. T. Eddy, in a lecture he gave at Achimota (Accra) in 1952, pointed out that, of the total of £3,654 being expended on Methodist schools at the close of the nineteenth century, Government grants amounted to £1,612 (just under 50%); Church sources £1,567 (49%) and fees £475 (·13%).[34] We have noted in the previous chapter the state of the Government and Mission schools that existed in 1880. The period after 1880 was marked by increased Government interest in education. The number of pupils in the Government schools for boys at Cape Coast and Accra in 1888 was 832. The pupils in the Government schools for girls at Cape Coast and Accra numbered 217, an increase of 185 boys and 39 girls[35] over the figures for 1887.

The number of pupils in schools other than Government schools also showed a total increase of 480, but there was a falling off in the girls' attendance by eighty-four. The actual numbers of pupils in 1888 were as follows:[36]

|  | Boys | Girls | Total |
|---|---|---|---|
| Government schools | 832 | 217 | 1,049 |
| Other than Government schools | 2,789 | 759 | 3,548 |
| Total | 3,621 | 976 | 4,597 |

There was a total increase of 704 pupils as compared with that of 1887. The Education Report of 1888 states: " The Report of the Inspectors of Schools shows a decided progress during the year, and there can be no doubt that the action of the Government in introducing the system of making grants to the various schools in accordance with the result of the examinations held has had a most beneficial effect."[37]

The following table indicates the average number of scholars of each sex in attendance at assisted schools of various denominations in each of the years 1888, 1889, 1890:[38]

|             | 1888 | | |
|-------------|------|--------|-------|
| Denomination | Male | Female | Total |
| Catholic | 150 | 57 | 207 |
| Wesleyan | 1,067 | 124 | 1,191 |
| German mission | 931 | 375 | 1,306 |
| Government | 626 | 160 | 786 |
| Total | 2,774 | 716 | 3,490 |

|             | 1889 | | |
|-------------|------|--------|-------|
| Denomination | Male | Female | Total |
| Catholic | 303 | 71 | 374 |
| Wesleyan | 1,071 | 109 | 1,180 |
| German mission | 976 | 383 | 1,359 |
| Government | 638 | 177 | 815 |
| Total | 2,988 | 740 | 3,728 |

|             | 1890 | | |
|-------------|------|--------|-------|
| Denomination | Male | Female | Total |
| Catholic | 297 | 59 | 356 |
| Wesleyan | 1,183 | 129 | 1,312 |
| German mission | 1,078 | 441 | 1,519 |
| Government | 512 | 153 | 665 |
| Total | 3,070 | 782 | 3,852 |

These figures, which include both primary and secondary schools, reveal a number of interesting facts. Firstly, it is clear that the various denominations (apart from the Basel mission, which is not included) maintained at this period a fairly consistent growth in the strength of their schools. The Government schools were the only ones which began to decline in 1890. The rate of growth and expansion of the German mission schools was remarkable at this time. Thus, by the beginning of 1890, the German missionary schools had overtaken the Wesleyan schools in many respects. It is interesting to note that of all the denominational schools, the German missions took the greatest interest in the training of girls. At no period between 1888 and 1890 did the inflow of the girls into the German mission schools ebb to even one-third of the boys' total numbers.

The table also confirms that the Catholics were off to a rather slow start, but their rate of growth was much faster than that of any other denomination.[39] Thus, by the 1890s the various denominations were represented in the Colony. The Basel mission—which the statistical tables relating to the Colonies and other possessions of the U.K. had omitted—had twenty-two male and eleven female European missionaries working on the Akwapim ridge and in Christiansborg, with experience in the Colony ranging from six to twenty-eight years. The Wesleyans had four European missionaries, and a number of African ministers. The Roman Catholics employed fifteen priests and nuns over an area about one quarter the size of the Wesleyan or Basel District.

The journals of Wesleyan ministers are also full of accounts of the mushrooming of schools. The distribution of Government and assisted schools between 1881 and 1901 was as follows:—[40]

| Controlling Body | 1881 | 1891 | 1901 |
|---|---|---|---|
| Government | 3 | 4 | 7 |
| Basel mission | 47 | 27 | 61 |
| Wesleyan | 84 | 17 | 49 |
| Bremen mission | 4 | 2 | 3 |
| Catholic | 1 | 3 | 12 |
| Total | 139 | 53 | 132 |

The table confirms the rather late entry of the Catholics and the Bremen missions into the educational race of the 1880s. It also shows that the Bremen mission started with much enthusiasm, which they were unable to maintain until the end of the century. On the other hand, the Catholics, after a slow start, were able to whip up their educational activity by the end of the nineteenth century. The Catholics were receiving aid from the Parliamentary grant, by virtue of a special "minute" in their favour. In fact, they had set up the Catholic Poor School Committee in 1847 to dispense the Privy Council grants to Roman Catholic schools.[41]

The table shows also that whilst the number of Government schools expanded, however slowly, from 1881 to the end of the century, the number of Wesleyan and Basel mission schools which the Government " assisted " fell sharply by 1891. During the ten years (1881-1891) about two-fifths of the Basel schools closed down, and the Wesleyans closed down two-thirds of their schools.

It is sometimes alleged that the Government grants might have been withdrawn during that period, and that that might have accounted for the fall. The facts, however, do not support this. For the Government grant, which had been £350 in 1888, had nearly trebled the following year to £916, whilst it jumped to over £1,423 in 1890, and to £2,167 in 1892.[42] It is more probable that the fall was largely due to the Ashanti invasions which might have driven parents into battle with the consequent wide-scale burnings of buildings both private and public, famine, death, and all the horrors of large-scale war.

The remarkable increase in educational activity after 1891 is striking. The Government doubled its schools in the twenty years that spanned 1881 and 1901. The Basel and the Catholic schools showed marked improvement. The Wesleyans, however, never came near to their pristine strength of 1881.

The figures, however, do not include the mission schools which were not receiving Government grants. Thus, judging from the efforts which the African missionaries in particular were making in education, the frequent appeals being made by the local people and the chiefs, it could be surmised that many schools not receiving Government grants were not included in the statistics. C. T. Eddy, for instance, has pointed out that the Methodist Church alone by the close of the nineteenth century had 100 schools with 202 teachers and 6,200 pupils.[43] The figures in the table, therefore, are an under-estimation of the number of educational establishments.

It cannot be doubted, however, that the story of national education in the second half of the nineteenth century was one of co-operation between the Government and the missionary bodies, a co-operation that has existed to the present day.

NOTES

1. W. Claridge, *A History of the Gold Coast and Ashanti*, Vol. I, pp. 479 ff. See also P.P. 1885, xxxviii (383), p. 83.
2. C.O. 97/1, Gold Coast Acts (1852-1864).
3. C.O. 96/25, H ll to Pakington, Despatch No. 75 of 1.12.1852.
4. H. O. A. McWilliam, *The Development of Education in Ghana*, pp. 27-28.

5. C.O. 100/8, *Blue Book for 1852*.
6. C.O. 96/23.
7. C.O. 96/111, Minutes of 1.6.1874 by A. N. Hemming.
8. D. Kimble, *A Political History of Ghana, 1850-1928*, p. 71.
9. C.O. 267/302, J. Hates, Minutes, West African Customs, 16.9.1869 (Richmond's Report).
10. M.M.S., Box 1868-76, Grimmer to Governor Ussher, 27.10.1870.
11. *Ibid.*
12. *Ibid.*, Governor Ussher to Grimmer, 8.11.1870.
13. M.M.S., Box 1868-76, Governor Ussher to Grimmer, 8.11.1870.
14. *Ibid.*, Penrose to Governor Stratham, 14.4.1875.
15. C.O. 96/127, Cape Coast Archives.
16. C.O. 96/136.
17. C.O. 96/130.
18. H. O. A. McWilliam, *The Development of Education in Ghana* (1960), pp. 30-31.
19. *The Gold Coast News*, 4.4.1885.
20. J. S. Maclure, *Educational Documents, England and Wales, 1816-1963*, pp. 98-105.
21. *Ibid.*, pp. 98 ff.
22. J. S. Maclure, *op. cit.*, pp. 149-153.
23. P.P. 1890, XLVIII, Report on the Blue Book for 1886 (Gold Coast), p. 74.
24. *Ibid.*, p. 80.
25. H. O. A. McWilliam, *op. cit.*, p. 31.
26. Kimble, *op. cit.*, p. 74 has indicated that the Ordinance made further educational expansion possible.
27. *Gold Coast Ordinance*, par. 7. Sec. I; Secs. 4 and 5; and par. 12.
28. W. J. Rottman, *The Educational Work of the Basel Missions on the Gold Coast*, Appendix AI to Special Reports, H.M.S.O. (1905), XIII, Part II, 301.
29. *Gold Coast Ordinance*, Rules passed (Para. 67).
30. *Ibid.*
31. J. M. Sarbah, *Fanti Customary Laws*, pp. 102, 244.
32. F. Wright, 'System of Education in the Gold Coast Colony', *Board of Education Special Reports on Educational Subjects*, London, 1905, Vol 13, Part II.
33. M.M.S., Box 1859-67, Solomon's letter of 12.6.1865.
34. D. Kimble, *Political History of Ghana*, p. 75 (Notes 4).
35. Gold Coast No. 74, Report on the Blue Book for 1888 (P.P. 1890, XLVIII).
36. Gold Coast No. 74, Report on the Blue Book for 1888 (P.P. 1890,
37. *Ibid.*
38. Statistical Tables, Part XX, 1888-1890, presented to both Houses of Parliament, pp. 366-370.
39. 'The Roman Catholic Tradition in Education', *The Year Book of Education (1938)*, pp. 745-776.
40. F. Wright, 'The System of Education in the Gold Coast Colony', *Special Reports on Education of Subjects*, London, 1905, XIII, Part II, 3.
41. *Census of Great Britain 1851*, p. lxii; see also 'The Roman Catholic Tradition in Education', *The Year Book of Education (1938)*, pp. 745-776.
42. *Statesman's Year Book, 1887-1893*.
43. D. Kimble, *op. cit.*, p. 75.

I

CHAPTER VIII

# AGRICULTURAL, INDUSTRIAL AND VERNACULAR TRAINING 1850-1900

The point was made earlier on that the climate of European opinion favoured new educational experiment—agricultural, technical and industrial training—and that the European educationists exhibited no desire to impose a purely academic system upon the traditional system. By the middle of the nineteenth century, for instance, Dr. Madden had proposed the establishment of a model farm at each settlement where a school existed, and also in the towns.[1] At the same time, some Wesleyan ministers such as Beecham and Freeman were also holding similar views. These men and others like them were of the opinion that all the instruction that could be given the African boys and girls would be of little value if they were not taught habits of industry[2]

The missionaries, therefore, never relaxed their efforts in the second half of the nineteenth century in this direction. The Rev. T. B. Freeman, for instance, was especially keen on obtaining supplies of seed and agricultural implements for distribution to local farmers, while giving them instructions on methods of cultivation, and in the 1840s the Committee of the African Slave Society had given £100 to Freeman to purchase implements of husbandry to be given to the Chief at Dominasi, and Mr. Forster had also added other tools to the value of £50.[3] Freeman, in his diary, had recorded how at Dominasi, a small Fanti town, about 25 miles in the interior, there was a little band of Christians, about sixty in number, with the young chief of the district at their head, who were anxiously awaiting his return with a supply of the tools.[4] There were also many of the natives of Cape Coast and Anomabu who had small plantations in the bush, at a distance of from three to ten miles, who were then turning their attention more fully than they had ever before done to the cultivation of the soil.[5] Freeman was so impressed that he decided, at the earliest opportunity, to establish two model farms so that he might " thereby have the means of teaching them the best methods of agriculture, and of showing them the great capabilities of the soil ".[6] These two farms were to be set up, one at Dominasi and the other at Manso, fifty miles away on the road to Ashanti. There was to be a residence for a missionary, who would instruct in the practical science of agriculture all those natives, "whether Christians or heathen, who might feel disposed to turn their attention to it ".[7]

Although the farms were not primarily intended to be used by the schools it is clear that Freeman realised that any interest in agriculture which he could kindle in the elderly Africans would indirectly influence the younger generations too. Freeman's success was soon to be felt. As he himself put it :

> "The moral improvement which has already taken place in Dominasi is beginning to have a powerful bearing on the social condition of the people; their houses are kept more clean and decent than those of the heathen, and they are imbibing a taste for those many domestic comforts and conveniences which are to be found in an European cottage. Several of them are beginning to wear European clothes and have requested me to take out a fresh supply on my return from England. . . . People in the surrounding areas call it 'whitemen's kurow' (town) and are now feeling in some measure, at least, a respect for that religion which has been the cause of such a beneficial change."[8]

Freeman's zeal lay equally in educating pupils in academic subjects as well as in agricultural techniques. And in the 1880s a small industrial school was set up to teach carpentry, blacksmithing and printing.

The Rev. Kemp too, when he was a Wesleyan minister in the Colony in the 1880s, tried to re-organise teaching in two day schools at Cape Coast and Accra. Each of the schools consisted of an Upper and a Lower Division. In the Upper Division (renamed the Higher Grade) advanced subjects like Drawing, Singing, Geography, Elementary Science, Household-work, Bookkeeping and Industrial instructions were taught. The subjects taught in the Lower Division were the familiar elementary lessons—Reading, Writing, Arithmetic and Needlework.

In 1892, Kemp opened a Technical Boarding School at Cape Coast.[9] He took on twenty young boys to train them in the handicrafts. They were to become joiners, blacksmiths, printers. A capable carpenter was also found in Cape Coast to teach the boys. It was arranged that they were to spend two half-days a week in the workshop with him, under the general direction of the Rev. Simon Hall of the Wesleyan mission. The boys made progress and in 1891 Kemp reported that about thirty boys had availed themselves of the opportunity of spending on an average, eight hours a week in the workshop.[10] Presumably Wesleyans like the Rev. Kemp were influenced by the success of the Basel missions at Accra and Akwapim in their training of artisans such as coopers and printers. For the Basel missionaries had earlier paid serious attention to agriculture and industrial training, on a scale greater than the Wesleyans ever attempted.[11] An Inspector of Schools, the Rev. Metcalfe Sunter, had in a Report of 1886 compared the Wesleyans very unfavourably with the Basel mission. He was of the opinion that " while the Wesleyans neglected altogether industrial training and oversight of the children out of school, only going in for the Bible in particular and such other secular books as may be thought necessary, the Basel mission recognised the importance of industrial training as a humanising influence ".[12]

The Basel mission tried to use the spade and other working tools side by side with the Bible, and they concentrated their school effort in the inland areas. In their schools the pupils' first three years of school were taken up with intensive agricultural and manual instruction as well as the normal class-room work. When pupils entered the higher schools, agricultural and industrial teaching continued to play a leading part in their activities. The last decade of the nineteenth century saw practically every school in the interior boasting a small plantation where the pupils grew such crops as coffee and sisal hemp.[13] In 1877 a three-year course was also started in Accra to train pupils in joinery, carpentry and iron works.

In this way, the Basel missionaries gave a boost to agricultural and industrial training, but their emphasis on residential institutions tended to isolate the African Christians from their traditional way of life.[14] Despite their interest in agricultural and industrial training, the products of their schools tended to exhibit a clear distaste for anything savouring of labour.[15] Thus, the fact that the products of the Wesleyan schools also came to look upon manual work with disdain, implies that the mere fact of emphasising agricultural and industrial training in schools could not (and did not), *per se,* produce scholars with that bent. Of course, this disdain for manual work was widespread. It has been reported that in Western Nigeria, for instance, the boys also disdained manual work.[16] And something similar happened in the early history of Zambia when the British South African Company began its trading and the Colonial Government set up offices. Here too it was the business and clerical careers that appealed most to the Africans; and even when, as late as the 1920s, more rural and trade-type education was recommended by the mission bodies and the Phelps-Stokes Commissions to East and Central Africa, the Zambians regarded this as an attempt to return them to the rural environment which they disdained. They preferred identification with the European prestige system.[17]

It is interesting to note that, in the last decade of the nineteenth century, attempts at agricultural or industrial training in the Gold Coast were also made from another direction—this time, through the establishment of botanical gardens. It was intended by this to broaden the basis of trade by the introduction of foreign plants and the exploitation of native growth-plants which have been found profitable in other countries. It was thought that no better means could be used than the establishment of experimental gardens under trained botanists to bring them to the knowledge of the people and to instruct them in the cultivation of such things. The gardens were also considered useful as training stations for young Africans to learn civilised methods of cultivation, to enable them either to cultivate the soil for themselves or to take charge of plantations established by others. It was felt that no greater boon could be bestowed on the country than such an opening for the employment of its youth who were then flooding the clerical market and had almost reduced the rate of wages below the means of living.[18]

So highly was this scheme of establishing botanical gardens regarded that it was suggested that each principal town in the Colony should establish one, so as to keep it under the attention of the greatest possible number of educated Africans " who were the portion of the community most likely to benefit by the example ".[19] The station should be in the charge of a skilled botanist whose duties were to study the native flora and ascertain its capabilities of development and industrial expansion, to make experiments in the cultivation and improvement of native production, to introduce foreign products, to make the station a distributing centre for new and useful economic plants, and improved varieties of the old, to afford information and guidance to persons actively engaged and interested in agriculture, to keep a regular meteorological record and to instruct and train young Africans in practical and scientific agriculture.[20]

In spite of all these efforts, manual work (e.g. agricultural or industrial) was disdained by the younger generation.[21] " All our towns ", reported a survey on Economic Agriculture in the country in the last decade of the nineteenth century, " are filled with young men seeking in vain a livelihood in clerical offices while vast fields of labour are left untouched."[22] Notwithstanding the attempts made to establish agricultural and industrial schools, there is little doubt, as we noted earlier, that the rationale upon which the policy stood was a mistaken one, especially since the financial and prestige rewards of such training did not measure up to those derived from academic studies. Moreover, indigenous handicraft, for instance, had little hope of survival in face of superior imported foreign articles such as chairs, tables, and so on, which people (especially the educated) generally preferred to indigenous articles. And even when the missions attempted to teach their converts superior European craftsmanship in brick-making, tailoring, boat repairing and masonry—this also involved importation of tools, an expensive undertaking. And as it is today, there was less respect for those who did technical jobs than white-collared workers. In any case, the charge often brought against missionary education that it has been solely " book learning " and not industrial training, is easily met. The Church was sent to African communities first and foremost to make Christians, and it could be required to devote money from its own inadequate resources to industrial and agricultural training only if that training could be proved to be the sole, or the best, means by which its members could live a consistent Christian life. The Church might experiment in industrial and agricultural training, but only in a small way, and to give an example of what could be done with more adequate financial resources.

It has to be pointed out, however, that a similar attitude was noticeable in the products of contemporary English society but for a different reason. " By an inversion of values," wrote H. C. Dent, " the clerk, who properly should be the amanuensis of the engineer or the skilled craftsman, had been falsely elevated to be his social superior and taught to regard him with disdain."[23]

In the Gold Coast Colony, generally, whether the curriculum stressed industrial, technical or agricultural training as in the Basel schools, or whether boys were tied hand and foot to a purely academic and bookish curriculum, as in the Wesleyan schools, similar results were achieved—namely, that the pupils detested manual work. The point needs stressing, however, that the intention of the missionaries was clearly to underpin the need to train Africans in agriculture and elementary technical skills. But it was pressure from the Africans themselves which shifted the emphasis onto the literary skills. And as L. J. Lewis was to point out in the 1950s, " formal instruction in agriculture in schools had little bearing on peasant farm practice, and the educated boy rarely saw himself earning his living as a farmer. Until investigation and experiment have been carried far enough to indicate clearly the lines along which technological development of the industry was possible, and until the social climate was such that large-scale farming was possible, there was little that could be done in the schools ".[24]

Another subject which received attention in the educational ventures of the second half of the nineteenth century in the Cape Coast area was vernacular teaching. A knowledge of the native tongue (written or spoken) was considered essential to any progress in evangelisation.[25] Many European ministers have recorded how greatly disadvantaged they were " through ignorance of the language of the people ". And they tried always " to devote a little time almost everyday to the study of their barbarous, whistling, difficult tongue ".[26] And earlier in 1836, the Rev. Wriggley had told of how he was " striving to learn the native tongue ". " It appears to me ", he wrote, " that a knowledge of the native tongue is quite necessary to any progress of divine truth among the people, and it is a question with myself whether it would be wisdom to proceed to any considerable extent in teaching English, except at Cape Coast and Anomabu."[27]

It has been noted already that the Basel educationists had made vernacular the medium of instruction. And among the Basel missionaries who had helped much to write down the Twi language of Akwapim was Johann Gottlieb Christaller, who served the Basel mission in the Gold Coast, 1853-1868. Among his translations were the *Four Gospels* (1859), the *New Testament* (1864), *Psalms and Proverbs* (1866) and the whole *Bible* (1871). His dictionary has been described as one which is in the first rank of dictionaries of African languages or indeed of any languages.[28]

African Church members of the Basel denomination were also encouraged to assist in the production of books in Twi for use in schools and by adults. The Rev. T. R. Picot, for instance, a Wesleyan minister, had written to the Secretaries of the Wesleyan Church in 1873 saying that his visit into the interior had afforded him the opportunity of seeing much of the work that was being done by the Missionaries of the Basel Missionary Society among the Akwapims and Akims.[29] He had been especially pleased with the pains taken in their schools to teach in the native tongue. The children read the Scriptures, studied their histories, learnt geography, ciphered, wrote and sang all in their respective dialects. And even adults who were candidates for baptism were first taught to read and learn their catechism, before they were baptised.[30] Picot regretted that English was not more generally taught in the Basel schools, " lessons being given to the first class boys, but once a week, in that tongue ". He concluded: " whilst we in the past have devoted too little time to the teaching of the native tongue in our schools, the Basel Brethren have gone to the opposite extreme."[31]

It should be pointed out, however, that some Wesleyan ministers had clearly realised the need to teach Fanti in the schools. The Rev. West, for instance, in a letter he wrote to the Rev. W. B. Boyce, one of the Secretaries of the Wesleyan Mission in the 1860s, stressed this necessity, and said: " if I looked upon the schools merely as institutions to teach English to a class of people never likely either to speak or to understand that language, I should have recommended the closing of them years ago ". West added that he regarded the schools as institutions in which " the mind becomes early impressed with divine truth ". The schools were " as truly the nurseries of the Church as any schools at home could be ". And he felt that this goal could be better achieved if school boys and girls were taught in their own language.[32]

Of course, the Wesleyans had earlier begun to spend more time learning and teaching the vernacular. Thus, the marked inefficiency of Methodist schools in introducing lesson books in the Fanti language had led the Wesleyans in 1859 to turn to a number of Twi school books obtained from the Basel missionaries for transcribing into Fanti for use in its schools.[33] Christaller's dictionary became an invaluable reference book when the Bible was being translated into Fanti. And in the 1840s, Mr. Smith, the African headmaster, had also attempted to compile a Fanti dictionary and an orthography of Fanti words.[34] There is no evidence, however, to show that he completed the task.

In due course, the Wesleyan missionaries—Africans and Europeans alike—began to write Fanti books on an increasing scale. By 1870, for instance, the Rev. T. Laing, a mulatto minister, had produced the first primer in the Fanti language to be used in the schools. His aim was " to assist school children to understand the meaning of the English books which they learnt to read ".[35] He was soon contemplating revising the Fanti Primer. The Fanti books proved to be so useful that supplies often fell behind demand. In 1874 the Rev. T. R. Picot had to point out that they " would suffer some inconvenience in their schools by their not having a sufficient number of the Primers ".[36]

By 1885, a European Wesleyan minister, the Rev. W. M. Cannell, had also set himself the task of compiling a Fanti Grammar. A local newspaper observed at that time that his effort was " surprising even to an abnormal degree, especially because Cannell had not been in Cape Coast for more than three years ".[37] Cannell had spent the first two years of his stay studying Fanti. By incessant labour in the intervals of a busy life of teaching and circuit administration Cannell succeeded in mastering the Fanti language.[38] And whilst he was the headmaster of a Wesleyan secondary school (Mfantsipim) he had stimulated a number of publications which included: *Fanti Reading Book for Beginners* (1884), a joint work by him and the Rev. A. W. Parker; *Fanti English Dictionary* (1886), a joint work with the Rev. Isaac Anaman, an African minister; Fanti Translation of John Bunyan's *Pilgrim's Progress* (1886), which he wrote jointly with the Revds. R. Hayfron and S. R. Attoh-Ahumah. And in 1888 a European, the Rev. A. W. Parker, also completed his Fanti Translation of the New Testament.[39] After Cannell's retirement in 1887, owing to ill-health, little more was done in vernacular work other than a translation of sufficient hymns into Fanti to provide the flowing congregations with the medium through which the African religious temperament could express itself.[40]

But a few dissenting voices could be heard among the Wesleyan missionaries calling for a greater use of English and the abandonment of Fanti in school and church. The Rev. Wharton, for instance, advocated more widespread teaching of English " since all the extensive town populations of the Gold Coast have been brought under the English flag, and English education thereby having become more than ever the increasing demand of the day ".[41]

This attitude is understandable partly because these missionaries who, despite the prospect of ruined health and even death, came because of their passion to teach the Gospel (which meant more than life to them), would naturally seek to reach the largest number possible in the quickest time and would use the means available. There were at this time in the Cape Coast area educated men like Smith, de Graft and others who could interpret for them, and these European ministers preferred to avail themselves of the means at hand. And, in fact, the amazing influence of the missionaries who lived for only a few months was largely attributable to the part played by the African interpreters. This factor in the explanation of missionary success is usually ignored.

The translations into Fanti were, nevertheless, not easy to achieve. An African minister, J. K. Solomon, wrote in 1869 to the Secretaries of the Wesleyan Mission in London to point out that " to have a Gospel in Fanti required a man who is well acquainted with Greek to translate it properly; and such a man we have not ".[42] The Rev. Carr, another African minister, has also told of how he had to spend nine long years turning his attention to the Fanti language.[43] And in fact, discussions regarding these translations were also sometimes acrimonious. The Rev. West's

*Journal,* for instance, was replete with some of such exchanges, and because of the frankness of its content one example is quoted here. He wrote in 1870:

> "The matter of the Fanti orthography gave us a good deal of trouble. A meeting was held consisting of all the ministers present at the District Meeting with Messrs, Cain and Brown. We held three sittings of about three hours each, but were not able to induce all parties to agree. The alphabet ultimately decided on was objected to by Mr. Laing on the ground of its containing a character representing the sound of ' u ' in the English word, but he maintaining in opposition to all the rest, that there was no such sound in the language. . . . Mr. Carr also, having formed an alphabet of his own, in which he had written his Grammar, was opposed to all change."[44]

Carr wrote to the Secretaries of the Methodist Church in 1871 to explain why he was opposed to the change. In his letter he laid stress on the fact that he could not afford to spend all his hard earnings and his health as well, on a concern which seemed to the very persons intended to benefit but an idle project. "It is really hard ", he wrote, " that now that I ought to be erecting super-structure, I should be perpetually to relay foundations destroyed ".[45] Carr added, however, that he was aware of the desirability for all Africa to have a universal alphabet, nevertheless, it was quite obvious that the sounds of even two different dialects could not be the same.[46]

The Rev. Carr did much to help the teaching of Fanti. When he completed translating St. Mark's Gospel into Fanti in 1871 he started work on St. Luke's Gospel.

It is noteworthy that when African translators came up against any difficulties in translating portions of the Bible into Fanti, they had to refer their problems to the headquarters in England, with notes on their suggestions. Thus, when the Rev. Laing, for instance, was finding difficulty with translating the clause " Their worm dieth not ", he had to write to London with the following note:

> "Our world for that species of worm that are bred in putrefying substances is ' nsiamba ', a word always used in the plural. Another kind is that which crawls upon the ground, and is always in the singular—susuma. Susuma also refers to the intestinal worm, sometimes the cause of griping in the stomach—a great tormentor. . . . This latter kind seems more consistent with the expression ' dieth not ' since the intestine heat is its proper element, and it can all the better endure fire, in as much as it is an inhabitant of the flesh."[47]

And Daniel Carr also wrote about " a few difficulties he had met with in the course of translating the English version of the Gospel according to Matthew into Fanti ", and then requested the secretaries of the Wesleyan Mission to help him to translate the words: " till ", " just ", " regeneration ", " hypocrites ".[48] Sometimes too the Africans referred the difficulties to their European colleagues. The Rev. West, for instance, has recorded that when Laing was preparing a Fanti Primer, he " came to town a day or two ago in order to show it to me; and I suggested a few improvements and urged him to try if possible to get it ready to send home by the next mail ".[49]

Thus, in spite of the difficulties in the way of the translators, there was a fair measure of co-operation between the European and African translators. In this way, much was done by them to write down the Fanti language for use in schools and church. And, in fact, by the 1860s an African minister, Solomon, was urging the need for translating the entire Bible into Fanti.[50]

## NOTES

1. P.P. 1842, Vol XII, Appendix No. 3, p. 19.
2. *Ibid.*
3. P.P. 1842, Vol. XI, p. 193, par. 3647-3648.
4. *Ibid.*
5. *Ibid.*
6. P.P. 1842, Vol. XI, par. 3648.
7. *Ibid.*
8. P.P. 1842, Vol. XI, pp. 186-192 (Beecham's evidence).
9. A. E. Southon, *Gold Coast Methodism—The First Hundred Years*, p. 122.
10. D. Kemp, *Nine Years on the Gold Coast*, p. 149.
11. W. J. Rottman, *The Educational Work of the Basel Missions on the Gold Coast*, p. 301.
12. *The Year Book of Education (1938)*, p. 716.
13. Wright, ' The System of Education in the Gold Coast Colony ', *Special Report on Educational Subjects*, H.M.S.O., London, 1905, p. 9.
14. H. O. A. McWilliam, *The Development of Education in Ghana*, p. 24.
15. W. J. Rottman, *The Educational Work of the Basel Missions on the Gold Coast*, p. 300.
16. M. J. Walsh, ' The Catholic Contribution to Education in Western Nigeria 1861-1926 (Unpublished M.A. Thesis). See also P. Mercier, ' The Evolution of Senegalese Elites ', *International Social Science Bulletin*, Vol. VIII, No. 3 (1956), p. 445.
17. R. E. Hicks, ' Similarities and Differences in Occupational Prestige Ratings ', *African Social Research*, June 1967, No. 3. See also L. J. Lewis, ' The Challenge of Education in Tropical Areas ', *The Modern Churchman*, Vol IX, No. 1, October, 1965.
18. The Gold Coast 110; Economic Agriculture on the Gold Coast 1889.
19. *Ibid.*

20. *Ibid.*
21. W. E. F. Ward, *Education in the Colonies,* p. 187.
22. The Gold Coast 110; Economic Agriculture on the Gold Coast 1889.
23. H. C. Dent, *A New Order in English Education,* p. 28. See also M. A. Dalvi, *A Historical Survey of Commercial Education in England 1543-1902.*
24. L. J. Lewis, ' Technical Change and the Curriculum ', *The Year Book of Education (1958),* pp. 421 ff. esp. p. 425.
25. M.M.S., Box 1836, Wriggley to Secretaries, 30.11.1836. See also A. E. Southon, *Gold Coast Methodism: The First Hundred Years,* pp. 136-138.
26. M.M.S., Box 1859-67, Taylor to Secretaries, 13.10.1863.
27. M.M.S., Box 1835-41, Wriggley to Secretaries, 30.11.1836.
28. C. P. Groves, *The Planting of Christianity in Africa,* Vol. 2, p. 229.
29. M.M.S., Box 1868-76, Picot to Secretaries of Wesleyan Mission, 6.11.1873.
30. *Ibid.*
31. *Ibid.*
32. M.M.S., West Africa 1859-1867, West to Boyce answering queries, February-April, 1863.
33. C.O. 100/4, *Blue Book for 1858.*
34. M.M.S., Gold Coast 1842-5, Smith to Beecham, 18.1.1842.
35. M.M.S., Box 1868-76, Laing to W. B. Boyce of the Missionary Committee, 2.2.1870.
36. M.M.S., Box 1868-76, T. R. Picot to Missionary Committee, 24.1.1874.
37. *The Gold Coast News,* 31.3.1885.
38. A. E. Southon, *Gold Coast Methodism—The First Hundred Years,* p. 136.
39. C.O. 100/4, *Blue Book of 1858.*
40. A. E. Southon, *op. cit.,* p. 137.
41. M.M.S, Box 1872, Wharton to Secretaries, 16.10.1872.
42. M.M.S., Box 1868-76, Solomon to Secretaries, 6.4.1869.
43. *Ibid.,* Carr to West, 4.3.1871.
44. M.M.S., Box 1868-76, West to Secretaries of Missionary Committee of 22.3.1871.
45. *Ibid.,* Carr to Secretaries, 4.3.1871.
46. *Ibid.*
47. *Ibid.*
48. *Ibid.,* Daniel Carr to Secretaries, 26.4.1870.
49. M.M.S., Box 1859-67, West to Secretaries, 12.9.1863.
50. M.M.S., Box 1868-76, Solomon to Secretaries, 4.12.1868.

# CHAPTER IX

# GIRLS' EDUCATION AND TEACHER TRAINING
## 1850-1900

The period 1850-1900 also saw increased interest in girls' education. By 1870 Mrs. Grimmer, " a lady highly esteemed by all who knew her, whether European or African ", was taking special interest in the education of the young females of the Cape Coast school. She used to meet them three days in the week at the Wesleyan Mission house, and gave them lessons in needle-work.[1]

An advanced girls' school was opened in 1874 with fourteen girls. The number soon increased to twenty. Admission was open only to girls who had been sufficiently long in the lower school to be able to speak English, to read and write. They were also taught various kinds of needlework, and as far as practicable were " exercised into civilised habits ". The average number of girls in attendance at schools of various denominations (apart from those of the Basel Mission) from 1888-1890 was as follows:[2]

| Denomination | 1888 | 1889 | 1890 |
|---|---|---|---|
| Catholic | 57 | 71 | 59 |
| Wesleyan | 124 | 109 | 129 |
| German Mission | 375 | 383 | 441 |
| Government | 160 | 177 | 153 |
| | 716 | 740 | 782 |

It is interesting to note the remarkable interest the German mission took in the training of girls. The others tried to maintain a fairly steady growth.

The need was also expressed for a Wesleyan boarding school where parents from the adjacent towns might send their daughters and where the girls would be entirely under the control of the Governors. It has already been pointed out that John Wesley believed that girls should be trained not in the large public schools but in a private school kept by a pious man or woman. The advanced girls' school was, perhaps, to be patterned to some extent on schools for middle class girls in England, where the " accomplishments " were the accepted core of a girl's education, where performance on the piano or the harp or drawing and painting were diligently practised together with a host of ornamental skills which could be effectively performed in the restricted life of the drawing room, and where the girl was to be brought up almost solely to shine on the social occasion. Needlework, Dressmaking, Fancy-work and Crochet were thus among the subjects taught the girls in the Colony.

The Director of Education in his Report of 1892[3] noted with satisfaction that a beginning had been made in teaching practical cookery. At that time all the girls in the Catholic mission schools at Cape Coast and Elmina (from Standard 3 upwards) were receiving a course of demonstration and practical lessons. The Director's Report noted further that the teaching of both the Theory and Practicals was thorough, and the girls also took keen interest in the sciences.[4]

The need was felt more than ever before that educated young men should be able to have for wives women who would match their educational attainments. But at the time of the Director's Report the Wesleyans had only eleven girls to every hundred boys, whilst the Basel mission schools had fifty-nine girls to every hundred boys, and the Catholic twenty-eight.[5] It was to meet this discrepancy in girls' education in the Wesleyan schools that Mrs. Kemp (wife of the Rev. Kemp) took on sixty-five girls aged between seven and seventeen, whom she taught from two to five times every week.[6]

Such was Mrs. Kemp's enthusiasm for improved education for girls that in 1893 she proposed to the Missionary Committee, among other things, a scheme to provide elementary and advanced education as well as training in domestic economy and handicrafts for girls. This scheme did not materialise.

In contemporary England as well girls' education ran side by side with that of boys. There, too, marriage appeared to be the main goal to which girls were educated to aspire, and stress was also placed upon behaviour, deportment and feminine skills. In 1890 in England, for instance, when grants for the 3 Rs were abolished, the needlework, singing and cookery grants were continued. Thus, feminine skills were encouraged.[7] In both England and the Gold Coast, therefore, girls' education seemed to have a rather specific and definite goal: that of marriage. Some of these girls nonetheless took up teaching. By 1856, for example, of the seventy teachers working in the Wesleyan schools, nine were women.[8]

The Government of the Gold Coast Colony did not seem particularly anxious to give special place to girls' education.[9] It was
the missions which attempted to help forward girls' education,
although the mission school managers often made direct appeals
to the Governors for financial assistance. It was quite evident that
as far as the European educators were concerned, the strongest
argument for the education of women was that of marriage. (" If
you educate men, you must give them educated wives " was
the cry.) The Europeans were apt to forget or to overlook the
fact—as I tried to explain earlier—that in the Gold Coast, as in
many other parts of Africa, woman, as woman, has a place of
her own, quite independent of her husband, in the social and
economic life of the tribe.[10]

One problem that continued to plague the efficient running of
the schools in the Gold Coast Colony was that of teachers. The
Basel missionaries, however, unlike the Wesleyans, had tried to
give systematic training to their teachers as well as preachers.
There was, however, generally a lack of proper training for them.
A Report of the Director of Education, even, in the last decade of
the nineteenth century, for example, had referred to teachers " who
wrongly supposed that their pupils were purely destructive
animals . . . their business being to counteract this innate tendency
by keeping them as much as possible perfectly still ".[11] The Report further stressed that if any higher ideal of education were to
be realised, " the bulk of the teachers should be better, more fully
educated; they must possess large stores of varied and well
digested knowledge, a truer view of what education stood for, and
a thorough acquaintance with the principles underlying the science
of teaching, and the best method of carrying them out ".[12] The
need was for more adult teachers, fewer pupil teachers.

This question engaged the minds of many people. For instance,
the Rev. Grimmer of the Wesleyan mission at Cape Coast thought
the answer lay in establishing a High Class School. " Such a
school ", he believed, " should be both a Training College and a
Grammar School to which native merchants can send their children."[13] Grimmer thought that an experienced European should
head it, assisted by an African. He considered also that either
Mr. Brown, the African school master at Cape Coast (the best
man in the District), or Mr. Solomon's son at Accra (reported
to be a steady young man who also had been educated in England) could be assistant to the Europeans.[14]

Apart from writing to the headquarters of the Wesleyan mission
about this subject, Grimmer also wrote to the Governor, His
Excellency H. J. Ussher. He informed the Governor that he was

negotiating with the Rev. W. B. Boyce (one of the Secretaries of the Wesleyan Mission) " as to the best method of improving Day schools and respecting the urgent necessity there is for establishing a school of higher class ".[15] He pointed out that the " present inefficiencies in our schools are explained by the fact that we have no good Grammar School from which to select our teachers ".[16]

Fifteen years before the Director's Report of 1892, the Wesleyans had also seen and expressed the need for establishing a Higher School where (among its other functions) " a better educated class of native youths as efficient school masters and teachers could be trained ".[17] This High School was to be established by the Wesleyans themselves, for (as Freeman argued) if the Government were to establish such schools, the influence of the Church of England and probably the dominance of High Church principles, would allow no reasonable hope of their receiving from such an institution, trained youths imbued with that true spirit of Methodist doctrine, discipline and spiritual warmth which should constitute their main value to the Wesleyan activities in the future. The Government, at best, should be approached only for a grant of money; but even then, great caution should be exercised.[18]

This school was not established. And the problem of laying hands on an adequate number of trained teachers remained unsolved. Some of the schools in the Colony, for instance, the Training Institutions and the Cape Coast Girls' school, had to suffer largely owing to lack of qualified teachers. The solution was, however, to be found in the twentieth century.

Another issue in the Gold Coast Colony tending to militate against educational expansion throughout much of the nineteenth century was that of truancy on the part of school children. There were instances of boys who, during school hours, found themselves casual jobs in order to get money to pay their school fees.[19] Some parents encouraged this. The problem of boys absenting themselves to earn school fees, books, or clothes is still a real one. There were some parents too who removed their children from school before they ever completed their schooling. So rampant was this that enlightened public opinion had to remind parents— through the colums of newspapers for instance—of the harm they were doing to their children, and the injustice and incalculable mischief that the practice entailed. Doubtless, some of the children did enjoy " the treat of leaving school early; the thought that a prospect would thus be opened up for him to wear high military colours, gold chains, with bunches of keys instead of watches, and long frock coats, which appeared to him as the only infallible proof of respectability or importance ".[20] This prospect gladdened their hearts. The Ordinance of 1887 had set out clearly to help solve some of these shortcomings in the educational system of the nineteenth century. But a more radical solution of the many-sided issue was to lie in the twentieth century.

It must be pointed out, however, that the educational welfare of the Africans in the Cape Coast area, and in the Gold Coast generally in the nineteenth century did not lie in the hearts of the Governors, missionaries and Africans alone. There were a number of independently-minded Englishmen in England—men not directly involved in the education process—who also in their own ways helped to bring as much understanding to bear on the educational process being enacted in the Gold Coast at that time as the educationists themselves.

This concern about the educational development in the Gold Coast generally is noticeable, for instance, in a pamphlet which its author—who described himself anonymously as " A Friend of Africa "—called wordily: " Hints on Education printed for School Masters in the Gold Coast Colony."[21] It is interesting to note that the style and content of this pamphlet come close to another pamphlet entitled " Hints to Teachers ", orginally written by H. L. Bradshaw and translated from English into Luganda by Ebisanira Abaigiriza.[22] However, it is difficult to see why the author of " Hints on Education printed for School Masters in the Gold Coast Colony " should publish it anonymously.

In this pamphlet the author set out the General Principles of Education, the Teachers' Qualifications, Discipline Maintenance, Theory and Practice of Questioning, the Best Methods of teaching Reading, Spelling and Dictation, Geography, History and Arithmetic. In its introduction, the author sums up what he considers to be the aims and nature of education:

> " The nature of education is often imperfectly understood. On the coast [i.e. Colony of the Gold Coast] it is generally supposed to consist of instruction in Reading, Writing and Arithmetic in order that its recipient may be prepared to act as a clerk in some Government Office, or to engage in trade. This is, to a certain extent right, but true education includes much more, for man is destined for two successive stages of being, namely, a brief period of probation in this life, and an immortal existence in another world. A complete education seeks to prepare him for both. The best education is the one which combines physical, intellectual and religious, a relationship with the body and mind, and the soul respectively."

K

After this rather abstract and tedious description of the purpose of education—a description that has clearly a religious ring—the anonymous author goes on to state what the duties of a good teacher must be. Apart from educating children "physically" (that is, helping them to preserve their health and promote the due development of their physical powers), and intellectually (that is, enabling them to acquire such knowledge as the ability to read, write and calculate), true education must also impart religious instruction, which includes a moral training. The author spells out the qualifications of any good teacher thus: He must possess Physical Qualification (that is, he must be in good health); Intellectual Qualification (that is, he must have knowledge of the subjects to be taught, an aptitude for teaching, and an ability to govern) and Moral Qualification (which means earnestness and diligence, kindness, and a love for children, truth and justice, punctuality and order, cleanliness, neatness and perseverance). The first duty of a teacher on taking charge of a school should be to secure proper discipline (that is to obtain a perfect mastery over the pupils). To this end, punishments were necessary, but they should be inflicted in every case with calmness, justice and impartiality.

The author further outlines the methods which a teacher should employ to enable him to teach effectively. The teacher must endeavour to place himself, as it were, in the place and in the condition of the children as regards the knowledge of the subject. He should help train pupils to work for themselves, and Music and Drawing should be encouraged in schools because the latter teaches habits of observation, helps to cultivate the taste, and is practically useful in many ways.

The author was also favourably inclined towards home work, in so far as it was the means of forming domestic habits and of inducing the children as they grew older to spend their evenings quietly with their parents, instead of lounging about in the streets, a custom which proved the ruin of many. Whilst learning home lessons, a boy would also find that he must depend in some measure upon his own resources. In this way the habit of self-dependence, and a resolution to overcome difficulties without seeking the aid of others, would be formed. Parents might also be led to take greater interest in their children's school work.

There is little doubt that the anonymous author was fully acquainted with some of the problems of running elementary schools in the nineteenth century Gold Coast setting. His ideas were certainly far-reaching, rich and thought-provoking. It is rather a pity that he did not seem to have followed the series up as he had intimated in his foreword.

Throughout the nineteenth century, therefore, many influences were at work, helping variously to shape the country's educational system towards that of the twentieth century. And in this venture, the missionaries, Governors and administrators, Africans (educated and uneducated, chiefs and commoners) and some independently minded Europeans—all of them played their part in planting firmly the seeds of elementary education in the Gold Coast soil in the nineteenth century. The mission schools were understandably oriented towards religious education, but did not neglect secular instructions. As Britain's commercial and political interests grew, education became increasingly secular in its objective. The new aim was to provide qualified Africans with a modicum of modern skills, in order to fit them into subordinate and routine tasks, such as clerks and book-keepers, in the British administration and commercial establishments. British educational policy never sought to educate an African ruling class. There was already a ruling class in existence: the chiefs on whom the British relied. There was a widening of the basis of recruitment. The expansion of British political interests, the generally improving economic situation, the relative peace in the country—all these added up to give a fillip to educational advancement.

## NOTES

1. M.M.S., Box 1868-76, Picot's letter to Perks, 10.5.1870.
2. Extracted from Statistical Tables, Part XX 1888-1890, pp. 366-370.
3. *The Gold Coast Chronicle*, 4.1.1893, Report of Director of Education, 1892.
4. *Ibid.*
5. *The Gold Coast Annual* (1892), p. 14.
6. M.M.S., Gold Coast 1876-93, Kemp, 4.9.1892.
7. Frank Smith, *A History of English Elementary Education*, pp. 33 ff.
8. F. L. Bartels, *The Roots of Ghana Methodism*, Appendix, p. 351.
9. Statistical Tables, Part XX 1888-1890, pp. 366 ff.
10. *The Year Book of Education (1940)*, p. 479.
11. *The Gold Coast Chronicle*, 'Report by the Director of Education', 11.2.1892.
12. *Ibid.*
13. M.M.S., Box 1868-76, Grimmer to Secretaries, 17.10.1870.
14. *Ibid.*
15. M.M.S., 1868-76, Grimmer to Ussher, 27.10.1870.
16. *Ibid.*
17. M.M.S., Box 1868-76, Freeman to Missionary Committee, 2.6.1874.
18. *Ibid.*

19. P.P. 1861, Vol. XXI (Part V), p. 9.
20. *The Gold Coast News*, 11.4.1885.
21. 'Hints on Education Printed for School Masters in the Gold Coast Colony', by a Friend of Africa (printed in 1876 by W. J. Johnson, 121 Fleet Street, London, E.C.).
22. A copy of this book is in the Institute of Education Library, Senate House, London, W.C.1.

# CHAPTER X

# HIGHER EDUCATION

It has been said that generally speaking more than "half the time and labour spent on primary instruction in the elementary day-schools will be spent in vain unless the educational process started there was continued afterwards; that by far the greater portion of the usual school-time is devoted to the acquisition of mere instruments for gaining knowledge, not the acquisition of knowledge itself; and that, if facilities are, therefore, not offered for the future application of these instruments—if reading and writing having been acquired, no opportunities present themselves for putting into useful exercise these means of information—then many would still remain uneducated ".[1] The truth of this statement was, perhaps, felt in nineteenth century Gold Coast. For although African parents did not put it into so many words, they acted by helping to give higher education to their offspring.

Throughout the greater part of the nineteenth century nearly all the Africans who had received anything beyond elementary schooling had had to seek it in Europe. A writer of the day noted the " not inconsiderable number of natives who managed, one way or another, to get enough money to send their children to England ".[2] An influential newspaper of the period proudly proclaimed its intense satisfaction at the fact that a number of boys belonging to the Colony were being trained in England. " Seldom had they got so many in England at the time " declared the paper.[3]

Public opinion was, however, divided as to the usefulness of this practice. A correspondent of the *Gold Coast Chronicle,* for example, pointed out in 1881 that " a great majority of parents, when sending their children to Europe, did not take the matter into the serious consideration the case demanded ".[4] To many parents the mere fact of their having sent their sons to England for education seemed sufficient without the afterthought of what the future careers of the children should be.[5] Because of this lack of foresight several promising young men had to return from England without calling or profession.[6]

Criticism of this practice was not confined to the Africans alone. Some Europeans, especially the missionaries, were equally critical of the practice. However, the Rev. W. West of the Cape Coast

Wesleyan mission disagreed with the Secretary of the Wesleyan Committee (Rev. W. B. Hayes) for having expressed disapproval of African ministers who were then sending their children to England to study. West argued as follows: " If on a salary of £100 a year . . . if in the course of years a Wesleyan minister could manage to save a little out of it and with the assistance of his friends contrive to send one child out of a numerous family to England for a few years (as a Scot peasant sometimes continues to educate a son for the Church), I do not see what objection can be taken to his doing so."[7]

The trips to England were often financed by parents, with the occasional assistance of the boy's immediate relatives. This was in consonance with the obligations expected of kinsmen. It was also possible that contributions by the extended family or lineage could have been made, the contributions being channelled through the lineage head. This must have formed one example of mutual aid.

Of course, help in sending a Fanti child to England sometimes came from friends as well. The Rev. W. West, for instance, has recorded that in the case of Mr. Laing whose son had just been placed at Holinfort, " a few friends in Anomabu paid the lad's passage and expense ".[8]

The Wesleyan Church also used to give financial assistance to church members who wished to send their children to England. This practice, however, stopped in the second half of the nineteenth century.[9] The Basel missionaries, on the other hand, still looking for methods of improving their work, had initiated a policy of further training in Europe in 1857 when four youths, David Dieterle (later David Asante), and Andrew Hall, both from Akropong, and Daniel Abose and Paul Fleicher from Christiansborg, were selected and sent to the Missionary Training Institution at Basel.[10] Fleicher and Hall had to return within a year on account of illness, but Asante completed a five year course and began his thirty years' ministry in the Gold Coast in 1862.

The most sought after profession at that time was law, considered more lucrative than medicine. As in most societies, the Africans adored successful lawyers. A local newspaper has described the joy that could greet the winning of a court case. " No sooner had the judgement been given in favour of the Chief of Assin than we saw the chief and his followers going through the streets of Cape Coast (with some of the latter in a state of intoxication) turning somersaults, springing up as if on the point of catching a passing bird, jumping in the streets and above all singing the songs and choruses of their country, which betoken triumph . . . their bodies were daubed with clay."[11] There was, in fact, an increasing volume of litigation connected with land alienation at this time. This was a chief source of income for the African lawyers; and this accounted for the popularity of the profession among early educated Africans. An African lawyer, Awooner Renner, for instance, had to turn down a senior Government appointment because he was earning well over £1,000 a year from his private practice.[12] Throughout this period, " the legal profession remained unique for both the political independence and the unprecedented income it offered to those who succeeded in qualifying ".[13]

Most of the African lawyers were found to be useful in the Gold Coast community. Governor Hill, for instance, on his appointment to the country in 1851 commissioned twelve Justices of the Peace, half of whom were Africans. The African lawyers proved themselves to be one of the important watchdogs of Fanti and African rights in the Gold Coast from the 1850s onwards. In 1883, for instance, a local paper—*The Gold Coast Assize*— was established to serve as the " legal spokesman of the people ". The paper was intended to contain leading articles on legislation and on legal matters generally. It was also to contain a full report of the most important cases decided in the courts. Foreign legal information, especially with reference to other colonies on the West Coast, and contributions especially on matters of native law and customs were also to be published.[14]

By 1885, however, it was reported that parents and guardians were beginning to make up their minds to give their youths a profession before allowing them to return to the Gold Coast. This was considered to be " a marked improvement on the old custom of bringing them out without professions and leaving them to do whatever they liked with the instructions they received ".[15]

The practice of giving higher education in Europe to children was not confined to boys alone. In 1886, for example, F. C. Grant, one of the principal and most influential members of the Wesleyan Church had a daughter who was being educated at the establishment of Mrs. Britten of Nantwich. An attempt was made to find her admission into Westminster Training College in order to give her a thorough training. Her father was to be responsible for her training, and it was expected that on her return to the Gold Coast she would be employed as a teacher or a mistress.[16] It is not clear what happened to Grant's daughter in the end—whether she became a teacher at all.

At this time, a few Fantis received further education in Sierra Leone, where at a very early date an institution for the training of teachers and catechists had begun. This institution—Fourah Bay College[17]—which was for many years the pioneer of higher education for all West Africa, had humble beginnings. It was first opened in 1816 as a school for boys and girls. Two years later, a proposal was made for its conversion into a fully-fledged college to take male pupils only. When this was accepted, it moved to Freetown, some ten years after its establishment. Then followed a period of measured growth in training teachers and preachers. In 1827, when a coloured American missionary, the Rev. Haensel, was appointed the first principal, six students were taken on. Some thirteen years later, in 1840, when another West Indian minister —the Rev. Edward Jones—was appointed principal, the number rose to twenty-one. And by 1847 there were thirty-seven students.

It was in 1876 that, under the principalship of the Rev. Metcalfe Sunter, the College was affiliated to the University of Durham.

The Church Missionary Society which had founded the Fourah Bay College also opened a school for the secondary education of boys and girls in 1845. The first intake numbered fourteen, but this was doubled within a few months. In 1874, the Wesleyans also opened a boys' secondary school in Sierra Leone.

In the second half of the nineteenth century, therefore, the need was felt for higher education. Those who could afford it continued to send their children over to England. But it was obvious that many parents could not afford to do this, and the pressing need, therefore, was for the establishment of a higher school in Cape Coast. This need was echoed in the letter of the Rev. Picot, who wrote to the Methodist Committee: " For many years past the cry of the people to us has been—' Give us better schools ' —and often has our own District Meeting requested that this great want of our Districts be supplied."[18]

In Accra too, the need for a higher school was urged. The Rev. W. Penrose wrote in 1875: " The educated people of the town [i.e. Accra] are asking for a higher school and a better class of instruction than can be obtained. . . . If this object could be gained we fully believe that many of the advanced scholars would draft into the higher school, and from here into the Church for it is through this channel that we must look for the men who as mission agents, are to break up the fallow ground."[19]

In 1870, the Methodist Synod recommended the immediate establishment at Cape Coast of a higher class school open to boarders as well as day pupils. This school was to be self-supporting. The Wesleyan Synod decided to look to Europe or the West Indies for an educationist to take charge of the school.[20] The school, however, was not established at that time.

Another attempt was made by the Governor, H. T. Ussher, by commissioning a West Indian chaplain of the Cape Coast Castle (the Rev. Thomas Maxwell) and a Sierra Leonean doctor, Dr. B. Horton, to draw up a scheme to raise educational standards. This Commission was to set up an Academy at Cape Coast, under the auspices of the Government, for the more advanced pupils to be drafted from the day schools.

This proposal did not materialise either, and it was left to the Wesleyan Church again to find out ways and means of giving effect to this need. But this was possible only when peace came after the Fomena Treaty of 1874. As Picot commented: " although the plea for a high school had been frequently made, it was not until last year—when immediately after the Ashanti War, a better form of Government was introduced on the coast than had hitherto existed, securing to the Protectorate paramount peace and pre- paring the way for extensive missionary enterprise—that we addressed ourselves to the task of converting the extensive Mission premises at Cape Coast into a High School ".[21]

This was a popular undertaking at Cape Coast. But thirteen years earlier, the Basel mission had started two secondary schools, one at Christiansborg and the other at Akropong. Students from the secondary school were to proceed to the College at Akropong where they were to receive theological training. It was soon obvious that the Basel Missions, with their liberal use of Twi in teaching, were turning out men who were proving educationally mature for the twin work of pastor and teacher. And already people were beginning to acknowledge the superior nature of the staff of the Basel schools. In 1874 the Rev. Picot, for example, was speaking of " our inferior men in point of education. . . . Our mission is not at all well spoken of either by the people in general or by the sister missionary societies, because we have not in the past paid sufficient attention to the education of our people ".[22]

Thus, when the Missionary Committee made a grant of £500 for starting a secondary school at Lagos, and increased the church's annual grant to £4,000, an immediate decision was taken to start a High School.[23] The Head was expected to have received training in England, and a European was preferred. It was also realised that for the establishment to be successful, African teachers (well- trained and qualified) would be needed. To this end, upon the recommendation of the General Secretaries of the Wesleyan Mission in London, " two young men " from Cape Coast were sent to Sierra Leone to train in the Wesleyan High School there in 1875.[24] Kofi Assam and E. J. Hayford were sent in April 1875 to the Sierra Leone High School to train for appointments at the school when it should be opened. Two months after the opening of the school, they returned from Sierra Leone at the request of the Wesleyan Church, and after a period of inservice training, they were appointed as Assistant Masters, the first African masters of the school. By the end of 1879, five more Africans were undergoing similar inservice training at the school.

It is noteworthy that Secondary School education, right from its inception, was seen as a joint enterprise involving African and European trained personnel. High standards were also envisaged as can be seen from the prospectus of the school when it was opened in 1876.[25]

The headmaster was James Picot, a brother to the chairman of the Wesleyan Mission at Cape Coast. Although he was then only eighteen years old (his teaching qualifications and experience limited to the College of Preceptors Certificate and a brief period as French Master at Claremont College at Blackpool)[26] Picot had the " laudable intention of making the school share the best European education with Africa ".[27]

Mr. Picot was able to attract intelligent pupils, amongst whom were J. Mensah Sarbah and J. E. Casely-Hayford, men who were both to make an impression upon the political and social scene of their country.

Among the first African teachers were as noted earlier, Kofi Assam and Ernest J. Hayford.[28] Others who followed later were W. S. Johnson, the Rev. S. Attoh Ahuma, G. E. Ferguson, the Rev. Egyir Asaam. Both F. E. Asaam and S. B. Attoh-Ahuma had been sent to Richmond College, England in 1886 for further training. And because the Wesleyan Synod of 1887 wished them to take up educational work on their return, the Missionary Committee further arranged lectures for them to attend at the Methodist Westminster Training College in London. " They conducted themselves with great propriety during their residence at Richmond, and won the respect and affection of the Governors and Tutors and of their fellow students."[29] They returned in 1888.

Six years after the school was opened, the students numbered forty. The same year, a girls' secondary school was opened with twenty girls, and was named Wesley Girls' High School. The subjects taught included Algebra, Arithmetic, French, Science, Geography, English Grammar and Composition, Scripture, Catechism and Needlework. The fact that a girls' school followed soon after the opening of the boys' school is indicative of the interest which was already being shown in girls' education.

The girls' school flourished, but the boys' school met with

difficulties. In 1889, *The Gold Coast Echo* as well as some church members wrote to the Wesleyan Synod asking that Assam or Attoh-Ahuma should be appointed Headmaster of the school.[30] Mr. Cannell, who was Headmaster at that time, recommended Attoh-Ahuma to the Missionary Committee, and asked that he should be encouraged to take a degree at Richmond. Mr. Cannell felt Attoh-Ahuma could do the work of the High School, but he could vastly improve by mixing a little in English society.[31] Both Attoh-Ahuma and Asaam had worked under him as Assistant Headmaster, the former at the High School in Accra, and the latter at the Cape Coast High School.

Meanwhile, however, from the time the training department of the school was discontinued in 1886, enrolment had begun to fall sharply and the school was therefore running at a loss. The Rev. Kemp, who was then in charge of the district, was all for closing the school down, and at the Wesleyan Synod of January 1889 a decision was taken to close the school.

The opinion of the leading personalities in Cape Coast was, however, dead against its closure.[32] It was felt that financial difficulties and a fall in student attendance were only part of the cause of its closure. Some believed that private personal feelings must have had much to do with its closure. A section of the Synod who had formed a group called "Reference Group"—a group which believed in the value of vernacular teaching in the church and detested certain dangerous African customs, a group made up largely of employees of commercial firms, merchants and elders of the church—were unhappy at the decision to close down the school, and so brought the matter up at the meeting of ministers.

The Rev. J. T. F. Hallingey, who was at that time in charge of the district from Lagos was of the opinion that, provided the people would accept financial responsibility, nothing should be placed in their way. This challenge was taken up, and a number of Africans, notably J. W. de Graft Johnson, John Sarbah, J. P. Brown and W. E. Pieterson, had the school reopened. The Revds. Kemp and Hall were dissatisfied with the reopening of the school, especially since they believed that the effective thing to do was to set up Industrial Schools.[33]

The reopening of the school received universal approbation. *The Gold Coast Echo,* for instance, was full of praise for the " gentlemen, the patriots who had come to the rescue ", and then reminded the Africans at Cape Coast of the benefits of higher education.[34] The time had come already, stressed the paper again, when the man whose attainments were of the ordinary elementary run must make way to the man who had attainments of sound learning.[35] The paper then hoped for great things from the school.

Egyir Asaam, meanwhile, had been appointed headmaster and, in 1891, the school came to be known as the Collegiate School. By January 1892, there were seventy-one pupils, including fourteen girls. The staff consisted of Mr. Asaam himself, and three un- trained teachers. The school tried to live up to the expectations of those who had helped to put it on its feet.

The Director of Education, F. W. Tuck, in his Report of 1892, praised the proficiency shown in the writing tests, both as regards accuracy and finish. " In the main," said the Report, " instructions proceeded on the right lines. The papers done in Mathematics and Latin were on the whole excellent, and the pupils presented in French showed a thorough mastery of the work professed."[36] The Director of Education also recommended that a Government grant should be made payable to the school in accordance with the new system of payment by results, as follows:[37]

|  |  |  |  |  |  |  | £ | s. | d. |
|---|---|---|---|---|---|---|---|---|---|
| 76 | passes in | Reading | at 2s. | per | pass | ... | 7 | 12 | 0 |
| 68 | „ | „ Writing | „ | „ | „ | ... | 6 | 16 | 0 |
| 68 | „ | „ Arithmetic | „ | „ | „ | ... | 6 | 16 | 0 |
| 64 | „ | „ Geography | „ | „ | „ | ... | 6 | 8 | 0 |
| 57 | „ | „ History | „ | „ | „ | ... | 5 | 14 | 0 |
| 57 | „ | „ Grammar | „ | „ | „ | ... | 5 | 14 | 0 |
| 6 | „ | „ Sub-standards (i) and (ii) at 1s. | | | | | | 6 | 0 |
| | Organisation and Discipline at 6d. | | | ... | | ... | 2 | 2 | 6 |
| | Merit Grant 90% at 2s. | | | ... | ... | ... | 39 | 0 | 0 |
| | Average attendance at 2s. | | | ... | ... | ... | 8 | 10 | 0 |
| | | | | | Total | | £88 | 18 | 6 |

The Rev. Kemp, however, looked upon development in the school with disquiet. The boys were dressing in European fashion and the girls were wearing " mortar-boards "; the headmaster was doing rather little pastoral work. Kemp grew very impatient with Egyir Asaam, whom he thought had been " petted and pampered and lionised until his head was turned, and was becoming un- manageable ". He thought little of the Rev. Attoh-Ahuma too. In 1893, at a Synod meeting held under Kemp's chairmanship, Egyir Asaam was transferred to Accra; George Main was to succeed Asaam and the Collegiate School was to be amalgamated with the Cape Coast school. The amalgamation was unsuccessful, for the boys of the former Collegiate School considered the move undignified and withdrew themselves. In 1893, the school was re-organised as a distinct and separate school, and an African,

J. L. Mayne was appointed headmaster, assisted by A. M. Wright of Cape Coast. Both of them had served in the Collegiate School. Mayne and Wright, however, could not maintain the high standards their predecessors had set, and the Report of the Director of Education was mostly unsatisfactory.[38]

From this time, the school's progress declined—there was a succession of headmasters up till 1898, when the enrolment fell to sixteen, and the school was precluded from earning any government grant. Many of the pupils were drawn away by the Cape Coast Grammar School, a rival institution which opened at the beginning of 1898, with Egyir Asaam as Headmaster, and reported an increase in the number of pupils from five in February to forty-six at the end of the term on June 15. The struggling Collegiate School was pushed further down the hill when it had to transfer in 1900 from the Mission House to Amoono's house in the town, which turned out to be sadly out of repair, and to worsen the fortunes of the school.[39]

It comes as no surprise, therefore, that when a scholarship scheme was instituted for the Collegiate School in 1895, by the end of the century (that is, five years later) " not a single student " had won this scholarship. The boys definitely had the ability, but the environmental conditions were not conducive to sound learning. The scholarship had been intended to prepare the students for the Cambridge Local Examination.[40] The scholarship, worth £200 a year, was to be tenable for three or four years, at the discretion of the Education Board, and subject to the sanction of the Secretary of State. It was to be granted out of public funds to natives of the Colony, aged not less than eighteen or more than twenty-two, or the children of residents of not less than ten years' standing. The scholarship was open to men and women. The examination papers were to be set and the choice of subjects made with a view to testing the fitness of the successful competitor to at once proceed to take up the study of law as a barrister or solicitor; medicine; or civil or mechanical engineering. The women would be tested for their fitness to be the mistresses of schools in the Colony. The tenure of the scholarship was conditional upon satisfactory periodical reports of tutors, good moral conduct and the passing of any of the intermediate examinations.

By the turn of the twentieth century, however, the Collegiate School had managed to turn out a number of scholars. In the words of a notable educationist of the era—words that perhaps appear exaggerated—" in the Collegiate School, Methodism had a record of scholastic successes of any school in Africa, possibly, of any school in the world. A great claim, but easily provable ".[41]

*Conclusion*

It has been said that in Africa, generally, the main factors that tended to militate against higher education in the nineteenth century were the paucity of candidates capable of profiting from such training, the scarcity of posts suitable to the trained products, and the little money available after the prior claims of primary education had been met. However, as far as the Gold Coast was concerned, there was no lack of potential scholars who could have profited by higher education. The Africans had the will, and all they required was the creation of suitable conditions in which higher learning could thrive. These suitable conditions for secondary as well as elementary education were to exist in the twentieth century. It was then that the aims of education were more clearly set out. As *The Education Policy in British Tropical Africa* put it:

> " Education should be adapted to the mentality, aptitudes, occupations and traditions of the various peoples, conserving as far as possible all sound and healthy elements in the fabric of the social life, adapting them where necessary to changed circumstances and progressive ideas, as an agent of natural growth and evolution. Its aim should be to render the individual more efficient in his or her condition of life, whatever it may be, and to promote the advancement of the community as a whole through the improvement of agriculture, the development of native industries, the improvement of health, the training of the people, in the management of their own affairs, and the inculcation of true ideals of citizenship and service. It must include the raising up of capable, trustworthy, public-spirited leaders of the people, belonging to their own race. Education thus defined, will narrow the hiatus between the educated class and the rest of the community whether chiefs or peasantry."[42]

This was the goal which twentieth century Gold Coast generally set out to achieve.

## NOTES

1. *Census of Great Britain (1851)*, p. lxviii (Report and Tables).
2. F. Hart, *The Gold Coast: Its Wealth and Health*, p. 139.
3. *The Gold Coast Times*, 20.1.1881.
4. *The Gold Coast Chronicle*, 30.7.1881.
5. *Ibid.*
6. *Ibid.*
7. M.M.S., Box 1859-67, West to Boyce, 12.7.1865.
8. *Ibid.*, 12.7.1865.
9. *Ibid.*, West to Secretaries of the Wesleyan Committee, 12.7.1865.
10. F. L. Bartels, *The Roots of Ghana Methodism*, p. 91.

11. *The Gold Coast News*, 21.3.1885. The article does not indicate whom the Assin chief was litigating against, nor whether jubilation was restricted to the Assin chief's supporters.
12. C.O. 96/200, Brandforth Griffith to Knutsford, 15.1.1890.
13. D. Kimble, *Political History of Ghana*, p. 96. See also M. Priestly, 'The Emergence of an Elite: A Case Study of a West Coast Family', in *Elites in Africa*, ed. P. C. Lloyd, pp. 88-96.
14. *The Gold Coast News*, 21.3.1885.
15. *Ibid.*, 28.3.1885.
16. M.M.S., Box 1859-67, West to Secretaries of Wesleyan Committee, 11.1.1866.
17. Dr. D. Nichol, 'West Africa's First Institution of Higher Education', *Journal of Education, Vol. I, No. 1 April, 1966*. A general discussion of the influence of Sierra Leone on affairs in Cape Coast will be found in A. Nicol's 'West Indians in West Africa', *Sierra Leone Studies*, June 1960, N. S. 13, pp. 14-23. They served mainly in commerce, Christian missions, army, as civil servants, barristers, and skilled artisans. See also F. H. Hilliard, *A Short History of Education in British West Africa*, p. 13 *et seq.*
18. M.M.S., Box 1868-1876, Picot to Secretaries of Wesleyan Committee, 7.5.1875.
19. *Ibid.*, 26.4.1875.
20. *Ibid.*, Grimmer to Missionary Committee, 4.5.1870.
21. *Ibid.*, Picot to Secretaries, 26.12.1874.
22. *Ibid.*, Picot, 26.12.1874.
23. M.M.S., District Minutes, 1876.
24. M.M.S., Box 1868-76, Picot to Missionary Committee, 7.5.1875. See also K. A. B. Jones-Quartey, 'Sierra Leone's Role in the Development of Ghana 1820-1930', N.S. No. 10, June 11, 1958.
25. M.M.S., Report of 1868-76 (see Appendix for Copy of Prospectus).
26. M.M.S., Gold Coast 1860-76, Picot, 28.12.1875.
27. A. E. Southon, *Gold Coast Methodism*, pp. 126-127.
28. District Minutes, 1877, Report on Cape Coast High School.
29. M.M.S., Missionary Committee letter of 14.12.1888 in Gold Coast Box 1876-93.
30. *The Gold Coast Echo* (1889).
31. M.M.S., Gold Coast 1876-93, Cannell, 11.6.1884.
32. *The Gold Coast Echo*, 26.10.1891. See also A. E. Southon, *Gold Coast Methodism*, p. 127.
33. M.M.S., Gold Coast 1876-93, Hallingey, 12.2.1889.
34. *The Gold Coast Echo*, 26.10.1891.
35. *Ibid.*
36. Mfantsipim Log Book (1892-1903), par. 9 (quoted by F. L. Bartels, *op. cit.*, p. 132).
37. *Ibid.*
38. *Ibid.*
39. F. L. Bartels, *The Roots of Ghana Methodism*, pp. 146-147.
40. Wood's *Gold Coast Almanack*, 1895 (Cape Coast Archives).
41. A. E. Southon, *Gold Coast Methodism, The First Hundred Years*, p. 126.
42. *The Education Policy in British Tropical Africa*, London, H.M.S.O., 1925, pp. 3-8.

CHAPTER XI

# NOTES ON TWENTIETH-CENTURY EDUCATIONAL DEVELOPMENTS

(i) *1900-25*

## PRIMARY EDUCATION

The turn of the century saw increased educational activity by the missions and Government: among the notable developments was the extension of education into Ashanti and the Northern Territories, as well as the opening of Government schools in places which were not served by mission schools.

### Basel Mission

The Basel Mission continued to expand its educational activities, and by 1917 there were 10,000 children in 176 schools throughout the country. They seem to have paid more attention to the provision of education for girls than the other missions or government for by 1918 there was 1 girl to about 3 boys in the Basel schools, whereas in the Government and Wesleyan schools there was 1 girl to 6 and 7 boys respectively.[1] The Basel Mission concentrated upon opening boarding schools, which they felt would produce the future leaders of the school, church and state. In these boarding schools, the pupils had a full time-table. The subjects studied included English Reading and Writing, Twi or Ga, Geometry, Natural History, Physics, Geography, History, Drawing and Bible Study, and there was also craft instruction and singing practice. Greek and Church History were taught to those in the upper classes desiring to go to the Basel Seminary. In addition to classroom work, the pupils worked on the farm or in the garden, and fetched water, washed their own clothes, and swept and looked after the compound.

The Basel Mission owed its considerable success to the careful selection of boys, the relatively small size of the schools, the Christian tone of the institutions and the enthusiasm of the teachers. However, in December 1917 and January 1918, for reasons connected with the war, most of the Basel missionaries—

150

who as German nationals were naturally suspected of being in sympathy with the German cause—were deported. Their schools and the teacher-training college at Akropong were taken over for some time by the Government, and were placed under the Education Department. However, the Scottish Mission took over the training college in 1919, and in the following year, it took over complete control and responsibility for the former Basel mission schools. The Basel missionaries returned in 1926 and with the Scottish mission formed the Presbyterian Church of the Gold Coast.

## Bremen Mission

The Bremen missionaries were also deported in 1916 during World War I, and the Government took charge of their schools and provided funds for the payment of teachers' salaries. Officers of the Department of Education were made responsible for their organisation and supervision. In June 1923, however, the Scottish mission took charge of the schools, and in August 1923, when the German Bremen missionaries returned to the Gold Coast with the permission of the Secretary of State, they began to work with the Scottish mission. In the same year the name of the mission was changed from " Bremen mission " to the " Ewe mission ", and four years later—in 1927—the name was changed again to the " Ewe-Presbyterian Church ".

## Ahmadiyya Movement[2]

In 1921 the Ahmadiyya Movement established a station in the Gold Coast, and opened its first school at Saltpond in 1923.

## Catholic Mission

The Catholic mission appeared to turn its main attention towards the Northern Territories of the Gold Coast. Soon after that area was established as a Protectorate in 1901, the Roman Catholic White Fathers Mission began to work in Navrongo and opened their first school there in 1910. Other schools were established later.

## Government Effort

The Government efforts were directed specifically at opening primary schools in those areas where the missionaries had made little or no progress at establishing schools. In 1911 a school was opened in Kumasi, and another one at Tamale. In the following year schools were established at Sunyani and Gambaga, and by 1914 there were nine Government schools. Between 1916-1918,

L

the Government's share of the educational cake was increased by the management of the schools belonging to the deported Bremen and Basel missionaries. By 1925 the Government had opened boarding schools at Lawra, Salaga and Wa and in the same year the breakdown of Government and Assisted schools and the total enrolment was as follows:[3]

| Year | No. of Government and Assisted Schools | Total Enrolment | Average Attendance |
|---|---|---|---|
| 1904 | 126 | 13,955 | 10,234 |
| 1909 | 158 | 16,711 | 11,968 |
| 1914 | 160 | 20,246 | 15,152 |
| 1919 | 213 | 27,318 | 21,928 |
| 1924 | 236 | 34,690 | 30,456 |

These figures do not include the non-Assisted schools which numbered 217 in 1911, and 308 in 1920. The approximate number of pupils in such schools in 1920 was 12,000 boys and 1,500 girls.

At this time pupils had to pay school fees. In Government schools, infants paid 3d. monthly whilst pupils in standard 1 to standard 7 paid 6d.; whereas the fees paid by pupils in Mission schools were higher, and ranged from 3d. to 1s. 6d. per month. The payment of grants by the Government continued as before, but from 1911 to 1914 a stop was put to this payment. It was continued up to 1925 and awarded only when the Director of Education had satisfied himself that a school generally conformed to certain stated standards in building, management, staff and teaching.

One of the serious drawbacks in the educational developments of all schools remained that of wastage. Before 1925 about one half of the children reached Standard 1, and only one child in ten reached Standard 7. There were a number of reasons for this. One common reason was that parents and guardians tended to consider that only a few years' schooling was necessary for children to be able to read and write. Moreover, boys in particular were expected to engage in full-time work from an early age, and young girls were expected to help their mother at home.

## POST ELEMENTARY EDUCATION

*Basel Mission*

The Basel missionary conference of 1905 had considered the opening of a secondary school; but it was generally felt by the

Church that secondary education should be the responsibility of the Government. However, the special Education Conference held in 1923 to plan for an enlarged Seminary at Akropong discussed the provision of academic courses to pre-University level. It was even hoped that the Seminary—to be housed in new buildings—would secure affiliation to a University in Scotland.

## Church of England Mission

The Church of England re-entered the field of education in 1906, after an absence of several years. In January 1910 they opened a grammar school, with 29 boys. The aim of the Anglican Bishop of Accra—Bishop Hamlyn—who founded the school (now known as Adisadel) was to establish a school which would produce teachers, catechists and priests for the English Church mission. One year after its establishment, the school received a government grant. The attendance then averaged thirty-seven. Some twelve years later the attendance averaged sixty-nine and a government grant of £268 was given to the school. In 1924 the mission opened a girls' school at Cape Coast which two years later was taken over by the sisters of the order of the Holy Paraclete. In 1930 these sisters opened a girls' boarding school at Mampong Ashanti.

## Wesleyan Mission

The Wesleyan Secondary School (now known as Mfantsipim) which had been established in 1876, had 91 students in 1910. During this year it moved into new buildings in Cape Coast town. In 1925 the present site of more than 80 acres was acquired. But it was not until 1930, when the foundation stone of the new buildings were laid, that the school began to settle down to a new period of growth and consolidation.

## Private Secondary Schools

During this period—1900 to 1925—private individuals made attempts to establish secondary schools in the country. Two of these, the Accra Collegiate and the Accra Grammar School, qualified to receive a government grant, but their standards did not improve over the years to justify their continued recognition, and eventually the payment of the grant was stopped.

## Girls' Secondary Education

By 1925 there were two well-established girls' schools—the Wesley Girls' High School, and the English Church Mission Girls'

School—both at Cape Coast. At first they were not strictly " secondary schools "; nevertheless, they were later to become so.

## Technical Education

From the 1850s attempts were made by the missionaries and the government to provide commercial as well as agricultural training to pupils in the elementary schools in the Gold Coast. In most of the schools which were receiving grants for manual work, this work constituted agriculture. And before 1909 a number of courses for teachers and students were held at the four agricultural stations in the Colony—namely, Aburi, Asuantsi, Kumasi and Tarkwa—in order to assist in the teaching of agriculture.

However, in 1909, the first serious attempt was made to establish a form of technical training, and Accra Technical School was opened. The chief purpose of the school was to turn out people who would take charge of the workshops the Government had set up. The technical school admitted persons who had attained Standard 5 or upwards and the course lasted two or three years. This school was transferred to Takoradi in 1939 to become the nucleus of the present Technical School.

In 1922, four junior trade schools were also established, two in Ashanti and two in the Colony. These schools were also expected to meet the " growing need for artisans of a reasonable general educational standard " and taught both literary and technical subjects. In the same year, technical classes were attached to the Gold Coast Railway, and were conducted twice a week in one hour periods. These classes were attended by engineering apprentices who were serving under bond. The course lasted five years, and was intended to augment the practical training the boys had received in the workshop. Among the subjects taught were practical mathematics, engineering and workshop practice.

## Teacher Training

One of the earliest institutions for training teachers was the Basel Seminary established at Abetifi in 1898. The intention of the Basel mission was to develop missionary and educational work in Ashanti, Akim and Kwahu, and the seminary achieved this goal. In 1924 it was merged with the Akropong Seminary.

In 1909, the Government opened a training college for teachers in Accra. The students were drawn from teachers, pupil teachers and pupils who had passed Standard 7 in a primary school, and after training for two years they were bonded to teach in a Government or Assisted school for five years. Their salary ranged from £20-£30; they were also to receive an additional yearly grant of from £5-£20, and the effect of this was to raise the total emoluments to a level well above that of the clerk in Government service.[4] This Government training college was the first institution of its kind established by a British West African Government, and it was to become the teacher training centre for the Government as well as all the missions except that of the Basel mission, which had already established seminaries for teachers and catechists at Akropong and at Abetifi.

During this period the Bremen mission had a small seminary at Ho, and the Roman Catholics built a college at Amisano, near Cape Coast. In 1924 the Wesleyan mission transferred its teacher-training college from Aburi to Kumasi. In the same year the Government established Achimota College where classes progressed from the kindergarten, through the lower and upper primary, to the secondary department, and where also teachers were trained for the Government and for those missions which had no training colleges of their own. The cost of training was met from funds under the control of the Director of Education.

The conditions of service of teachers in mission schools were less attractive than those of teachers in Government schools, and from 1914 onwards there were many resignations in the mission service. It was the introduction of the 1925 Education Ordinance—which we discuss later—that began to help solve this problem by the introduction of new salary scales.

By the close of 1925 the distribution of teachers was as follows:

| Teachers | Men | Women | Total |
|---|---|---|---|
| Certificated | 972 | 37 | 1,009 |
| Uncertificated | 1,084 | 104 | 1,188 |

## Organisation of Schools

Throughout the period 1900-1925, it was the Educational Ordinance of 1887 which formed the basis of the educational system. Under that Ordinance, a system of managerial control was set up in place of the Local Boards. The local governing body of a mission society became the Board of Management of its school, but it was responsible to the Government for its efficiency. The managing body appointed Local Managers, who, normally ministers in charge of the Church, assumed control of each school, and were accountable to the central managing body in Cape Coast or Accra. The General Board of Education, which had been reconstituted before 1900, remained until 1925. This Board consisted of members of the Legislative Council and eight nominated members and its chairman was the Governor or his representative.

*Educationists Committee*

One of the important developments that had helped the growth of education in the 1920-1925 period was the appointment of the Educationists Committee set up by Governor Guggisberg[5] on March 5, 1920. This Committee had been charged to investigate past educational efforts in the country, and the reasons for their success or failure, and to report on the methods, principles and policy governing the progress of education in the country. The Committee's recommendations, which had touched upon the entire field of education in the Gold Coast, were (1) that since boarding facilities were crucial, more Government Middle Schools should be opened; (2) that a Secondary Boarding School for boys and one for girls should be opened (this recommendation led to the establishment of Achimota); (3) that a Training College should be opened near this Secondary School; and (4) that increased financial provision should be made to cover the proposed expansion and improvements.

Such was Guggisberg's interest in the conclusions of the Educationist Committee that he had begun to implement some of their urgent recommendations even before the report had come out, and the tremendous educational strides that characterised the 1920-1925 period were largely attributable to the Committee's Report, which stands as a document embodying a clearly defined, detailed policy for the expansion of educational work at a time when a great change in the fortunes and outlook of the people made the need for such a policy crucial. Thus was opened a new chapter in the educational history of the country.

*The Phelps-Stokes Commission*

Another important event which also helped to give a fillip to educational expansion was the visit in 1920 of the Phelps-Stokes Commission on Education in Africa, which included among its members Dr. J. E. K. Aggrey, a Fanti from Anomabu who had spent about twenty-two years studying and teaching in the United States of America. The aim of this Commission was to assess the nature and quality of the education of Negroes both in Africa and the U.S.A. The importance of the Commission for this country lay not only in its recommendations, but also in the fact that it focussed attention on the needs and problems of African education and encouraged local administrators to study the experiments that had been made among American Negroes.

The report of the Commission, published in 1922, stressed the need for girls' education, character-training, rural improvement, secondary schools and the co-operation of the Africans themselves. The Commission stressed the fact that education must conserve whatever was sound in the African's life and transmit the best that civilisation and Christianity had to offer. Moreover, it emphasised the point that African education must cater both for the masses and for the leaders, but that the latter must be trained directly for service to the community. The Commission felt that " every people must have some of its own to serve as leaders ".

The Phelps-Stokes Report whipped up much interest, and in 1923 the Colonial office formed a permanent Advisory Committee on Native education in the Tropical African Dependencies. This Committee urged the need for continuity of policy and fuller cooperation between Government and missions.

(ii) *1925-30*

*Education Ordinance 1925*

A new Education Ordinance was passed in 1925. Under this, the Board of Education comprised the Governor, the Colonial Secretary, three nominated officials, the Directors of Education, the Principal of Achimota College, and four nominated African members, one of which was to be a head chief. The Board was empowered to make detailed rules, subject to the approval of the Legislative Council, for the control of education. The rules laid down by the Board stipulated that all schools, Assisted or non-Assisted, shall be open to inspection by the officials of the Education Department. Provision was also made for schedules of curriculum, certificates of teachers, minimum standards of attendance and so on.

The Ordinance made it possible for any school to qualify for a grant by attaining certain standards of efficiency. Grants were paid on a scale determined by the efficiency of the school, and the Government expenditure on grants-in-aid rose steadily.

*Enrolment in Schools*

The Education Ordinance of 1925 sought to multiply as rapidly as possible the number of schools classed as efficient. This aim was achieved and the number of schools on the assisted list rose year by year. In 1927 for instance, 234 schools received grants-in-aid, and by the following year the number had risen to 241. In addition, eighteen primary schools were maintained entirely from Government funds. The missions continued to increase their educational activities. The enrolment in Government and Assisted Schools for the period 1926-28 was as follows.[6]

| Description of School | Enrolment | | |
|---|---|---|---|
| | 1926 | 1927 | 1928 |
| Presbyterian | 10,278 | 10,468 | 11,062 |
| Wesleyan | 7,999 | 8,231 | 8,436 |
| Catholic | 4,137 | 4,020 | 4,067 |
| Government | 4,625 | 4,651 | 4,689 |
| Ewe Presbyterian | 2,636 | 2,808 | 2,914 |
| A.M.E. Zion | 1,103 | 1,020 | 1,077 |
| English Church Mission | 941 | 1,064 | 1,277 |
| Ahmadiyya | 58 | 73 | 81 |
| Undenominational | 416 | 426 | 518 |

There were a number of non-Assisted schools at this time: by the beginning of 1925, there were some 155 of them, with a total enrolment of 3,604. The number of non-Assisted schools increased over the years; in fact, by 1938 there were about 477 such schools, with a total enrolment of 20,851 pupils.[7]

*Technical Education*

During this period, there were three junior trade schools situated at Asuantsi (near Cape Coast), Kibi (in Akim Abuakwa) and Mampong (in Ashanti). The number of pupils in training in these schools was as follows:

| Town | Number of Pupils in Agriculture | Number in Masonry | Number in Metalwork | Number in Woodwork | Total |
|---|---|---|---|---|---|
| Asuantsi | — | 29 | 28 | 40 | 97 |
| Kibi | 14 | 23 | 25 | 38 | 100 |
| Mampong | — | 23 | 16 | 38 | 77 |
| Total | 14 | 75 | 69 | 116 | 274 |

In these junior trade schools care was taken to correlate the literary, practical and theoretical work. Apart from evening and early morning work, about one-third of school time was devoted to such literary subjects as Arithmetic, Drawing, Hygiene, Nature Study, History and Geography. The rest of the time was spent on the theory and practice of the pupils' trade. Employment was found for those who successfully completed their training.

At this time the Government technical school in Accra continued to show marked progress. By 1930 there were 84 pupils in training, 52 of whom were trained as wood-workers and 32 as metal workers. The practical training of the wood-workers was devoted to joinery and cabinet work, with instruction in arithmetic, geometry and building construction. The metal workers received training in fitting, turning and smithery, in addition to mechanical drawing, applied mechanics and the theory of internal combustion engines.

## Teacher Training

During this period, teacher training was seriously undertaken by both the Government and the missions. The Government—in addition to the direct grants awarded to the missions—also undertook the training of a number of mission and Government teachers. It was reported at this time that teachers who left the Government's training colleges at Accra and Achimota endeavoured to put into practice much of what was taught them during the period of training and that they often showed initiative in dealing with local school problems. This improved efficiency was attributed partly to the extension of the period of training to four years.[8]

The main teacher training colleges were the Presbyterian Training College at Akropong, Wesley College at Kumasi and Achimota Training College which trained teachers mainly for Government schools. All the students underwent a four year course of training. At Akropong College and Wesley College some students stayed on for an extra year to study theological subjects. By 1927 there were 464 students in these three teacher training colleges. The number of students in each year of the 4 year course was as follows:[9]

| Training College | Number of Students in Year 1 | Number in Year 2 | Number in Year 3 | Number in Year 4 | Total |
|---|---|---|---|---|---|
| Akropong | 49 | 49 | 45 | 50 | 193 |
| Wesley | 34 | 29 | 31 | 30 | 124 |
| Achimota | 62 | 29 | 30 | 26 | 147 |

The Roman Catholic mission also continued to show interest in training teachers for their schools. At this period they adapted certain mission buildings at Bla in Togoland to make them suitable for use as a training college. The first students were admitted in 1930, but the college closed in 1933 and its students transferred to Cape Coast in 1933. The Catholic mission was engaged also in building a training college for teachers at Amisano, near Elmina. A part of the college was opened in 1930. These two colleges— St. Augustine's College at Amisano and St. Nicholas College at Cape Coast were to play a leading role in teaching activities.

Another Catholic training college was established by Roman Catholic sisters at Cape Coast at this time, and the students were housed in a separate block of buildings, which enabled them to live a corporate life as students. In 1928, in its efforts to aid the training of female teachers, the Government decided to assist this small training college for women and to award grants to those missions which trained girls as teachers.

### (iii) *1930-35*

*Education Review Committee (1930)*

In 1930 the economic depression which had engulfed the British Government had its chilling effect on development projects in the Gold Coast. The Government, therefore, appointed a Committee to consider the cost of education and to recommend measures by which reductions in expenditure amounting to £50,000 might be made. But even before the publication of the Committee's Report in 1933, cuts of £38,000 had been made in the estimates for the year 1932. As expected, the Report contained recommendations which provided for a reduction of £30,000 in expenditure by the Education Department on all items except grants-in-aid in respect of training colleges and secondary and primary schools. In the end, however, it was not found necessary to make such a large cut in education expenditure, and the reduction in the Colonial estimates in respect of it amounted to only £18,421.

The Education Rules for the Colony were also re-drafted with a view mainly to introducing a system of awarding block grants-in-aid instead of the then existing system of payments in respect of individual schools.

The cost of education to the Government in 1932-33 was £175,085. This was exclusive of expenditure on Achimota College. In fact, the largest item of expenditure provided for in the Colonial estimates was the grants-in-aid for the maintenance of primary and secondary schools, training colleges and the European staff of the missions.

The total Government expenditure on education for the period 1928 to 1933 was as follows:

|  | Year | | | | |
|---|---|---|---|---|---|
|  | *1928–1929* | *1929–1930* | *1930–1931* | *1931–1932* | *1932–1933* |
| Amount | £92,000 | £117,135 | £125,975 | £97,260 | £96,688 |

## Secondary Education

In spite of reduction in expenditure on education, secondary education showed marked progress. Secondary education continued to be provided by the Prince of Wales College (Achimota), and by two schools which were receiving grant-in-aid from the Government, namely, Mfantsipim and St. Nicholas Grammar School, and the number of students who entered these schools continued to rise. In 1932 the number of pupils at Mfantsipim was 244, 150 of whom were boarders. Achimota had 93 pupils all of whom were boarded; and St. Nicholas Grammar School had 189 pupils, of whom 89 were boarders.

By 1935, a number of privately owned secondary schools had been opened at Kumasi, Koforidua, Sekondi and Accra. Although they did not appear to have attained a high standard generally, Accra Academy seemed to have been well organised with the enrolment at 469.

## Fees

Tuition fees at Mfantsipim varied from £2 to £4 per term, the boarding fee (including charges for laundry and medical attention) was £6 per term, and for stationery and sports, an extra fee of ten shillings was charged.

At St. Nicholas Grammar School fees were gradually reduced in accordance with the number of years the student had been in attendance. This was intended to encourage students to complete their secondary schooling. Thus, for the first and second years, the fees per term were £2 15s; for the third and fourth years the fees were £2 5s per term and for the fifth and subsequent years, £1 15s. The boarding fees were paid at a flat rate of £7 2s 6d per term. At Achimota the fee for the secondary department was £50 per year, and this covered board, tuition and supply of sports materials.

## Duration of Course

The duration of the course at Mfantsipim and St. Nicholas remained six years up to the School Certificate Examination whilst at Achimota it was four years. The average age at which students were admitted into these secondary schools was about fifteen years.

## Curriculum

Apart from the usual subjects such as mathematics, English and Latin, commercial subjects were taught at Mfantsipim. At St. Nicholas, special courses in commercial subjects were arranged upon request for students who had reached the post-matriculation stage. At Achimota vernacular, music, art, hygiene, practical woodwork and metal work were made compulsory subjects.

In 1932 the two Akan languages of Twi and Fanti—and by 1938 Ewe and Ga—were accepted by Cambridge University Local Examination Syndicate as examinable subjects equivalent to other languages, and they were included in the curricula for all three schools. Agriculture was also re-introduced as a subject of the School Certificate Examination.

## Scholarships

At the end of 1933, the Education Department instituted four Secondary Education Scholarships of £25 value per year, to be awarded on the results of the Standard 7 examination. The scholarships were open to boys and girls. Those for girls were tenable at Achimota, and those for boys at the Government Technical School, at Achimota, at Mfantsipim and at St. Nicholas. Character and age were to be taken into account in making the awards; the maximum period of an award was four years, and the tenure itself depended on satisfactory reports on character and progress. There were eight scholarships for 1935.

## Examination Successes

The record of passes at the Cambridge School Certificate Examination was modest. In 1929-30 there were twelve passes; of these ten were from Mfantsipim and two from St. Nicholas Grammar School. Achimota had three passes in 1930-31. Some eight years later, 82 out of the 179 pupils in secondary schools in the country were successful.

## Vocational (Technical) Education

A scheme for re-organising the junior trade schools was adopted by Government in 1932. Hitherto, apart from a slightly vocational bias given to certain subjects in primary schools, vocational training in masonry, carpentry and metal work was given in the three Government Middle Boarding Schools at Kibi, Asuantsi and Mampong (Ashanti). The re-organisation of the junior trade school consisted of the establishing of four classes, corresponding to Standards 4, 5, 6 and 7 of the elementary schools. Pupils were required to maintain school farms of between twenty-five and thirty acres, so as to provide food for their own meals, and to demonstrate, as part of the training, the value of scientific agricultural methods, especially the advantages of the system of seed selection, crop rotation and manuring.

In the re-organised Vocational (Technical) Schools, sheep and poultry (and sometimes pigs) were kept, and lessons on animal husbandry were given. In the first two years the pupils worked through a graduated syllabus of exercises arranged to give practice in the correct methods of handling tools and to ensure that each stage of practical work was taken in its proper order. Lessons in theory and drawing were related to the practical work of the course. The pupils were also engaged on the construction of permanent buildings, which helped to provide useful training for all three trades: masonry, woodwork and metalwork. At Asuantsi between 1932 and 1933 the pupils built a bungalow for the accommodation of an European Agricultural Officer. They also made alterations and minor additions to existing school buildings. At Mampong the pupils erected a dining hall in dressed stone and also constructed a drain about 135 yards long and two bridges. And at Kibi the pupils completed a set of quarters for the African staff. They also built an incubator house, an agricultural store and office, and made alterations and additions to existing buildings.

The pupils in these schools received proficiency pay which was dependent upon the conduct, work and ability of the individual. They were expected to place about half of this amount in the school Savings Bank, and from the money thus saved, the pupils were to meet half the cost of the kit of tools supplied to them by the Government.

## Government Technical School at Accra

At first this school provided courses of three years' duration in Engineering, Motor Mechanics and Building Construction, for pupils with Standard 7 Certificate or its equivalent or even a higher educational qualification. However, after 1932, the first two courses (Engineering and Motor Mechanics) were combined as Mechanical Engineering and the subjects taught included English, Mathematics (Mensuration, Algebra, Geometry, Trigonometry), Mechanics, Experimental Science, Engineering and Building Science.

During this period part-time courses in drawing design, building construction, heat and heat engines, and workshop processes were also instituted, mainly for the employees of various Government Departments. Later, the courses were expanded to enable the pupils to take the intermediate technological examinations of the London City and Guilds Institute. By 1935, the courses were being brought into line with requirements for the examinations for the National Certificates in Engineering and Building, awarded by the Institute of Mechanical Engineers, the Institute of Builders and the English Board of Education.

In the part-time courses too, the theoretical teaching given was kept in close touch with the practical work. Students of carpentry and building were engaged throughout the year on the erection of buildings in Accra, and at the same time that they worked on constructional detail in the school workshops. Students also diagnosed engines and electrical equipment faults and their repair, and attempted the complete servicing of motor cars. They also visited local workshops, sheds and buildings in the course of construction.

The school always kept in close touch with the various commercial firms which had suitable vacancies for the students. In 1933, for instance, of the thirty-five pupils who completed their training, thirty-one were secured suitable employment before they left the school.

*Teacher Training*

The training of teachers by the Government and the missions continued and by 1933, the total number of male teachers in training was 478. Achimota was training 115, Akropong Training College 171, Wesley College 109, Amisano Training College 54, and Bla Training College 29, and of the total number (478), 161 successfully completed their training. Moreover, by 1933 four of the missions had each established a training centre at one of their girls' schools. The Presbyterian Church opened theirs at Aburi Girls' School in 1930, the English Church mission at the Convent of St. Monica at Cape Coast, the Methodist mission at Mmofraturo, Kumasi and the Roman Catholic mission at the Girls' School in Cape Coast. A training college for women was also opened by the Basel at Agogo in Ashanti in 1931. This was to serve Akim and Kwahu in Ashanti. The female students underwent a two-year course of training which led to the award of " Preliminary Third Class Certificate ". Girls who were employed as " student teachers " in the kindergarten and girls' departments of Achimota College received a training which qualified them to teach mainly infant and junior standards, and they sat for the Teachers' Certificate Examination.

An external examination for women teachers was annually conducted by the Education Department on the same lines and at the same time as the external examination for men. Candidates were tested in practical teaching at the schools in which they were employed. Domestic science, needlework, theory of teaching and arithmetic were compulsory subjects in the examination and candidates were also expected to choose two subjects from the following: English Language and Literature, Hygiene and Nature Study, History and Geography, Drawing and Handwork. Of the forty women students presented in June 1932, twenty-seven of them passed and secured the " Preliminary Third Class Certificate ".

Up to 1935, the great majority of the schools, and all the training colleges but one, were under the control of the missions. And there was cordial and close co-operation between them and the Government in the administration and improvement of education and in the development of further facilities for it.

## Post-Secondary and University Education

Achimota College was the only institution which—prior to 1933—provided post-secondary or University education in the country. The courses covered the syllabuses for the Arts, Science and Engineering Intermediate Degree Examinations of the University of London held overseas. Arrangements were later made by which students took the entire course for the University of London B.Sc. degree in Engineering.

After graduating, they often underwent three years' training with the Public Works Department or four years with the Gold Coast Railway, prior to being appointed as Assistant Engineers in these branches of the Government Service. By 1933, five students had started on the course.

In July 1935 one candidate obtained his degree in Mechanical Engineering. The number of scholarships available for engineering students was increased through the generosity of the larger mining companies which were operating in the country, and there were five such awards by 1935. Students sometimes received financial assistance from the King Edward VII Scholarship Fund.

In 1935 the University of London—after an inspection of Achimota—decided that the College should be recognised for the purpose of preparing students for External Degrees in Engineering. Such students were permitted to take the degree examinations in the Gold Coast.[10]

Thus, by 1935 the overseas examinations of the University of London were Matriculation, the Intermediate and Degree Examinations in Arts and Science, and the Intermediate Examination in Engineering. Sometimes Intermediate Examinations in Economics and Diploma in Theology were also taken.

## (iv) 1935-41

### Elementary Schools

At the beginning of 1935 there were a total of 215 Assisted and non-Assisted schools in the Eastern Province, 164 in the Trans Volta, 107 in the Central Province, 43 in the Western Province,

8 in the Northern Territories, and 141 in Ashanti. In the Northern territories the Native Authorities began to take a practical interest in education, and in 1935 Native Administration schools were opened at Yendi, Lawra, Bawku, in addition to schools which already existed at Salaga and Wala. Qualified teachers who were also natives of the Northern Territories continued to be in short supply but it was hoped that at least four Northern Territories teachers would be available each year after training at Achimota.

However, progress continued to be made in elementary education as in all other fields of education. By 1938 there were 439 Government and Assisted schools with an enrolment of about 60,000, and at the same time, there were 477 non-Assisted schools with an enrolment of nearly 20,000.[11] The number of Government and Assisted Primary Schools at the end of 1940 was 464, and 466 in 1941. Most of these schools were co-educational but at least 25 of them admitted girls only. There were about 46,000 boys and 15,500 girls in the Assisted Schools in 1941. In the non-Assisted schools in the same year there were 22,900 boys and 5,100 girls, but the figures for the non-Assisted schools are by no means complete due to lack of information.

*Vernacular Schools*[12]

An interesting feature of elementary education at this time was the prevalence of vernacular schools, conducted by catechists of some of the missionary bodies. In this type of school, which was generally established in villages remote from a regular school centre, vernacular instruction was given with a view to furthering the spread of religious education among those who were unable to attend ordinary primary schools, either because of distance or because of the lack of funds necessary to pay school fees. The Director of Education usually had to issue a special certificate on the recommendation of the head of the mission, authorising the person named on the certificate to conduct such a school. This certificate was valid for service only in the school for which specific approval had been given, and if the mission wished to employ the holder of the certificate in another school, then the written authority of the Director of Education had to be sought. At the beginning of 1935, 27 persons held certificates of this kind.

*Agricultural Education*

Progress continued in agricultural education, particularly in Ashanti and the Western Province. At Asikuma, for instance, the Methodist School maintained a farm on which were grown sugar cane, corn, cassava and plantain. By 1938, a scheme had been started by which every pupil cultivated a small farm of his own with some help from his family when the physical labour involved was great. The object of the scheme was partly to give the pupils practice in agriculture and partly to enable them to earn part of their school fees from the sale of their produce. And in Ashanti, the Sunyani Government school constructed an up-to-date cocoa bean fermentory and drying shed, which were used during the cocoa season, and which helped to produce eleven bags of well fermented and thoroughly dried beans of an unusually high standard of purity.

Another interesting feature of agricultural training was that in the senior classes, pupils formed themselves into syndicates for the purpose of farming their jointly-owned plots, marketing the crops and keeping detailed accounts. At the end of the season, profits would be shared and each syndicate would be asked to pay into the school fund a small sum to cover the cost of replacement of tools and purchase of seed.[13]

*Secondary Education*

In 1935 Wesley Girls' High School at Cape Coast began to add secondary classes to its primary section. In 1936 St. Augustine (Catholic Boys' Secondary School) at Cape Coast was given Government recognition and received its first grant-in-aid. In 1938 the Presbyterian Church opened a new secondary school at Odumasi, some fifty miles from Accra. Within a month of its opening there were eighteen boys on the roll and a staff of three trained and certificated teachers. The fees were £24 a year. At Achimota the enrolment reached the maximum capacity of 744 in 1940.

Modest successes were achieved. In 1938, of the 179 candidates presented for the School Certificate Examination 82 passed. And for the Junior School Certificate Examination, 153 out of the 287 candidates presented passed in 1938, and the following year 191 out of 326 candidates presented passed.

It was reported by the Director of Education that "Mfantsipim maintained its reputation for outstanding examination results. Of the thirty-four candidates presented for the School Certificate Examination in 1939, twenty-nine passed, and of these, twelve secured exemption from the Matriculation Examination. One candidate secured an "A" (i.e. Very Good) mark in all eight subjects he presented".[14]

*Teacher Training*

In 1937 the White Fathers' mission instituted a small teacher-training course in connection with the senior primary school at

M

Navrongo. The course was of two years' duration. No special provision was made at this time for the training of teachers for secondary schools.

By 1938, a special course for training teachers of Arts and Crafts was instituted in connection with the teacher-training department of Achimota College. The course was to be of three years' duration and selected students were to receive a thorough training in drawing, painting, and sculpture, with instruction by African craftsmen in indigenous crafts. Particular attention was paid to the local craftwork, and the chief weaver and the chief wood-carver attached to the household of the Ashantehene had been lent by him for the purpose of teaching the students those arts. An European expert in pottery was also appointed.[15]

The number of certificated teachers in primary schools rose to 3,000 in 1938. Of this number, more than two-thirds were trained. The ratio of trained to untrained teachers, which had been approximately one to one in 1927, had by 1938 increased to nearly two to one.[16]

*Medical Training*

The Government began to recognise the need for training more local people in the medical profession, and a decision was taken to award medical scholarships to suitable candidates between the ages of 17 and 20, to enable them to obtain registerable qualifications in medicine in the United Kingdom. The value of each scholarship was £300 a year, and it was tenable for five years. It included, in addition, an outfit allowance of £50 and a grant not exceeding £50 for medical expenses during the period of the scholarship. Travelling expenses were also to be paid. Such scholarship holders were chosen by a Board of Selectors. These students had to take the first part of their course at Achimota College where they were prepared for the First Bachelor of Medicine Examination of the University of London. After this they proceeded to the United Kingdom for the rest of their course. Successful candidates were expected to return to West Africa and to practise there.

*World War II and its effect on Education*

With the outbreak of the war in 1939, educational development was affected to some extent. The Inspectors, Principals and Masters of Schools and Colleges were mobilised for military service. The Basel mission supervisor of schools, the headmistress of the Basel mission girls' school at Agogo, and the secretary of the Ewe Presbyterian Church were all deported from the country. However, the Scottish mission took charge of the schools of both missions.

It was during this time that Mr. V. A. Tettey, B.A., M.B.E. was appointed the first African Deputy Director of Education. As has been the case throughout the educational history of this country, there was close and systematic co-operation between the Presbyterian and Methodist Churches in order to avoid harmful rivalry and wasteful competition in the location of schools. The Roman Catholic Church found itself unable to co-operate in this way, but a step forward was taken at Aduamoah in Kwahu, where the English Church Mission had joined the Methodists and Presbyterians to form a United School, which had on its staff one teacher from each of the three main churches in the locality. And in the following year—1942—a joint test was held by the Supervisors of the Presbyterian and Methodist Schools for the admission of pupils into their primary schools.

## 1942-57

### The Education Committee Report (1942)

At the request of the Board of Education, a Committee had been appointed in 1937 to examine the existing educational system in the Gold Coast and to make recommendations where necessary for its modification. The Committee was made up of representatives of the Education Department, the missions, Achimota College, Teachers' Union and two leading citizens, namely, Nana Sir Ofori Ata I and Sir Arku Korsah. The Committee's Report, which had come out in 1941, set out the general lines of educational development to be followed, but the war delayed the full implementation of the Report, and progress was made only after the war, particularly in 1951 when the Accelerated Development Plan for education was published.

The Education Report set out what it considered were the proper aims of education which, among other things, were (1) that the child must be the focus of the whole educational policy; (2) that the school must provide an environment in which the child can grow; (3) that the quality of the school will depend upon the provision of suitable and well-trained teachers; (4) that education should be adapted to the mentality, aptitude, occupations and traditions of the various peoples, conserving as far as possible all sound and healthy elements in the fabric of their social life.

Having set out these aims, the Report then tried to consider the needs of the existing system at all levels from the Primary to the University. Some of the Committee's recommendations were that Primary education should be organised first on the basis of a six-year infant-junior course, of which two years should be devoted to infant work and four years to junior work. The second phase—the senior primary—was to be four years, and to be organised around a central group-subject, such as agriculture, fishery or a craft or crafts, with emphasis on domestic science for girls. At the end of the senior primary course an examination should be held as hitherto, but it should be called the " Primary School Leaving Examination ".

The Report also recommended that Government should give full assistance for the establishment of good secondary schools and particularly of girls' secondary schools. The secondary school curriculum should be brought into closer relation with the national life and needs, and furthermore, teachers should be trained in a two-year course for infant-junior, and a four-year course for senior primary schools. Successful students should be awarded Certificates B and A respectively. Special training should be provided for secondary and middle boarding school teachers. The Report urged the immediate development of University work, recommended a generous provision of scholarships to residential universities in Great Britain, and stressed the need for a Board of Public Instruction for further adult education.

The financial recommendations the Report made included new salary scales for teachers in Assisted schools, increased grants-in-aid to training colleges and an improved contributory pension scheme for non-government teachers. The administrative measures recommended also included an increase in the senior staff of the Education Department, a system for the registration of schools, and the establishment of a Central Advisory Committee and District Education Committees. As a result of this last recommendation, a new Central Advisory Committee was duly established and it held its first meeting in 1942. It consisted of the Director of Education and the Principal of Achimota, three representatives of missions and other educational bodies, one female for women's education, and four Africans of whom one was a paramount chief, one teacher and one person who was an Ashanti representative. Moreover, the first experimental District Education Committee met soon afterwards, and by the end of 1945, fourteen District Committees had been established which were made up of representatives of the Government, the Native Authorities, the educational agencies and the teachers.

*Adult Education*

The year, 1942, saw an " experiment " in adult education which started at Kibi, where classes in cookery and child welfare for the women of the town were held after school hours by the Domestic Science Mistress of the Government Senior Primary School.

*Elementary Schools*

The exigencies of the 1939-45 war, had led to a drastic cut in money and staff which made it difficult even for the existing system to function adequately, and there was a growing and insistent demand for schools. In the rural areas, a considerable number of small primary schools—many of them badly housed, equipped and staffed —sprang up, and by 1944-45 there were 143,000 children in schools of various kinds—an increase of over 30,000 on the known total for 1943-44. There were also about 2,018 non-Assisted primary schools in being.

The Government continued to show increased interest in the growth and expansion of primary schools. In 1944 the sum of £25,000 was granted to the Native Administrators and other local authorities to provide new primary schools and improve the existing ones. The Local Authorities themselves contributed about 9% of their revenue—an amount of £25,000 to education.[17]

Girls' education began to engage the serious attention of the Government at this time, and there were 16,197 girls at the end of 1942, compared with 15,382 at the end of 1941. Of the known non-Assisted schools there were 6,454 in 1942, and 5,087 in 1941. And of the 96,643 children known to be attending primary schools in 1942, 22,651 (i.e. 23.5%) were girls.[18]

*Secondary Education*

Secondary school education continued to receive increased financial assistance from Government. The percentage of the approved salaries paid by Government grant was increased from 60% to 80%. There was also a marked increase in the number of students. In 1941, 344 candidates sat for the Cambridge School Certificate, and 273 for the Cambridge Junior Examination. At the beginning of 1942 it was decided to discontinue holding the Junior Examination in the country. By the end of 1943 the number of passes in the Cambridge School Certificate obtained in the schools had increased to 205—of which 10 were obtained by girls. The result is remarkable if one realises that only five years before the number of passes had been 82.

Between 1943-44, the Wesley Girls' High School at Cape Coast, hitherto essentially a primary school, began to develop its secondary department. The number of girls who enrolled at the end of 1943 was 46. At this time too, at Achimota—the only other institution which then provided a recognised course of secondary education for girls—the enrolment was 53 at the end of 1943.

After the Government's acceptance of the Educational Report of 1944, secondary education continued to receive increased Government aid. And by 1945, in addition to Achimota College (which was co-educational and Government-endowed) there were four grant-aided schools for boys. At the beginning of 1946 there were 1,085 boys in these institutions.

There were at this time 18 non-Assisted secondary schools, most of which were situated in the larger centres of the population, with a total enrolment at the beginning of 1946 of 1,969 boys and 212 girls. Although most of the non-Assisted secondary schools were of "indifferent quality", one of them in particular—Accra Academy, founded in 1930 by a group of public-spirited men was an exception. By 1945, the Academy had acquired a stability and a degree of efficiency which differentiated it sharply from the other non-Assisted secondary schools. At the beginning of 1946 467 boys were enrolled in the Academy.

On the whole, the secondary schools showed better results. Of the 366 boys presented for the School Certificate in 1945, 238 were successful.

The existence of the many secondary schools was proof of the strong and growing demand for secondary education which was stimulated about two decades earlier partly by the prescription of the Cambridge School Certificate as the minimum qualification for admission to the clerical branch of the Junior Civil Service, and partly by the institution of many Government scholarship schemes for post-secondary education and training.

By 1950 there were eleven Assisted secondary schools. Accra Academy, which had made excellent progress over the years, was added to the Assisted list in 1947. Two years later, the first Assisted school for boys in Ashanti—Prempeh College—was opened. In 1950 the first secondary boarding school was opened at Ho and named Mawuli Secondary School.

The number of non-Assisted secondary schools also continued to increase over the years, and in 1950 further changes were effected upon the recommendation of the Central Advisory Committee, which had wanted to see (1) the improvement of existing staff by means of scholarships; (2) the provision of more libraries; (3) the payment of salaries of teachers selected for further training and (4) the provision of science equipment.

In December 1950, 743 candidates, including 177 private candidates, were entered for the Cambridge School Certificate Examination, of whom 533 passed, including 39 private candidates.

*Teacher Training*

Numerous amendments were made to the Education Rules in 1944. Some of these amendments called for (1) substantial increases in grants-in-aid in respect of teacher training colleges (and secondary and senior primary boarding schools); (2) the introduction of grants-in-aid to enable allowances to be paid to teachers who were put in charge of Government-assisted primary schools; (3) the establishment of new schools in " backward " areas which as yet possessed inadequate facilities for education, and (4) the introduction of the approved two-year post-primary course for teachers for infant-junior schools.

Teacher-training had been showing signs of improvement in the Colony and Ashanti. The Methodist Women's Training College in Kumasi had introduced the four-year course advocated by the Education Committee in 1943, and at Achimota such a course had been in operation for some years. At the end of 1943 there were in all 170 women teachers undergoing training. In 1943 Government opened a Training College in Tamale. Until that time—apart from three teachers training at Navrongo—the North had relied largely on Achimota for the training of teachers.

By the end of 1943, 120 students had completed their course at the four teacher-training colleges. It was decided to re-organise the External Examination for the Teachers Certificate, the intention being to broaden the scope of the examination and make it more in touch with contemporary developments.

In 1944 a new Training College for women to provide the two-year post-primary course was opened by the Scottish Mission at Odumasi, in the Eastern Region, with full Government support. The same year saw opened at Tamale a new Government-owned Men's Training College, which provided a two-year post-primary course adapted to the needs of men of Northern Territories birth, who would teach in infant-junior day schools.

The Ewe Presbyterian Church also built a post-primary teacher training college for men at Amedzofe in 1946, with 30 students on its register. In the same year, a similar training college with 30 students was opened at Akropong, under the joint management of the Methodist and Presbyterian Churches.

At the end of 1945, the four training colleges which were providing 4-year post-primary courses had 532 students in training. Another 169 students enrolled for training at the beginning of 1946.

At the close of 1946 there were six two-year colleges for men and one for women, with 150 men and 43 women in residence. At Tamale in the North, the Government Training College had 48 men students in training. There was a total of 571 in the older established men's colleges, whilst there were 272 women in women's training colleges. Thus, by the end of 1946, there were 1,084 teachers in training, rising to 1,696 some two years later.

By December 1950 there were in all the primary schools in the country, 2,529 teachers with Certificate A and 762 with Certificate B. At the same time there were about 5,000 untrained and uncertificated teachers in the primary schools.

### Wastage

Wastage in the schools continued to be considerable, especially in Infant classes 1 and 2, and there was not sufficient accommodation in the Junior Schools for all the pupils who had passed through Infant Class 3. It appeared that a number of children were sent to school merely to be under supervision at an age when they needed much attention, and that their parents tended to withdraw them when they were better able to look after themselves. But despite the fact that statistics were kept in respect of wastage in the Government and Assisted Schools of particular areas, they could be misleading. For the school-going population was fluid, and transfers from a school in one district to a corresponding school in another were numerous. To be of real value, therefore, statistics would require to take into account the enrolment not only in Assisted and Government Schools but also in non-Assisted ones, and there still remains the difficulty of estimating the wastage during a particular period, of giving due weight to such factors as the steady increase in the number of schools and consequently, in the number of infant pupils, and also the practice of pupils leaving school for a period and returning when they were able to do so.

In the Northern Territories, however, there was much less wastage than elsewhere. This was largely due to the fact that almost all the pupils were boarders and therefore, better fed and maintained in school. Added to this was, of course, the free education which the White Fathers' mission was giving.

### Progress in 1944

By all accounts the year 1944 was a progressive one for educational advancement in this country. It was in that year that the Education Department invited all Educational Units to draw up plans for the development of their organisations in the ten years following the end of World War II. The Education Units were asked to envisage the achievement, within a period of 20 to 25 years, of facilities for a six-year infant-junior course of education for all children of school-going age.

It was in 1944 also that the Education Department, in close collaboration with other Government Departments, initiated a series of education surveys in the Colony, Ashanti and the Southern part of Togoland under British Mandate. These surveys were designed to give detailed information of all schools, " no matter how indifferent their quality ", and to ascertain the number of additional infant and infant-junior schools required in each region. It was planned to use the required information in choosing localities in which to establish new senior primary schools for the further education of the more promising products of the infant-junior.

It was in 1944 that, in order to help education in the " backward " areas, the Government decided to make a grant of £25,000 payable direct to the Native Administration, or other local Governments, to augment the funds which these administrators were able to devote to education.

*Higher Education*

In 1944 the Government approved a scheme drawn up by the Education Department to provide the large staff of highly qualified African men and women who would be required to work in training colleges and secondary schools, and for supervisory duties. The scheme provided for the higher education and professional training at Achimota, in the United Kingdom or both, for men and women recommended by the Educational Units and interviewed by the Central Advisory Committee on Education and the Education Department. A total of £96,000 was to be spent on the scheme in seven years. Accordingly, ten men and one woman were selected for courses in the United Kingdom in October 1944. At the same time a number of people were selected for the Intermediate University Courses at Achimota.

By the end of 1945, of the total of 582 students at Achimota, 156 of them were undertaking the Intermediate Degree or Special Courses. A number of successes were recorded at this time. Of the 80 candidates presented for the Intermediate Examinations in Arts, Science, Engineering, Commerce, Law, Economics and Divinity, Achimota alone presented 49. Of this number 25 passed; and of the 16 candidates presented for the Divinity, Economics, English, History and Engineering, 7 passed; this included the 5 out of the 12 entered by Achimota.

Of course, a few also turned to Europe for further training. In 1945, for instance, there were 136 students undergoing courses in the United Kingdom. These included 66 individuals with scholarships awarded under Government schemes, and 12 with scholarships from other sources. There were at the same time, 58 students supported by their own families.

The courses and the number of students taking them by 1945 included the following: Law (12), Medicine and Dentistry (43), Engineering (4), Arts and Economics (26), Education, including Diploma in Education and Domestic Science (19), Science (7), Agriculture (3), Accountancy (5), Pharmacy (3), Nursing (4). Of the total of 126 students, 12 were women.

The University College of Ghana was established as a result of the recommendations of the Asquith Commission on Higher Education in the Colonies and those of the Elliot Commission on Higher Education in West Africa, the reports of which were both published in 1945. The Elliot Commission's report put forward a minority recommendation that there should be one university, to be sited in Ibadan, for all the then British territories in West Africa, and territorial colleges in Nigeria, Sierra Leone and the Gold Coast, and this minority view was readily accepted by the Colonial Office. But objection was raised, largely by the African members of the then Legislative Council of the Gold Coast, and a change of heart came about in Colonial circles; and the University College of the Gold Coast came to be established as part of the general development of university education in West Africa.

In 1948, by an ordinance, the University College of the Gold Coast was established " for the purpose of providing and promoting university education, learning and research", and it expanded rapidly. By 1950 there were 213 students, 80 of whom were in the Arts, Economics or Science faculties, 103 were reading for Intermediate Examinations, and 30 were at the Institute of Education.

In 1950, a grant of £1,000,000 was made by the Cocoa Marketing Board (in addition to the £900,000 already provided from cocoa funds) to found a large teaching and research Department of Agriculture with facilities for the study of the associated sciences. The Government gave another £1,000,000 towards the capital cost of some of the College's permanent buildings, and with the Colonial Development and Welfare Act, another £400,000 was given. The construction of the first permanent buildings at Legon Hill, near Accra, began at this time.

The Government continued to award scholarships for training abroad. Between 1944 and 1950, 508 scholarships were awarded. The courses were varied, and included Accountancy, Agriculture, Architecture, Dentistry, Ecology, Pharmacy, Domestic Science, Engineering and other professional courses.

## Technical Education

Technical education did not expand as fast as was anticipated. However, it limped on, providing secondary courses in Engineering, Building Construction and Handicrafts. At the beginning of 1951 there were 64 students on the Mechanical Engineering course and 54 teachers in training taking the handicrafts course. And the same year a College of Technology was established at Kumasi in order to train a diversity of personnel required for the economic, technological, educational and social development of the country. The Principal was appointed in 1951 and a number of semi-permanent buildings were completed in that year to accommodate the first element of the College, a teacher-training department, which was formerly the Achimota Teacher-Training College. Other courses which were then to be provided at Kumasi College included Civil Engineering, Mechanical and Electrical Engineering, Accountancy, Pharmacy, Secretarial Studies and Agricultural Machinery. In addition, a course in Surveying and a special Accountancy course for Government officers were projected. Both of these institutions at Achimota and Kumasi as well as other developments in education and other social services were made possible by grants made from the United Kingdom funds under the Colonial Development and Welfare Acts of 1945 and later years.

## The Accelerated Development Plan for Education, 1951

When a new Constitution came into being in the Gold Coast in 1951, an Accelerated Development Plan for Education was laid before Parliament. The main objective of this Plan was " to help develop a balanced system working towards universal primary education as rapidly as consideration of finances and teacher-training allowed, but maintaining at the same time proportionate facilities for further education for those most fitted to receive it ".

Some of the main proposals were the following:

1. A six-year basic primary course for all children at public expense; primary school fees to be abolished as from January 1st, 1952.

2. Infant-junior schools were to be known as primary schools. Senior primary schools were to be known as middle schools, and were to be regarded as part of the post-primary system.

3. Facilities for the training of teachers were to be increased by the addition of ten new colleges and the doubling in size of the six existing ones.

4. Additional secondary day schools were to be provided, and certain non-Assisted secondary schools were to be assisted.

5. Four secondary-technical schools were to be provided, including the conversion of the Government Technical School at Takoradi. Technical institutes were to be established at Tarkwa, Accra, Kumasi, Sekondi-Takoradi.

6. All teachers-in-training, except those possessing a School Certificate, were to take the Certificate B course, and entry to the Certificate A course was to be made from among Certificate B teachers who had taught for a period.

7. The middle schools in the Northern Territories were to be increased in number as quickly as possible, and more potential teachers were to be provided. A new training college was to be opened at Pusiga. Primary schools in the North were to be increased in numbers as teachers became available.

8. The salaries of teachers—training and untrained were to be reviewed. It was proposed that in future all teachers in training would be treated as if on Study Leave, and would draw the salaries they would have received if they had been teaching in a school.

9. Considerable increases in scholarships to secondary schools, technical and trade schools were recommended.

The period 1944-1951 was marked by increased Government spending on education. The annual grant was as follows:

|        | 1946-1947 | 1947-1948 | 1948-1949 | 1949-1950 | 1950-1951 |
|--------|-----------|-----------|-----------|-----------|-----------|
| Amount | £467,000 | £742,000 | £744,000 | £902,000 | £1,065,000 |

In 1951 the first secondary school for the Northern Territories opened in Tamale. Entry to the school was open to all boys in Middle Form 2 who were clearly not more than 14 years old. In the same year a Trade Training Centre was opened at Tamale which provided the Northern Territories with a type of vocational training already being supplied at Mampong in Ashanti and at Asuantsi in the Colony.

The limiting factors in the rate of educational expansion were finance and an inadequate supply of trained teachers. Of course, by 1951 some progress had been made. New training colleges were coming into production, and existing colleges to which extensions had been made were contributing an increased number of trained teachers. Native Authority grants for educational purposes remained substantial, and there was an increasing realisation that education had to be paid for and was worth paying for.

The various types of school—Government, mission and Native Authority—were subject to the general control of the Government, in accordance with the provisions of two Education ordinances, one for the Colony and Ashanti, and the other for the Northern Territories.

The curriculum of the basic and senior primary courses corresponded broadly to that of similar schools in the United Kingdom. But the need was recognised to relate teaching to the community, and this was reflected in the syllabus of instruction. Special attention was given to the teaching of the Vernacular, Hygiene, Crafts, Agriculture, and—in the case of girls—Housecraft, including Nutrition and Child-Welfare. Secondary, and teacher training education was being given firm foundation; and closer attention was also being paid to post-secondary and university education. The stage was then set for the educational advance which characterises the second half of the twentieth Century.

For the six years up to the Declaration of Independence in 1957 educational facilities rapidly expanded to almost all parts of the country. By February 1958 there were, in the entire country, 3,402 primary schools and 1,030 middle schools. Because one of the most pressing needs was the provision of a sound primary education for every child of school-going age, the government had to introduce compulsory primary education after the payment of fees for primary education had been abolished.

Between 1951 and 1957 the number of secondary schools rose from 12 to 38; and by February 1958 there were 10,423 students in secondary schools. When the Accelerated Development Plan for Education was prepared in 1951, it was recognised that the key to the whole problem of educational expansion was the production of as many trained teachers as possible. The plan aimed at a total enrolment of 3,500 in the Certificate A and Certificate B training colleges. The enrolment in 1958 reached the record figure of 4,055. And in the same year, the number of untrained teachers in primary and middle schools fell below 10,000 for the first time since 1952, whilst certificated teachers for the first time exceeded the number of pupil teachers in primary and middle schools.

The requirements of industrial and governmental expansion called for an increase in technical education at and below university level. The need was seriously felt to expand the lower levels of technical training, both to provide skilled workmen for industry and to provide a field for the selection of students for more advanced technical training. Soon after Independence a reorganisation of technical education was envisaged. Technical Institutes were to be reorganised to provide additional Junior Institute training as well as their own courses. It was soon realised also that the efficiency of every establishment in the country rested with the clerical staff, and an attempt was made at an expanded programme for training clerical and commercial personnel. In fact, soon after Independence, the government provided nearly two million pounds for the reorganisation of technical and commercial courses.

## NOTES

1. McWilliam, *The Development of Education in Ghana, p.* 20.
2. There are two kinds of Islam in Ghana; one forbids any adaptation of Islamic Law to modern conditions and the other is known as the Ahmadiyya movement—a sect centred in Pakistan and founded by Mirza Ghulam Ahmad who died in 1908. The missionary activity of the Movement is patterned after Christian missionary methods.
3. Education Department Report 1923-24, Appendix E.
4. F. H. Hilliard, *A Short History of Education in West Africa,* p. 82.
5. For an account of the educational activities of Gov. Guggisberg, see McWilliam, *op. cit.,* Ch. 7.
6. Gold Coast Colony: Report on the Education Department 1928-29, p. 5.
7. Hilliard, *op. cit.,* p. 93.
8. *Ibid.,* p. 12.
9. *Ibid.,* p. 91.
10. Report of Education Department, 1935-36, p. 36.
11. Hilliard, *op. cit.,* p. 93.
12. Report of Education Department, 1935-36.
13. Report of Education Department, 1937-38, p. 31.
14. Report of Education Department, 1939-40, p. 5.
15. Hilliard, *op. cit.,* p. 45.
16. *Ibid.,* p. 95.
17. Report of Education Department, 1943-44.
18. *Ibid.*

# CHAPTER XII

# CONCLUSION

Elementary education in the Gold Coast (and in England too) was the result of a slow process of evolution characterised by experiment, by successes and by failures. But whereas in England education started with the express aim to " save " the poor, in the Gold Coast, education was originally intended for children of Africans in the upper segments of the society—mulatto children, the children of chiefs and of the rising class of wealthy merchants, traders and professionals. However, the concept of an elementary education, more or less common to all sections of the community, did not take long to emerge in the Gold Coast.

In both England and the Gold Coast the provision of education, especially in the nineteenth century, started as acts of philanthropy, largely undertaken by the Church and individuals; and in the Colony especially, by Merchant Companies, who desired to gain economic advantage from the products of the schools. Because the administrators worked parallel with the missionaries, one result was the emergence of a dual structure—Government and missionary schools, a feature that has persisted even to the present day. Moreover, the missionary bodies, especially the Wesleyan and Basel missions, adopted different methods. The Wesleyans used English as the medium of instruction, and the Basel missionaries preferred to use the vernacular. Moreover, the Wesleyans concentrated on the coastal towns, whereas the Basel mission chose to work mainly in the smaller towns in the Akwapim area, about twenty miles from Accra.

Much of the structure and content of education in contemporary England—the curriculum and the monitorial system, for example—was brought over into the Gold Coast educational setting. However, strenuous efforts were made to adjust some aspects of the educational process to suit local conditions, notably, the attempts at agricultural and industrial training. The failure of these experiments was due largely to the fact that the Africans themselves appeared to desire European-type education based on Reading, Writing and Arithmetic. It might be added here, in fact, that the use of English models and their adaptation was continued into the

181

present day, as is seen in the use of Ordinary and Advanced Levels, and School Certificate Examinations.

It may be said also that the charge that the Europeans who were directly involved in the educational venture in the nineteenth century Gold Coast failed to recognise the dangers of total culture borrowing is not fair. In fact, most educationists in England were themselves eager to reform their own educational system, and were certainly aware of the fact that any educational innovation within the cultural pattern might have deleterious effects, owing to the close relationship between various institutions.

Although both Europeans and Africans pressed for more schools in the Gold Coast, they desired them largely for different reasons. The European administrators wanted African education mainly in order to train human tools for their economic and administrative machinery. (References to "education" in the Despatches and Reports of the nineteenth century clearly show that the conception of the aims of education was one of exploitation and development largely for benefit of the people of Great Britain.) The African, on the other hand, desired European-type education in order to attain equality with, and even perhaps challenge the Europeans.

In the Gold Coast (unlike many other African societies), girls' education from the very beginnings of the educational process, was regarded as important. The woman's place was considered to be the home and the curricula in girls' schools had Domestic Science appended (as was done in England too). But not as many girls commenced education as boys, and not as many continued; a girl was more likely to receive some education if she had an educated father.

Among those who have recently traced the growth and development of the early educational system in the Gold Coast is P. J. Foster. He has rightly pointed out that the overall expansion of the Gold Coast system of education was neither directly in the hands of the Government nor subject to effective government policy; that its development was largely autonomous and uncontrolled; and that the pattern of distribution of schools closely followed the pattern of differential demand, itself becoming an indirect index of the extent to which indigenous social structures were already undergoing transformation as a result of European contact.

More specifically, Foster argues that in the nineteenth century there was no popular demand for education, that in spite of repeated efforts on the part of the missionaries for example, schools failed to enrol enough pupils to ensure their survival, and that it was only after certain changes in the traditional societies had taken place (changes initiated by the gradual growth of commerce on the

Coast at the close of the nineteenth century, and the development of cash crops and mining inland) that formal schools had any success at all.

Foster's observation, though certainly true of some towns in the Colony generally, is untenable as far as Wesleyan schools in the nineteenth century Fanti area were concerned. True, the Fanti chiefs in and around Cape Coast had to be prodded on by the Wesleyan missionaries, but the missionaries' efforts met with a considerable measure of success, as their letters and journals indicate. Indeed, it is even probable that these chiefs, far from seeing the schools as a threat to the traditional beliefs that upheld their status, might perhaps themselves have fostered the missionaries' educational endeavours as a means of enhancing their own superiority. Education at this time was prestigious, and some of the chiefs probably desired to be associated with it. A close examination of the number of schools and the intake of pupils, particularly in Cape Coast town, in the last decade of the nineteenth century, shows that the intake, especially into the Wesleyan schools, was appreciable. In fact, in the Colony generally, by 1851 there were eighty-four Wesleyan schools with a total enrolment of over three thousand pupils, and over one hundred teachers; and, by the close of the nineteenth century, the Wesleyans had a hundred schools, more than six thousand two hundred pupils and over two hundred teachers.

These figures become still more significant if they are looked at against the background of the total population at this time. The point is that judging from the efforts the African missionaries in particular were making in education, and the frequent appeals being made by the local people and the chiefs generally—as an examination of missionary letters and journals shows—it can be surmised that many schools not receiving Government grants were omitted from the official statistics to which Foster had access. And this accounts for his error in judgment.

Western-oriented education in the Gold Coast tended to open the door to new occupations, and with this often came wealth and prestige, and by the beginning of the twentieth century emerged the educated elite, fluent in English, a number of whom had European names, and tried to live in European-type houses and wear European attire. This educated elite formed a relatively small group which tended to follow such professions as law, medicine or commerce. In the Gold Coast, hopes of achieving higher standards of living depended almost directly upon the ability to train the men and women it required for services at all levels in the administration. There is little doubt that education is

N

related to productivity and economic growth. A nation, like an individual, must decide to devote time and resources to education in order to reap the benefits later. Moreover, national survival requires countries to invest in education as an investment in the future.

It is possible to argue, however, that in the Gold Coast resources were limited, so capital and labour invested in education were not to hand for investment in other types of development, and that education was invested in, thereby delaying economic gains in the hope of maximising them at a later date. But even if this is true—and assuming that the various attempts made later in the nineteenth century to introduce agricultural and industrial training lent support to this contention—it is nevertheless true also that the economic consequences of Western education were far less satisfactory than the early protagonists of agricultural and industrial education had ever thought possible. And far from giving an impetus to economic growth in agriculture and industry, education tended to reflect the bias of occupational structures towards clerical employment. The Africans preferred academic education, a situation which is a sure reflection of their realistic perception of the differential rewards and prestige accorded to Europeans.

Indeed, one of the problems of Ghana today is that technological education is not keeping pace with technological advance; and one of the paradoxes of post-independent Ghana is that independence has speeded up modernisation, but the latter has created a greater dependency on expatriate technological assistance. This is a major problem for all developing countries.

When Independence was achieved, however, some of the aims set out in 1925 in the *Education Policy in the British Tropical Africa*[15] had been realised through educational development. The achievement of Independence was itself proof that the country had trained men and women who were ready to manage their own affairs, that the ideals of citizenship and service had been inculcated, and that public-spirited leaders had been raised.

Over the years, education in Ghana came to be adapted to the traditions of her peoples. Much was done to conserve, as far as possible, the healthy elements in the fabric of social life and, whenever necessary, attempts were made to adapt these elements to changes in society. Education had led also to an over-all improvement in the provision of social services such as health and housing, though more could have been done at the time to raise standards through the improvement of agriculture and the development of local industries.

Despite the ideals envisaged in the *Education Policy* of 1925, education did not necessarily help to "narrow the hiatus" between the educated group and the rest of the community. But although an important factor in the stratification of Ghana was education, there was nevertheless a measure of co-operation, particularly between the educated people and the illiterate chiefs. Many illiterate men—in so far as they became aware of any specific political, social or religious grievance—did not fail to give whatever support they could.

The post-Independence period was marked by a clearer awareness of the part education should play in an independent African society. This realisation was given expression in subsequent educational reforms and governmental policies that were formulated from time to time.

# APPENDIX A

TIME TABLE FOR A TYPICAL MONITORIAL SCHOOL
(about 1888)*

*Morning*

| Time | 1st Class | 2nd Class | 3rd Class |
|---|---|---|---|
| 9.15 a.m. | Catechism | Collects | Lord's Prayer |
| 9.30 a.m. | Reads and spells to the master | Reads and spells from lesson to teacher (i.e. monitor) | Reads spelling cards to teacher |
| 10.00 a.m. | Repeats tables cyphers and spells from cards | Spells from cards; writes from copper-plate cards to teacher. | Reads and spells to the master; goes out |
| 10.30 a.m. | Reads and spells from lesson to teacher | Reads and spells from the lesson to master; goes out | Writes copper-plate cards sitting |
| 11.00 a.m. | Spells on the cards to the master; goes out | Writes a lesson from the spelling cards | Writes tables and figures; goes out again |
| 11.30 a.m. | Writes in copybook or if girls, sew | Goes out 5 mins.; writes tables; repeats them from cards. | Reads and spells to master |

This sets out the "occupations" of the different classes, the length

186

of lessons, and the way in which the master distributed his time. Birchenough culled it from "A Small Manual for the Use of Village Schools, to assist Masters and Mistresses to understand, to adopt the Rev. Dr. Bell's System" by W. Burkwell Leeck (about 1888).

*From Birchenough, *History of Elementary Education*, p. 246.

# APPENDIX B

## SYLLABUS FOR THE 3 Rs. (1870)*

| Subject | Class<br>Standard 1 | Class<br>Standard 2 | Class<br>Standard 3 |
|---|---|---|---|
| Reading | Narrative in Monosyllables | One of the narratives next in order after monosyllables in an elementary reading book in the school | A short paragraph from an elementary reading book used in the school |
| Writing | Form on blackboard or slate, from dictation, letters, capital and small manuscript | Copy in manuscript a line of print | A sentence from the same paragraph, and slowly read once, and then dictated in single words |
| Arithmetic | Form on blackboard or slate, from dictation, figures up to 20: add, subtract figures up to 10 orally, from examples on blackboard | A sum in simple addition or subtraction, and the multiplication table | A sum in any simple rule as far as short division (inclusive) |

| Subject | Class | Class | Class |
|---------|-------|-------|-------|
|         | Standard 1 | Standard 2 | Standard 3 |
| Reading | A short paragraph from a more advanced reading used in the school | A few lines of poetry from a reading book used in the first class of the school | A short ordinary paragraph in a newspaper, or other modern narrative, slowly dictated once by a few words at a time |
| Writing | A sentence slowly dictated once by a few words at a time, from the same book but not from the paragraph read | A sentence slowly dictated once by a few words at a time, from a reading book used in the first class of the school | Another short ordinary paragraph in a newspaper, or other modern narrative |
| Arithmetic | A sum in Compound Rules (money) | A sum in Compound Rules (Common Weights and Measures) | A sum in practice or bills of parcels |

Every scholar for whom grants were claimed must be examined according to the above standards.

*From Birchenough, *History of Elementary Education*, pp. 292–97. See also J. S. Maclure, *Educational Documents* (1816–1963), p. 80.

# APPENDIX C

## TYPICAL SYLLABUS IN GEOGRAPHY, HISTORY, AND ENGLISH LITERATURE*

| Class | Geography | History | Class | English Literature (as a specific subject) |
|-------|-----------|---------|-------|--------------------------------------------|
| Standard II | Definitions, points of compass, form and motion of the earth, the meaning of a map | Not taken below Std. IV | 1st year | 100 lines of poetry, got by heart, with knowledge of meaning and allusions. Writing a letter on a single subject. |
| Standard III | Outlines of Geography of Great Britain with special knowledge of the country in which the school is situated | | 2nd year | 200 lines of poetry not before brought up, repeated; with knowledge of meaning and allusions. Writing a paraphrase of a passage of early prose |
| Standard IV | Outlines of Geography of Great Britain, Ireland and the Colonies | Outlines of History of England to Norman Conquest | 3rd year | 300 lines of poetry, not before brought up, repeated, with knowledge of meaning and allusions. Writing a letter or statement, the heads of the topics to be given by Inspectors |

| Class | Geography | History | Class | English Literature (*as a specific subject*) |
|---|---|---|---|---|
| Standard V | Outlines of Geography of Europe—physical and political | Outlines of History of England from Norman Conquest to accession of Henry VII | | |
| Standard VI | Outlines of Geography of the world | Outlines of History of England from Henry VII to death of George III | | |

*From Birchenough, *History of Elementary Education*, p. 318.

# APPENDIX D

PROSPECTUS OF THE COLLEGIATE SCHOOL
(19th March, 1876)

WESLEYAN HIGH SCHOOL—CAPE COAST

PRINCIPAL: James Picot, Esquire.

The Boarding Department of the above school will open on Monday, 3rd July.

TERMS: Three Guineas per Quarter.

The following subjects are taught in the school, viz:
I ENGLISH: In all its branches. A thorough instruction will be imparted at a charge of one guinea per quarter.
II EXTRA STUDIES: for each of which an extra charge will be made of seven shillings and sixpence per quarter as numbered.

| | |
|---|---|
| *Classics:* | (1) Latin; (2) Greek. |
| *Mathematics:* | (1) Geometry and Mensuration; (2) Algebra; (3) Trigonometry. |
| *Sciences:* | (1) Chemistry; (2) Animal Physiology; (3) Natural Philosophy. |
| *Modern Languages:* | (1) French. |

N.B.—1st: All applications and payments must be made to the Superintendent, the latter to be Quarterly, in advance. No child will be admitted by the Principal who cannot produce her Quarterly receipt for the payment of all fees.

2nd: The academical year consists of two sessions, with a vacation of two weeks at the end of the first in June, and of four weeks at the close of the second. No Boarders will be allowed to remain on the premises during the vacation.

3rd: Parents desiring their children to belong to the Boarding Department must first correspond with the Superintendent on the subject.

Cape Coast, 19th March, 1876.

By 1891 the scope of the syllabus had widened to include subjects such as Fanti and Bookkeeping (*The Gold Coast People*—Supplement, p. 1, 26/10/1891).

# BIBLIOGRAPHY

## Abbreviations

| | |
|---|---|
| P.P. | Parliamentary Papers |
| B.T. | Board of Trade and Treasury Papers |
| C.O. | Colonial Office Records (Despatches, Sessional Papers) |
| C.C.A. | Cape Coast Archives |
| G.N.A. | Ghana National Archives |
| M.M.S. | Methodist Missionary Society Archives |
| S.P.C.K. | Society for the Propagation of Christian Knowledge |
| S.P.G. | Society for the Propagation of the Gospel |

## A. *Primary Sources*

### (i) *Great Britain Parliamentary Papers*

Parliamentary Papers, 1801–1852, Africa 3 (Miscellaneous).
— —' 1816, Vol. VIIB.
— —, 1820, Vol. XII.
— —, 1826–1827, Vol. VII (Part II).
— —, 1835, Vol. VII.
— —, 1842, Vol. XI.
— —, 1842, Vol. XII.
— —, 1842, Vol. XXX.
— —, 1843, XLVII (472).
— —, 1845, Vol. XXV.
— —, 1847–1848, Vol. XLVII, No. 130.
— —, 1861, Vol. XXI, Part I and Part V.
— —, 1865, Vol. XXXVIII.
— —, 1890, Vol. XLVII.
— —, 1896, Vol. XII.
— —, 1894 (Statistical Abstract, No. 317).

### (ii) *Reports*

*Reports* from the Committee of the House of Commons (Miscellaneous), Vol. X, 1785–1801.
*Report* of the Select Committee on Papers relating to the African Forts (London, 1816 and 1842).

*Report* of Colonel Ord, the Commissioner appointed to inquire into the conditions of the British settlements on the Gold Coast (London, 1865).

*General Report* on the Schools of the Gold Coast Colony for 1886 (Accra, 1887).

*Report* on the Economic Agriculture of the Gold Coast (London, 1890), No. 110.

*Report* on the Census of the Gold Coast Colony for the Year 1891 (London).

Educational Work of the Basel Missions on the Gold Coast, Appendix A.I. to *Special Reports on Educational Subjects* (London, 1905), Vol. 13, Part (ii).

The Educational Policy in British Tropical Africa, London, H.M.S.O. (1925).

(iii) *Board of Trade and Treasury Papers*

B.T. 70/66. Royal African Company (1/7/1720).
B.T.70/30. Melvie to Committee (11/3/1753).
B.T.70/29. Committee to Charles Bell (4/11/1756).
B.T.70/71. Committee to Governor and Council.
B.T.6/10. Tarleton to Privy Council (16/4/1788).

*Public Records Office* (*Despatches, Sessional Papers*)

CO.267/54. Letter of 17/4/1821.
CO.267/56. (No. 277), Macarthy's letter, 20/5/1822.
CO.267/56. (No. 273), Macarthy's letter, 15/2/1822.
CO.267/93. Denning's letter, 18/9/1826.
CO.96/4. Governor Hill to Colonial Office, 20/3/1844.
CO.96/4. Colonial Chaplain's Quarterly Report, 24/7/1844.
CO.202/43. (No. 132), Russell to Gipps, 25/8/1840.
CO.268/35. Russell to Doherty, 30/9/1840.
CO.97/1. Gold Coast Acts (1852–1864).
CO.100/8. Blue Book for 1852.
CO.100/8. Blue Book for 1858.
CO.100/4. Bird to Newcastle (No. 24), 13/2/1860.
CO.267/302. J. Hates, Minutes, West African Customs, 16/9/1869 (Richmond's Report).
CO.96/111. A. N. Hemming, Minutes, 1/6/1874.
CO.96/200. B. Griffith to Knutsford (15/1/1890).
CO.267/14.
CO.267/171.
CO.96/126.
CO.96/25, No. 20.

CO.90/14. Minutes of Council.
CO.96/143.
CO.96/23.
CO.96/136.
CO.96/130.
CO.96/45. Bird's letter of 11/6/1859.

(iv) *Statistical Tables*

(a) Relating to the Colonial and other Possessions of the
U.K. (Part XX), 1888–1890, presented to both Houses of
Parliament, pp. 366–370.

(b) *Accounts and Papers*, 1890–1891, LV.

(v) *Census Reports*

(i) Great Britain 1801–1931: Guide to official sources No. 2.
(ii) Great Britain 1851 (Education) XII–LXX.
(iii) Great Britain 1861 Vol. 3, General Report.
(iv) Nigeria—Report on the Census of Eastern Region, 1952.
(v) Ghana—Report on the Census of Population: G.C. 1948.

(vi) *Year Books, Annuals, etc.*

A Bibliography of the Gold Coast (Accra), 1931.
The Gold Coast (1931), Accra, 1932.
The Gold Coast Year Books (1884–1895).
The Gold Coast Annual (1892).
The Gold Coast Almanack (1895), by Wood.
Great Britain—Blue Books, 1851, 1852, 1856, 1861.
Statesman's Year Book 1887–1893.
Ketties Year Book 1898.

B. *Cape Coast Archives and Ghana National Archives*

Despatch of 25/2/1824.
C.C.A.CO.96/127.
C.C.A.CO.96/4, 20/3/1844. Gov. Winniet to Colonial
Secretary.
C.C.A.CO.267/56.
C.C.A.CO.297/135. Campbell to Wood 8/2/1836.
C.C.A. Gold Coast Education Ordinance par. 7, Sections
1, 4, 5; para. 12.

C. *Other Primary Sources* (Archives of Missionary Bodies)

(i) *Methodist Missionary Society*

*Gold Coast Box 1835–1841*

Dunwell to Secretaries, 2/1/1835, 8/1/1835, 1/4/1835.

Dunwell's Diary, 23/4/1835.

Wriggley to Secretaries, 30/11/1836, 17/10/1836.

Trustees of Methodist Church to Secretaries, 11/7/1841.

Freeman to Secretaries, 10/1/1838, 23/1/1840, November, 1841.

Brooking to Secretaries, 9/4/1841.

Freeman's Journal, 23/1/1840.

Thackaray's Journal, 20/2/1841, 22/3/1840.

Governor Maclean's instructions to Ashanti Princes, 1840.

Maclean to Colonial Office, 28/1/1840.

J. Nicholls, 10/4/1840.

Freeman to T. F. Buxton, July, 1840.

Waldron to Secretaries, February, 1841.

de Graft to Secretaries, November, 1841.

*Gold Coast Box 1842–1845*

de Graft's Notes, 4/3/1842.

Freeman's Report on Beulah, 28/2/1852.

Freeman to Secretaries, 17/4/1842, 9/5/1842.

de Graft to Secretaries, 4/3/1842.

Smith to Beecham, 18/1/1842.

Beecham's evidence before Select Committee on West Coast of Africa (copy), 31/5/1842.

Addison to Secretaries, 13/5/1847.

Allen to Committee, 10/5/1842.

Methodist Leaders (Cape Coast) to Maclean, 1843.

Minister of State (Netherlands) to Secretaries, 23/6/1843.

Smith to Secretaries, 18/2/1843.

District Minutes, 1842–1865; 18/1/1844, 4/2/1846.
   Report, 1845.

Freeman to the London *Times*, 1/11/1844.

Freeman's Diary ⎱ 1843
Freeman to Committee ⎰

Freeman's Statement of Accounts left to Brooking, Letter of 9/2/1842

de Graft to Secretaries, 22/9/1845.

Declaration by African Leaders on Pawning, March, 1845.

Martin to Secretaries, December, 1845.

Graham to Freeman, December, 1845.

*Gold Coast Box 1850–1857*
Freeman's Journal and Diary, 1850.
Report on the Deputation of Methodist Conference to examine accounts, December, 1856–July, 1857.

*Gold Coast Box 1859–1867*
Trustees of Methodist Missions to Secretaries, 11/7/1861.
Otu-Ansah's letter, 11/4/1860.
Taylor to Secretaries, 13/10/1863.
Laing's introductory note to R. Ghartey, 11/7/1861.
Ghartey to Secretaries, 13/12/1861.
West to Boyce, 12/2/1863, 12/7/1865.
Laing to Secretaries, 12/6/1863.
Solomon's letter, 12/6/1865.
West to Secretaries, 11/1/1866.12/7/1865, 12/9/1865.

*Gold Coast Box 1868–1876*
Taylor to Secretaries, April, 1868.
Solomon to Secretaries, 4/12/1868, 6/4/1869.
West to Secretaries, 23/3/1869.
Solomon to Secretaries, 26/9/1870, 26/4/1875.
Grimmer to Ussher, 27/10/1870, 8/11/1870.
Ussher to Grimmer, 8/11/1870.
Laing to Boyce, 2/2/1870.
Carr to West, 4/3/1871.
West to Secretaries, 22/3/1871.
Carr to Secretaries, 4/3/1871, 26/4/1870.
Picot to Perks, 10/5/1870.
Grimmer to Secretaries, 17/10/1870, 4/5/1870.
Wharton to Secretaries, 16/10/1872, 10/6/1873, 28/11/1872.
Freeman to Secretaries, 2/6/1874.
Rose to Laing, July, 1872.
Picot to Secretaries, 11/12/1873, 6/11/1873, 24/1/1874, 7/5/1875, 26/12/1874, 28/12/1875.
Penrose to Stratham, 14/4/1875.
Penrose to Secretaries, 26/4/1875.
Waite to Secretaries, 24/4/1872.
(Prospectus of Collegiate School, Methodist Missionary District Minutes, 1876, and Report on Cape Coast High School, 1877 are also in this Box.)

*Gold Coast Box 1876–1893*
Cannell to Secretaries, 11/6/1884.
Hallingey to Secretaries, 12/2/1889.

Kemp to Secretaries, 4/9/1892.

Missionary Committee's letter (concerning Cape Coast Scholars at Richmond College, England in 1886), 14/12/1888.

*MMS—West Africa* 1859–1867—West to Boyce answering queries, February–April, 1863.

*District Minutes* 1876, 1877.

(ii) *Society for the Propagation of Christian Knowledge* (S.P.C.K.)

S.P.C.K. Reports, 1823–1825.

Abstract Letter Box, Summary of Letters, 4833–5263.

Standing Committee Minutes, 1713–1718, p. 182.

(iii) *Society for the Propagation of the Gospel* (S.P.G.)

S.P.G. Letters: No. 8 (Quaco), 27/2/1766.

S.P.G. Committee Minutes, 21/12/1752.

S.P.G. Records, p. 259.

S.P.G. Letter Book, Vol. 1, pp. 61–65, Letter, 25/4/1795.

S.P.G. No. 11–59.

D. *Primary Sources Continued*

Gold Coast Newspapers in the 19th Century (British Museum Newspaper Library at Colindale):

*The Gold Coast News*, 21/3/1885, 27/3/1885, 28/3/1885, 31/3/1885, 11/4/1885.

*The Gold Coast Times*, 15/11/1880, 20/1/1881, 17/12/1881, 1/4/1882, 30/9/1897.

*The Daily News*, 26/10/1883.

*The Western Echo*, 9/13/1885, 28/11/1885, 18/12/1886.

*The Gold Coast Echo*, 26/7/1888, 16/1/1888, 10/9/1888, 26/10/1891.

*The Gold Coast Free Press*, March, 1899.

*The Gold Coast Chronicle*, 4/1/1893, 14/1/1893, 11/2/1892, 11/3/1893, 18/3/1893, 30/7/1881, 25/2/1893.

*The Gold Coast Methodist Times*, 31/3/1897, 15/10/1898.

*The Methodist Recorder*.

*The Gold Coast People*, 26/10/1891.

*The Gold Coast Aborigines*, 8/1/1898, 15/1/1898, 12/2/1898, 5/3/1898.

*The Gold Coast Assize*.

E. *Other Primary Sources*

(*a*) *Unpublished Thesis*

Walsh, M. J. "The Catholic Contribution to Education in Western Nigeria, 1861–1926." M.A. thesis, London University.

Bartels, F. L. "Provision and Administration of Education in the Gold Coast 1765–1865." M.A. thesis, London University, 1949.

Graham, S. F. "History of Education in Relation to Development of the Protectorate of Northern Nigeria, 1900–1919". Ph.D. thesis, London University, 1955.

Inyang, P. E. M. "The Provision of Education in Nigeria with reference to the work of the Church Missionary Society, Catholic Missions and the Methodist Missionary Society." M.A. thesis, London University, 1958.

Ackah, C. A. "An Ethical Study of the Akan Tribes of Ghana." Ph.D. thesis, London University, 1959.

(*b*) *Journal, Periodicals, Articles, Etc.*

Anderson, D. "Geographic and Economic Factors and the Development of Educational Systems in Western Europe," *Comparative Educational Review*, June 1965, Vol. (9), No. 2.

Bagley, A. "Seventeenth Century Childhood Education, reflections from Venus and Adonis", *History of Education Quarterly*, Dec. 1965, pp. 224–235.

Balandier, G. "Social Changes and Social Problems in Negro Africa", in *Africa in the Modern World*, ed. by Stillman, C. W. (Chicago, 1955).

Bartels, F. L. "Philip Quaque 1741–1816", *Transactions of the Gold Coast and Togoland Historical Society*, Vol. I, 1955, part (v), pp. 153–171.

Belshaw, H. "Religious education in the Gold Coast", *International Review of Missions* (London, 1945), Vol. 34.

Bernard Blankenheimer. "Economic Policy in Emergent Africa", *S.A.I.S. Review* (Winter 1959).

Bevin, H. J. "The Gold Coast Economy about 1880", *Transactions of the Gold Coast and Togoland Historical Society*, 2, 1956; pp. 73–86.

Brown, G. N. "British Educational Policy in West and Central Africa", *J.M.A.S.* (2), 1964, pp. 365–377.

Busia, K. A. "The Ashanti", in *African Worlds*, ed. by Forde, C. D., 1954.
"The Present Situation and Aspirations of Elites in the Gold Coast", *International Social Science Bulletin*, Vol. 8, No. 3.

Clark, F. "The double mind in African education", *Africa*, Vol. 5, No. 2, pp. 158–168.

Clignet, R. "Ethnicity, Social Differentiation, and Secondary Schooling in Western Africa", *Cahier d'Etudes Africaines*, VII, 26/2/67.

Clignet R. and Foster, P. "Potential Elites in Ghana and the Ivory Coast: a preliminary comparison", *American Journal of Sociology*, Vol. 70, 1964, pp. 349–362.

Cotgrove, S. "Education and Occupation", *British Journal of Sociology*, I, 13, March 1962, pp. 33–41.

Floud, J. "Educational Sociology" in *A Dictionary of the Social Sciences* (ed. Gould-Kolb).

Foster, P. J. "Ethnicity and the schools in Ghana", *Comparative Educational Review, 1962*, pp. 127–135.

Foster, P. J. "Secondary Schooling and Social Mobility in a West African Nation", *Sociology of Education*, Vol. 37, pp. 150–171.
"Status, Power and Education in a Traditional Community", *School Review*, 1964, Vol. 72.

Fyfe, C. H. "The Sierra Leone Press in the 19th Century", *Sierra Leone Studies*, New Series 8, June 1957.

Ginsberg, M. "Social Change", *British Journal of Sociology* (3), Vol. 9, September 1958.

Hall, J. and Jones, C. "Social Grading and Occupations", *British Journal of Sociology*, 55, 1950, pp. 533–543.

Hicks, R. E. "Similarities and Differences in Occupational Prestige Ratings", *African Social Research*, June 1967, No. 3.

Holst, R. "Polygamy and the Bible", *International Review of Missions*, Vol. 56, 222, April 1967.

Jahoda, G. "Aspects of Westernisation: a study of Adult-class students in Ghana", *British Journal of Sociology*, Vol. 12 (1), March 1962, pp. 44–53.

Johnson, H. H. "British Missions in Africa", *Nineteenth Century*, Vol. 4, 1887.